ALAN ROGEF

Good Camps

G000320555

FRANCE 19

Contents

Reports on Selected Sites

Published by: **DENEWAY GUIDES & TRAVEL LTD**
Chesil Lodge, West Bexington, Dorchester, Dorset DT2 9DG
Tel/Fax: (0308) 897809

Printed by: Friary Press, Bridport Road, Dorchester, Dorset
Covers: Jayne Homer - Maps: Charles Broughton
Cover Photograph is of Camp du Domaine, Provence

Sales: **Derek Searle Associates**
Burlington House, 14 High Street
Slough, Berkshire SL1 1EE
Tel: (0753) 539295 Fax: (0753) 551863

Distribution: **Bookpoint Ltd**
39 Milton Park
Abingdon, Oxon OX14 4TD
Tel: (0235) 835001 Fax: (0235) 861038

FOREWORD

to the 1994 edition

Amongst the many tributes we were pleased receive last year was one in French Traveller Magazine describing our France Guide as "considered by many to be the 'bible' of camping in France". Such an accolade is not won without a lot of hard work and every year we visit literally hundreds of sites, both existing ones (i.e. those already featured in our Guides) and potential new ones. In this last context, we always welcome readers comments and suggestions for new sites to include, which provide a source of valuable information.

Not only do we make a point of following up readers' suggestions and investigating their complaints, but we always endeavour to acknowledge every letter individually, even if at times our response is a little slow, particularly in the Autumn when our visit programme is complete and our three full time staff are busy planning and typesetting our Guides for the following year. In fact, most of the letters we receive now relate to potential new sites rather than to complaints about existing ones, but those complaints we do get nearly all relate to problems caused by overcrowding in the peak season, particularly between mid-July and mid-August, when the vast majority of the French take their holidays; such a short peak period makes it uneconomic for many sites to provide really adequate facilities to cope with the numbers of campers at that time, and our comments are often met with simply a Gallic shrug of the shoulders and a wry smile! If you can avoid the period mid-July to mid-August, our advice would be to do so.

The 1993 season in France was characterised by an apparent lack of any coherent pattern - some sites enjoyed a good season, others a very indifferent one - and the weather in the early part of the summer in many areas of France was distinctly changeable to say the least, which didn't help either. We would like to think that the more professional sites enjoyed the better season, and to an extent this does seem to have been the case; those sites which have tried to economise on staffing levels, maintenance, etc. seem to have done worse than those which, despite a difficult economic climate, nevertheless sought to provide really good value for money. We have been pretty ruthless in removing a number of sites which, we felt, were exploiting the situation to the detriment of their clients.

For 1994 we have for the first time included a few sites in CORSICA as well as those in mainland France. We don't expect a mad rush of readers to Corsica, but we have had a number of enquiries about that island in recent years, and would appreciate any readers comments or suggestions on our Corsican selection in particular.

For our 1994 edition we have also sought to address another potential problem, namely the tendency of some sites to provide more and more 'facilities' (not all of which are necessarily to our readers' taste) and use these as a justification for substantial price increases. We believe that the majority of our readers are looking for a good standard in terms of the 'basics' (i.e. good pitches, adequate, well maintained and clean sanitary facilities, an hospitable reception, and, where these exist, a good standard of catering, swimming pool maintenance, etc) rather than the provision of 'all singing, all dancing' facilities. We are therefore particularly keen now to identify and select those sites representing the best value for money.

An innovation for 1993 was the launching of the Alan Rogers Travel Club, details of which can be found on page 7 and which proved to be of particular interest to readers of our France and Europe Guides. The range of benefits now includes discounts and/or other special offers at many of the sites featured in this Guide (which we have marked with a small Alan Rogers' logo).

In response to numerous requests, we are also now including a little more 'destination information' on the areas where selected sites are situated, but we do not see our camp site Guides as Travel Guides per se - so far as France is concerned our personal favourites in terms of travel guides are French Leave, and French Leave Encore, both written by Richard Binns, and published by Chiltern House Publications.

We hope that you will find our 1994 edition to be even more useful and interesting, and take this opportunity to wish all our readers happy and enjoyable holidays in La Belle France, favoured by good weather.

Clive Edwards BEd, FTS, M.Inst.TT
Lois Edwards MA, FTS
Sue Smart DMS   (Directors)

The Guide's Aims and Principles

Our selective site guides are designed to provide the sort of information and guidance which we, as campers and caravanners ourselves, would wish to know before committing ourselves to staying on a site which we did not know personally. In assessing our sites (all of which are inspected by us before selection, and regularly monitored by further visits, usually unannounced, questionnaires, etc.) we pay particular attention to:

- the site itself, and its individual pitches
- the sanitary facilities
- the 'hospitality'

Only after satisfying ourselves that these basic necessities are of a good standard do we consider a site for selection, irrespective of whether or not it has an extensive range of other facilities. If a site does have additional facilities then of course these too must all be of an at least acceptable standard.

Of course most site guides provide at least some information on these subjects, often by reference to symbols and a key, a system which many people don't seem to like, and which is often difficult to operate in a moving vehicle, but the most important difference with our approach is that it allows us far more freedom to comment on QUALITY than does a system of stars or other symbols, which are really designed only to inform the reader (decoder!) whether or not a particular facility is provided, without any reference to the quality.

Every site in our Guides is known to us personally; they are not selected from official lists, or written about at second-hand. Even when we get readers' suggestions couched in glowing terms we only include a site after we ourselves have visited it - this ensures a degree of uniformity in our reports, as what appeals to one person may prompt an opposite reaction in another.

All our sites are chosen on merit alone, the only criterion being that they meet our standards; no payment is required of a site for inclusion in the Guide, so no site can buy its way into the Guide.

Reference has already been made to our rigorous inspection process, but of course we are not infallible, and occasionally we get caught out by an unexpected mid-season change in ownership or management of a site, so we do appreciate the invaluable feedback we receive from readers each year. Unlike some other guides we do not have an army of inspectors operating what seems to be an essentially bureaucratic approach to assessment, but rather we have a small dedicated team of Site Assessors, all of whom are experienced campers/caravanners themselves, with a breadth of relevant individual expertise.

The many positive readers' letters which we receive suggest that our choice of sites meets with general approval; we always try to visit sites in the season, and if staying overnight, to stay under exactly the same conditions as our readers, but obviously we cannot visit every site between mid-July and mid-August when there is the greatest pressure on both staff and facilities; so far as seaside sites in particular are concerned, our advice would be to avoid this period if you possibly can - the French themselves tend to holiday in that period, and for those restricted to school holidays the last two weeks of August and first week of September are usually quieter than the previous four weeks.

THE REGIONS AND DÉPARTEMENTS OF FRANCE

THE ALAN ROGERS'
Good camps guide

Thinking of travelling further afield?

Remember the GOOD CAMPS GUIDE - EUROPE

HOW TO USE THE GUIDE

In this Guide, France is divided into REGIONS, each of which is described briefly with an introductory paragraph. Each of the 24 Regions contains one or more of the official French DÉPARTEMENTS, (which correspond approximately to our counties). The Regions, listed alphabetically (followed by Corsica) with the Département(s) contained within each are:

ALSACE:	Bas-Rhin, Haut-Rhin
AQUITAINE:	Dordogne, Gironde, Lot-et-Garonne, Landes, Pyrénées-Atlantiques
AUVERGNE:	Allier, Puy-de-Dôme, Cantal, Haute-Loire
BRITTANY:	Ille-et-Vilaine, Côtes d'Armor, Finistère, Morbihan
BURGUNDY:	Côte d'Or, Sâone-et-Loire, Nièvre, Yonne
CHAMPAGNE-ARDENNE:	Ardennes, Marne, Aube, Haute-Marne
CÔTE D'AZUR:	Alpes-Maritimes
DAUPHINY ALPES:	Isère
FRANCHE-COMTÉ:	Tre.de Belfort, Haute-Sâone, Doubs, Jura
LANGUEDOC-ROUSSILLON:	Lozère, Gard, Hérault, Aude, Pyrénées-Orientales
LIMOUSIN:	Creuse, Corrèze, Haute-Vienne
LOIRE VALLEY:	Eure-et-Loir, Loiret, Cher, Indre, Indre-et-Loire, Loir-et-Cher
LORRAINE VOSGES:	Moselle, Meurthe-et-Moselle, Vosges, Meuse
MIDI-PYRÉNÉES:	Lot, Aveyron, Tarn, Haute-Garonne, Gers, Ariège, Hautes-Pyrénées, Tarn-et-Garonne
NORD/PAS-DE-CALAIS:	Pas-de-Calais, Nord
NORMANDY:	Seine-Maritime, Eure, Orne, Calvados, Manche
PARIS/ILE DE FRANCE:	Paris, Seine-et-Marne, Yvelines, Essonne, Val d'Oise Hauts-de-Seine, Seine-St-Denis, Val de Marne
PICARDY:	Somme, Aisne, Oise
POITOU-CHARENTES:	Deux Sèvres, Vienne, Charente, Charente-Maritime
PROVENCE:	Hautes-Alpes, Alpes-de-Haute-Provence, Var, Vaucluse, Bouches-du-Rhône
RHÔNE VALLEY:	Ain, Rhône, Drôme, Ardèche, Loire
SAVOY:	Haute-Savoie, Savoie
WESTERN LOIRE:	Mayenne, Sarthe, Maine-et-Loire, Vendée, Loire-Atlantique
CORSICA:	Corse-Sud, Haute-Corse

Page Headings, in alphabetical order by Region, indicate the Region and Département in which sites featured on that page are situated, whilst the site title line at the start of each report gives the site number (also indicated on the Site Map, see pages 186-187) and a combination of nearby village/adjacent town. This system should enable the reader to quickly identify the approximate location of any site.

Notes on Information Provided in Camp Site Reports

'Site' and 'Pitch'

Throughout the reports we have used the word site in the sense of a camping site: that is to say the camp itself, not your own individual place in the camp. The latter we have called a pitch (called 'emplacement' by the French). We try to tell you if the site does **not** take any particular type of normal touring unit - caravans, motorcaravans and tents - however if you have an unusual type of unit (e.g. American motorhome, commercial vehicle or motorcycle) it is advisable to **check** with the site first to make sure that there are no special restrictions.

Distances

Distances are given in kilometres and metres to correspond with those on continental maps and signposts.

Opening dates

We give the **advertised** opening dates of camps. If we know that the shops or meals service (if they exist) are open for a shorter period than the site itself, we have so indicated. However on occasion site owners will close/open earlier or later than stated, and it is wise to check with the site if you intend to visit in the period immediately following the stated opening date, or immediately prior to the stated closing date.

Sanitary facilities

Here we have tried to give the most important and variable information on sanitary facilities without expanding it into a detailed survey. All the sites featured in our guide have at least some 'pedestal' type WCs although these are often without a lifting seat (described as 'seatless'), The word 'Turkish' is normally used to mean the squatting type with hole at ground level and two raised foot stands; if you're tempted (or forced) to use this type of loo, beware of the flush, which often resembles a small tidal wave! In regard to personal washing facilities, on the plus side we mention particularly if private cabins are available and on the minus side if there are not individual basins or if the facilities are not under cover. All the sites included in this guide have at least some hot showers, and also special sinks for washing-up dishes and for washing clothes, and normally also points for electric razors. If there is free hot water in the washbasins, then generally we mention it in the text and, in the absence of such information you can expect to find only cold water in basins. If we say that the showers are 'fully controllable', this means that they have either two taps or a multipurpose tap which enables the temperature and flow to be controlled (as distinct from premixed hot water with pushbutton or chain control).

Electrical connections

The vast majority of sites featured in this guide have at least some electric hook-ups, although the amperage may vary from 2A to 10A - with the introduction of more and more electrical gadgets, we have started to give details of the current rating (i.e. amperage) where possible, but we would warn readers to be careful to avoid using domestic electrical appliances, such as household electric kettles, that are not specifically designed for use in caravans etc. as in many cases these will seriously overload the supply and blow the fuse in the connection box. Similarly readers should note that many sites in France, and elsewhere in Europe, have non standard two-pin sockets, requiring the use of an adaptor.

Charges

Few French campsites fix their prices for the following year before our press date and most charges refer to 1993. Where 1993 or 1994 prices were not available we try to give an indication of their usual level by providing latest available charges. The prices are given in French Francs. We would emphasise that the prices which we quote are merely a guide, as many campsites have complicated charging systems, and the limited space available to us means that we cannot do more than provide a summary or outline of charges - if you need to get an exact quotation you should write to the site specifying your precise requirements, and ask for a quotation.

Reservations

This is somewhat complicated subject, and difficult to deal with comprehensively in terms of the variety of different systems operated by individual campsites in our reports. What we have done, therefore, in our reports is to indicate whether or not the camp will make reservations, and if so to give any important special features of their system, such as whether they keep a particular place, whether there is any minimum period of stay, and whether any deposit or fee is payable. A fee of course is lost if the booking is cancelled whereas a deposit is deducted from your bill, though there could be cases where a camp objects to returning your deposit - for example, if you book for a precise period and then want to leave early because it starts to rain. Because of the many different systems and conditions, it is best not to send any money until the site has confirmed your reservation. Write first to the site asking for a reservation, and if they can offer you what you want they will normally write back confirming it and telling you how much they want in the way of deposit and fee. Then arrange either for your bank to make the necessary payment or simply send the site a Eurocheque for the required amount, in French Francs. If you are concerned about losing a substantial deposit, or of incurring cancellation charges our advice is to take out travel insurance including cancellation cover - travel insurance is a wise precaution anyway, and if you wish to take out cover you can arrange this through your travel agent, motoring organisation or through the Publishers, who are agents for the highly regarded and very popular `GOLD COVER' Scheme, details of which are given in a colour advertisement in this guide.

UK Reservations services

Several organisations offer a service in the UK for booking pitches at French sites. We have worked very satisfactorily with Select Site Reservations for some years, and their address and telephone number can be found in their advertisement in this Guide. Several organisations also offer a reservations service for booking the range of `static' accommodation which has become a feature of many French sites; again you will find advertisements for several of these organisations in the guide, all of whom we have found to provide a satisfactory service.

THE ALAN ROGERS TRAVEL CLUB

Last year we launched our TRAVEL CLUB, the benefits of membership being geared mainly to those travelling abroad. During the past year we have been able to extend the range of benefits significantly; in particular, many of our Alan Rogers Selected sites, in France as well as in the British Isles and other European countries, now provide our Travel Club members with some kind of `special offer', often in the form of specially reduced site fees, particularly out of season.

 Our Logo below the Site Report indicates which sites in this Guide provide such offers.

To summarise, the benefits of membership of the Alan Rogers Travel Club in 1994 include:

- Special reductions at many sites in Britain and Europe

- Discounts on our range of Guides and maps

- Special member's discount on Gold Cover Travel & Breakdown Insurance

- Camping Carnet Service (in conjunction with Gold Cover Insurance)

- Access to a range of discount and/or promotional ferry fares

The membership subscription for 1994 will be £5.00, plus an initial joining fee also of £5.00 (for new members) - if you would like to join, please send us a cheque (made payable to Deneway Guides and Travel Ltd), together with your full name, address and number of family members to:

Deneway Guides, Chesil Lodge, West Bexington, Dorchester, Dorset DT2 9DG.

TRAVEL INFORMATION

The following is a resume of some of the more important considerations in connection with travel to France. Those seeking more detailed advice and guidance on specific subjects should contact:

The French Government Tourist Office, 178 Piccadilly, London W1V 0AL, Tel: 071 491 7622

Passports

Visitors to France must hold a valid passport which can be either a standard British Passport or a British Visitors Passport (obtainable from a main Post Office); notwithstanding the `open market', in practice passports are still required. British Passport holders do not require a visa.

Health

There are no obligatory inoculations and, as Britain enjoys reciprocal agreement with France for health care, it is possible to obtain treatment in France by producing Form E111, obtainable in advance in the UK through post offices. As only about 80% of the cost of treatment is covered in this way, personal travel insurance, including medical expenses cover, is a wise precaution.

Insurance

Third party motor insurance is obligatory, and a Green Card is strongly recommended; you should contact your motor insurance company or broker. Comprehensive personal travel and breakdown insurance, including cancellation cover, is a sensible precaution - several organisations can arrange cover to suit virtually every need; details, and a proposal form for `GOLD COVER' insurance, a comprehensive but flexible scheme at a very competitive price, with special discounts for readers, are included in this Guide.

Finance

There is no limit to the amount of Sterling which you may take into France and you can change Sterling notes at banks or bureaux de change once there. Most holidaymakers prefer to take French Currency or Travellers Cheques with them, and most banks in the UK provide a foreign currency service, although smaller branches may need a few days notice of your requirements. Eurocheques, backed up by a Eurocheque Card, are accepted at many establishments and can be used to obtain cash at most banks in France. French banking hours differ from the UK - they are normally open Monday - Friday, between 09.00-12.00 and 14.00-16.00, but close either on a Saturday OR on a Monday. Bank Holidays in France are different from the UK; details can be obtained from the French Government Tourist Office in London. The major (i.e. Access, Visa, American Express and Diners Club) credit and charge cards are acceptable at many establishments throughout France.

Shopping

French shopping hours vary considerably, although shops are often open later than in the UK, and many close for lunch, often for up to two hours. Supermarkets and hypermarkets are normally open until 8-10 pm (20.00 - 22.00 hrs).

Customs

With the introduction of the open market in 1993, formalities for EC residents travelling between the UK and France are now minimal - it is however important to distinguish between `duty free' goods (where the limits are more or less unchanged) and `duty paid in the EC' goods which are no longer subject to strict limits.

Motoring Information

Both the AA and the RAC can provide full details of continental motoring regulations, including those applying in France, but the following points should be borne in mind in particular:

Documentation: it is advisable to carry your vehicle registration document and/or, if the vehicle is not registered in your name, a letter of authority signed by the registered owner to the effect that you have permission to take the vehicle abroad. A valid full (not provisional) UK driving licence is required and car drivers must be over eighteen years of age. An International Driving Licence (obtainable from the AA or RAC) is not required for France, but may well be necessary if you intend to make excursions into neighbouring countries, such as Spain.

Documentation (continued):
You must have valid third party insurance cover as a minimum requirement. An International Green Card (obtainable from your insurers) is strongly recommended and comprehensive breakdown insurance is also a wise precaution. An International Camping Carnet is not essential but can usually be deposited at Site Receptions as security if you dislike handing over your passport for this purpose. Camping Carnets are obtainable from the motoring organisations, from the G.B. Car Club, PO Box 11, Romsey, Hants (see advertisement in this guide) or, for members of the Alan Rogers Travel Club, we can provide a free short-term Camping Carnet in connection with a Gold Cover Insurance policy.

Vehicle: You should display a GB plate or sticker on the rear of your vehicle and you should carry a spare set of light bulbs and a red warning triangle for use in the event of an accident or breakdown. Similarly you should ensure that your headlights dip to the RIGHT (conversion kits are available from motor accessory shops). Riders and passengers of motorcycles exceeding 50 cc. must wear crash helmets and special speed limits apply to machines up to 80 cc.

Taking your caravan: Touring caravans may visit France for up to six consecutive months without formalities, but the following regulations apply:
- any vehicle towing a caravan must be fitted with adequate mirrors
- maximum dimensions are 2.5 m. wide, 11 m. long (for vehicle and trailer, maximum length is 18 m).
- no passenger may be carried in a moving caravan.
- outside built-up areas the driver of the towing vehicle is required by law to keep a distance of 50 m. between him/herself and the vehicle ahead.
- vehicles towing caravans are not allowed into central Paris, or in the outer lane of 3 lane motorways.
- on narrow roads you are required to give way to vehicles wishing to overtake by slowing down or pulling into the side.
- in case of breakdown you MUST display a warning triangle at least 30 m. behind you (irrespective of hazard lights).
- if the caravan is hired or borrowed, you must have written authorisation from the registered owner.
- if the maximum gross weight of the caravan does not exceed the kerb weight of the towing vehicle, speed limits are the same as for cars. If the weight of your caravan is greater than this, graduated speed limits, from 65 kph. apply according to the caravan/car weight ratio.

Overnight parking
Strictly speaking, overnight parking is not allowed in lay-bys, but in the case of fatigue you should pull off the road and stop to rest. On Autoroutes you should not look upon the rest areas (Aires de Repos) as alternative camp sites, and your toll (péage) ticket is only valid for 24 or 48 hours, depending on the particular Autoroute concerned - check your ticket for details.

Roads
France has a comprehensive road system, ranging from motorways (Autoroutes), Routes National (N roads), Routes Departmental (D roads) down to purely local C class roads; the Autoroute system is extensive but expensive! The use of Autoroutes nearly always involves the payment of substantial tolls and it is a matter of personal choice as to whether you prefer to use the normally much faster Autoroute, and pay the tolls, use the equivalent N road, or even avoid main roads altogether. Autoroutes are expensive, but they are fast and some savings in terms of the cost of overnight stops can sometimes offset the cost of tolls on a long journey. Up-to-date information on the prevailing toll charges is available from the French Government Tourist Office.

Post
Post Offices and many Tabacs (tobacconists) sell stamps; charges are roughly similar to those in the UK.

Telephone
To telephone the UK from France you will need to dial 19 44, followed by the UK exchange code MINUS the first 0, followed by the subscriber's number. e.g. to telephone our office from France you would dial 19.44.308.897809. Most French 'phone boxes now take 'phone cards not coins; 'phone cards (Telecartes) can be bought at post offices, tabacs and at most campsites. To call France from the UK, the code is 010 33 followed by the local number in full. All Paris numbers are prefixed by '1'.

NATURIST SITES

In recent years we have received an increasing number of enquiries regarding Naturist Sites in France, where naturist holidays are far more popular, and we therefore first decided to include a number of these sites in France in our 1992 Guide. During the past two years we have had very favourable feedback from readers concerning our choice of Naturist Sites, and have now added a few more, including, for the first time, one in Corsica.

Apart from the need to have a `Naturist Licence' (see below), there is no need to be a practising naturist before visiting these sites. In fact, at least as far as British visitors are concerned, there seems to be a trend towards what might be described as `holiday naturism' as distinct from the practice of naturism at other times. The emphasis in all the sites featured in this guide at least, is on naturism as `life in harmony with nature', and respect for oneself and others and for the environment, rather than simply on nudity. In fact nudity is really only obligatory in the area of the swimming pools. There are a number of `rules', which on reading prior to our visits we found somewhat daunting, but which in practice amount to sensible and considerate guidelines designed to ensure that no-one invades someone else's privacy, creates any nuisance or damages the environment. Whether as a result of these `rules', the naturist philosophy generally or the attitude of site owners and campers alike, we were very impressed by all the naturist sites we have visited. Without exception they had a friendly and welcoming ambience, were all extremely clean and tidy, and in most cases, provide much larger than average pitches.

The purpose of our including a number of naturist sites in our guide is not to provide a comprehensive listing or analysis of naturist sites in France (of which there are many) or to set up in competition with the several specialist naturist site guides, but rather to provide an `introduction to naturist camping in France' for British holidaymakers; we were actually surprised by the number of British campers we met on naturist sites, many of whom had `stumbled across naturism almost by accident' but had found, like us, that these sites were amongst the nicest they had encountered.

We mentioned the Naturist Licence - French Law requires all campers over 16 years on naturist sites to have a `naturist licence'. These can be obtained in advance from either the British or French national naturist associations, but they are also available on arrival at any recognised naturist site. The cost (in 1993) is FFr 90 per person (or about £10 in the UK) and a passport type photograph is required.

CAR FERRY SERVICES

The number of different services/routes from the UK to France provides a wide choice of sailings to meet most needs. The actual choice is a matter of personal preference, influenced by factors such as where you live, your actual destination in France, cost, and whether you see the channel crossing as a potentially enjoyable part of your holiday, or, (if you are prone to seasickness) as something to be endured!

In terms of providing helpful information concerning ferries in this Guide, we have provided a summary of the services likely to be operating in 1994 on information available at the time of going to press (October 1993), together with a number of reports on those services which we have used ourselves during the last two years. Detailed up-to-date information will be available from the Ferry Operators themselves, the Motoring Organisations and Travel Agents early in the New Year when the 1994 schedules are finalised; the information produced here is intended only as a provisional guide.

ROUTE	OPERATOR	SEASON	FREQUENCY	TIME
Dover-Calais	P&O Ferries	all year	up to 15 daily	75 mins
Dover-Calais	Stena-Sealink	all year	up to 18 daily	90 mins
Dover-Calais	Hoverspeed	all year	up to 27 daily	35 mins (hovercraft) 50 mins (Seacat)
Folkestone-Boulogne	Hoverspeed	all year	up to 6 daily	55 mins
Ramsgate-Dunkirk	Sally Line	all year	up to 5 daily	150 mins
Newhaven-Dieppe	Stena Sealink	all year	up to 4 daily	4 hours
Portsmouth-St. Malo	Brittany Ferries	Mar-Dec	up to 2 daily	9/11 hours*
Portsmouth-Caen	Brittany Ferries	all year	up to 4 daily	6/7 hours*
Portsmouth-Le Havre	P&O Ferries	all year	up to 4 daily	5¾ hours
Portsmouth-Cherbourg	P&O Ferries	all year	up to 4 daily	5/9 hours*
Southampton-Cherbourg	Stena-Sealink	all year	up to 3 daily	6/8 hours*
Poole-Cherbourg	Truckline	all year	up to 4 daily	4/7 hours*
Plymouth-Roscoff	Brittany Ferries	all year	up to 3 daily	6/8 hours*

* the longer crossing time is for night sailings

Addresses and Telephone numbers:

Brittany Ferries
Millbay Docks, Plymouth PL1 3EW
0752-221321

P & O European Ferries
Channel House, Channel View Road,
Dover CT17 9TJ
0304-203388

Stena Sealink Line
Charter House, Park Street, Ashford TN24 8EX
0233-647047

Sally Ferries
Argyle Centre, York Street, Ramsgate CT11 9DS
0843-595522

Hoverspeed
Maybrook House, Queens Gardens,
Dover CT17 9UQ
0304-240241

FERRY REPORTS

Introduction:

Visiting some 300 sites throughout Europe ourselves every year we use ferries extensively, and the most striking feature is the general improvement in facilities and service over the past few years; standards have improved dramatically and most ferry crossings, in all but the worst of weather, are a comfortable and often enjoyable experience. Even though we travel a lot, we do not use all the various services every year and our reports therefore cover those services which we have used over the past two years

 ## HOVERSPEED SEA-CAT SERVICE - Folkestone/Boulogne

The speed and comfort of the Sea Cat makes it a realistic competitor to the Tunnel. The professionalism and courtesy of the staff is impressive. Embarkation is quick and efficient, obviously facilitated by the comparatively small number of vehicles accommodated. Once aboard there is a certain resemblance to air travel in terms of the seating arrangements is noticeable, but there is plenty of space, and although we travelled at a peak period, we had no trouble getting a seat, buying our 'duty frees' or getting a snack and a drink from the bar. Admittedly the range of products is limited, but in view of the speed of the crossing, and the extensive facilities (including a good duty free shop) at Boulogne, this is no great problem.

The staff (18) were all pleasant and helpful, and the journey sped by in well under the hour (the Sea-Cat holds the cross channel record for the quickest passenger vessel crossing, other than by hovercraft) and the safety procedures were well demonstrated by an audio-visual presentation. There are two excellent observation areas onboard - at the stern, and immediately behind the bridge, where you can see the captain and crew at work navigating across the busiest sea lane in the world. A word of caution - don't stand on the stern observation deck when the engines are being started, especially if you're wearing light-coloured clothing! Disembarkation at Boulogne is quick and efficient and this crossing makes a most relaxing stress-free start to a holiday.

NDR

 ## STENA-SEALINK LINE SERVICE - Newhaven/Dieppe

The two ships on this four hour crossing, the Stena Londoner and the Stena Parisien, are both comfortable with a wide range of facilities including a casino and children's play area (Londoner) and a good a la carte restaurant (Parisien). There is a spacious feel about both ships and on two recent trips, one extremely busy, the staff were friendly and helpful. In all areas the ships were very clean.

Embarkation at Newhaven was quick, efficient and stress free. It was nice to travel through a small port with a few sailings each day, and one felt less like being on a conveyor belt. Obviously there were fewer facilities than at larger ports. Within a few minutes of arrival at Dieppe, following clear signposting, we were out of the town and on the way to our holiday destination. This route is ideal for those visiting Paris, less than three hours steady driving away, and the Département of Seine Maritime, a beautiful and interesting part of Normandy.

Dieppe itself is well worth investigating, so perhaps on the return journey leave a couple of hours or so to look round. The port area parking, on the sea front, adjoins the pebbly beach and is only a ten minute walk from the town centre and the quay side with its extensive and excellent range of reasonably priced sea food restaurants. If you are returning on a Saturday, a visit to Dieppe market, which seems to sprawl right through the town centre, is an enjoyable way of passing your time - an opportunity to make some last minute purchases before catching the boat home. There are limited port facilities at Dieppe.

Road works this year (1993) have made access to Newhaven difficult and the considerably longer crossings than those further east might not suit the less enthusiastic sailors, particularly in bad weather.

NDR

TRUCKLINE SERVICE - Poole/Cherbourg

To be honest this is our favourite service, partly because we live less than an hour's drive from Poole, which is a small and easily accessible port, with facilities that are adequate and friendly.

Since it started some years ago, this service has offered good value for money, comfortable onboard facilities and good restaurants, and the introduction of the brand new 'Barfleur' onto the route last year introduced a degree of luxury to rival any cross channel service. The main restaurant for example provides a variety of set menus, in very pleasant surroundings, and a standard of food and service which we thought was excellent, and which represented good value. The self-service cafeteria is also good, with reasonable prices, but tends to become more crowded. The ships, the good facilities and service, the interesting voyage along the Dorset coast for some miles, and the very competitive fare structure combine to make this service well worth serious consideration.

CE

 ## SALLY LINE - Ramsgate/Dunkirk

For those who prefer a more leisurely crossing with less crowded ports and for whom travel to Ramsgate is convenient, Sally Line provide five crossings in each direction daily at competitive prices. The pride of the Sally Line is the excellent Smorgasbord restaurant where, for a set tariff, one can eat as much as one likes. Depending on the time of day (or night), different menus are offered at different prices. For those who desire snacks or smaller meals, self-service restaurants provide an alternative. The duty free shop is well stocked with all the goodies we now expect to find on cross channel journeys. Improvements to Autoroute links at Dunkirk make for an easy get away to holiday destinations.

GO

 ## P & O EUROPEAN FERRIES - Dover/Calais

With the introduction of the new 'Pride of Burgundy' and the enlargement of the 'Prides' of Kent and Bruges, P & O now have five Super ferries on this route and advertise a shuttle service with 25 sailings (at peak times) in each direction at 45 minute intervals. The check in time has also been reduced to 20 minutes and, although it is advisable to book beforehand for peak times, it is generally possible to turn up without a booking and sail on the next ferry. No doubt the expected competition from the channel tunnel route has encouraged improvements and these have been made on board as well, with better shopping and refreshment facilities. Using this route several times each year, one is also struck with the excellent and courteous service by all employees.

The Club Class lounges, available for a small supplement, provide a haven of peace and quiet away from the bustle on the decks below, with steward service, free coffee, tea and newspapers. Two loading ramps operating simultaneously ensure a minimum of delay for boarding and disembarkation and the autoroute connection at Calais provides a quick departure from the port.

GO

14

BOOKING AT A CAMPSITE

Although France probably has more campsites than any other country in Europe, it can sometimes be difficult to find a pitch at a popular resort in peak season. You are advised to write direct to your selected site preferably enclosing an international reply coupon (obtainable from any post office). You may find it helpful to use the form below. A few sites do not accept advance bookings - if not, arrive before 11 am. to be sure of a space. The Good Camps Guide indicates where advance booking is advised.

For general enquiries to camp sites we have included (on page 181) some slips which may be used to request information from the sites in this guide.

Monsieur le Directeur

Camping: . . . .

At: . . . . **Date:** . . . .

Ayant obtenu votre camping par le ALAN ROGERS' GOOD CAMPS GUIDE
I have selected your site from ...

Je vous serais obligé de me communiquer rapidement vos conditions et tarifs correspondant au séjour suivant:
Please let me know at your earliest convenience your conditions for the following stay:

Arrivée le . . . . **Départ le** . . . .
Arriving on ...   *Departing on ...*

Nous sommes . . . . **adultes et** . . . . **enfants agés de** . . . .
We are   *adults and*   *children aged*

Nous désirons réserver un emplacement pour: **une voiture** *(a car)*
We wish to book a pitch for: **caravane** *(caravan)*
                                                         camping car
                                                         (motorcaravan)
                                                         tente *(tent)*
(delete as appropriate)   **avec l'electricité**
                                                         (with electricity)

Veuillez me répondre directement á l'adresse ci-dessous:
Please reply to my address below:

Mr/Mrs/Miss . . . . **Avec mes remerciements**

. . . . *Yours faithfully*

. . . .

Hoverspeed
Experience
the difference

Take a trip to France with Hoverspeed and you'll be spoilt for choice.

Will it be the dramatic, twin-hulled SeaCat, or the elegant hovercraft, at just 35 minutes the fastest service from Dover to Calais?

It's a tough call. Now, both SeaCat and hover-craft depart from the

Hoverport in Dover. So rest assured that whichever craft you choose, our exclusive port facilities mean a fast check-in and make queues or hold-ups a thing of the past.

For more information and booking details, see your travel agent or call direct on:
(0304) 240241

HOVER*SPEED*
The New Wave.

Dover – Calais & Folkestone – Boulogne. Up to 26 return crossings per day.

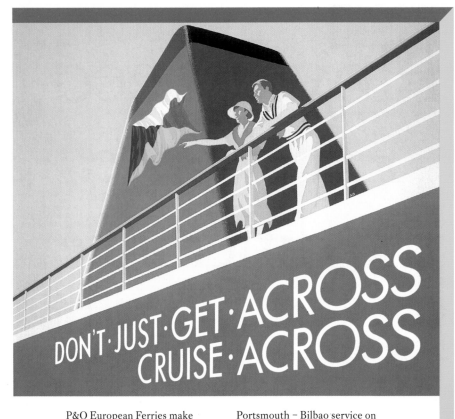

DON'T·JUST·GET·ACROSS
CRUISE·ACROSS

P&O European Ferries make taking your caravan to the Continent anything but a drag.

With our new high speed, high tech check-in system at Dover and superferry sailings to Calais every 45 minutes at peak periods, you can cruise straight through.

Wherever you're heading, we've a route and a sailing to suit you. Our Portsmouth service to Le Havre and Cherbourg take you direct to holiday France. And now you can even cruise all the way to Spain on our Portsmouth – Bilbao service on Britain's largest, most luxurious cruise ferry.

While our Felixstowe – Zeebrugge service sets you well on the way to all parts of Europe.

We still offer unbeatable value for carvans – especially if you travel off peak.

Find out more about cruising your caravan to the Continent. See your caravan club, travel agent or call P&O European Ferries direct on (0304) 203388.

P&O
European Ferries

DOVER-CALAIS, PORTSMOUTH-CHERBOURG, PORTSMOUTH-LE HAVRE, PORTSMOUTH-BILBAO, FELIXSTOWE-ZEEBRUGGE, CAIRNRYAN-LARNE.

HOLIDAYS & SALLY

FERRIES

THE ART OF SMOOTH SAILING

One of the joys of going to France is the food. Its one of the joys of going to France on Sally Ferries too.
Our Smorgasbords are justifiably famous.
Wonderful food at a delicious price.
And no matter how many times you go back for more you won't another penny.

FOR BOOKING OR MORE INFORMATION **TELEPHONE 0843 595522**
OR CONTACT YOUR TRAVEL AGENT.

HOTEL - OPEN AIR CLUB
LE COL VERT

MINI-CLUB, JUNIOR CLUB, SWIMMING POOLS (ONE INDOOR), TENNIS, GOLF AND ORGANISED ENTERTAINMENT FOR 7 TO 77 YEAR OLDS An exceptional position on the banks of Lake Léon

Chalets, Mobile-homes and pitches for tents and caravans for hire.

DOMAINE DU COL VERT
LAC DE LEON 40560 VIELLE ST-GIRONS
Tel : 58 42 94 06 Fax : 58 42 91 88

Direct access to the beach

EURO-PACT

La Paillotte
Hotel-Open air club

Private beach, swimming pools, bar and restaurant for your enjoyment. A Mini-club and a Junior-club for children.
A variety of entertainment is organised both daily and in the evenings for parents. Chalets and Mobile-Homes for hire.

LA PAILLOTTE LAC DE SOUSTONS 40140 AZUR
Tel.: 58.48.12.12 Fax: 58.48.10.73

EURO-PACT

ALSACE
Bas-Rhin - Haut-Rhin

Louis XIV referred to Alsace as `the garden of France' and this bright and friendly region certainly lives up to this description. It is a region of colour, with houses bedecked in flowers, outgoing and talkative people and countless festivals. The Alsatians certainly know how to enjoy themselves. At the `crossroads of Europe' and bordered by the Rhine, Alsace has had an interesting and turbulent past. History abounds, and there are plenty of places to visit - museums, castles, and the picturesque Medieval towns and villages on the famous `Route des Vins'. This is a fascinating trip for lovers of white wine, and there are plenty of opportunities for degustation (tasting) - do visit Strasbourg - a truly international city.

6701 Camping Eichelgarten, Oberbronn, nr Niederbronn
Inexpensive municipal site in northern Alsace, with good facilities.

This is an attractive and well run site, set amidst the mountains and forests of northern Alsace, not far from the German border. There are good views over the valley to one side with trees sheltering the other. The circular internal road has pitches around the outside, some on terraces, as well as space in the centre where there is also a good children's playground. There are two well appointed sanitary blocks which are heated in cool weather, with British WCs, washbasins, with free hot water dispensed through a push button tap, with shelf and mirror - some private cabins for ladies; good showers (hot water also free); washing machines and dryers. Baby room and facilities for the disabled.

The solar-heated swimming pool (open June-Sept) and children's pool are of excellent quality (possibly not opened on cooler days). There is a general purpose room with billiards, table tennis and table football. Minigolf, Children's playground. 2 hard tennis courts on site and there is a fitness circuit in the nearby forest. There is a small shop with very basic foodstuffs although bread can be ordered and drinks, ices and sweets are sold at reception. Supermarket in village 1 km. distant and baker and butcher visit regularly. The local authority have obviously gone to much trouble to provide this good quality site which has reasonable charges. It is very much a family site and good for overnight or longer stays. Bungalows to let.

Directions: Travel northwest from Haguenau on N62 for approx. 20 km. Near Niederbronn turn left onto D28 for Oberbronn-Zinswiller.

Charges 1993:
-- Per person Ffr. 12.00; child (under 7) 7.00; pitch 8.60; car 6.00; electricity (per A) 4.40; dog 5.40.

Open:
February - December

Address:
67110 Oberbronn, Zinswiller, Niederbronn.

Tel:
88.09.71.96.

Reservations:
Advised for high season. Write with precise dates; no deposit required.

6801 Camping de l'Ile du Rhin, Neuf-Brisach, nr Colmar
Well kept site in pleasant situation by Rhine, between the Vosges and the Black Forest.

The site contains many seasonal static caravans but there are also tourist pitches: individual plots which vary in size, all on flat grass with good shade and many electrical points. The three good sanitary blocks are well kept. They have free hot showers, British toilets and individual basins (cold water) with shelves, mirrors and separators. Amenities include washing machines, a shop, sports ground, table tennis, tennis and boule. Restaurants near. Good overnight stop or for exploring the area.

Directions: Site is close to bridge into Germany. Turn off N415 road close to French frontier post and proceed along river to north. Well signposted.

Charges 1993:
-- Per person Ffr. 12.00; child (under 7) 5.80; pitch 7.00 - 18.00; car 5.50; electricity 14.50 - 27.95.

Open:
All year.

Address:
68600 Neuf-Brisach.

Tel:
89.72.57.95.

Reservations:
Only for longer stays.

AQUITAINE
Dordogne - Gironde - Lot-et-Garonne - Landes
Pyrénées-Atlantique

This large sunny southern region extends from Périgord in the north to the Pyrénées in the south. Aquitaine is a diverse region of mountains and vineyards, vast beaches and fertile river valleys, rolling grasslands and dense forest. Within its boundaries are the beautiful valleys of the Dordogne and Vézère, the forest of the Landes, stretching from the Gironde estuary to the Basque Country on the Spanish border, the Pyrénées, some of the world's most famous vineyards around Bordeaux, and the wonderful Atlantic Coast beaches - truly a region with something for everybody.

2401 Castel Camping Château Le Verdoyer, Champs Romain (St Pardoux)

Dutch owned site developed in the park of the restored Château le Verdoyer.

Le Verdoyer is situated in this lesser known area of the Dordogne sometimes referred to as the Périgord Vert, with its green forests and small lakes. The 22 acre estate has two lakes, one in front of the Château for fishing and one accessed by a footpath, with sandy beach and safe swimming area where canoeing, windsurfing, sailing are also possible. There are 150 marked, level, terraced pitches (ground a little rocky) of good size (100-150 sq.m). All have electricity, with a choice of wooded area or open field, where hedges planted and have grown well; 24 are 'grand confort' pitches. Swimming pool complex with two pools (25 x 10 m. and 10 x 7 m.) and sand pit for children. In July/August activities are organised for children (3-12 yrs). The modern toilet block housed in the old barn buildings is good with free hot water, showers with dividers and hooks and washbasins in cabins. Another equally good, well appointed new block opened in 1993. Both have facilities for the disabled and baby baths. Hot water in dishwashing and laundry area (4 washing machines). Fridges to rent. Motorcaravan service point. Multi-purpose shop. Bar with snack bar and TV. Takeaway facilities in courtyard area. Good value bistro. All weather tennis court, volleyball and badminton. Table tennis, minigolf and mountain bike hire. Children's play area. Small library. Barbecues. Bungalows and mobile homes to rent. The Château has rooms to let, and public restaurant, open all year. Used by British and Dutch tour operators (only 20 pitches).

Directions: Site is 2 km. from the Limoges - Chalus - Nontron road, 20 km. south of Chalus and is well signed from the main road.

Charges 1994:
-- Per person Ffr. 28.00; child (2 -7 yrs) 19.00; pitch and car 41.00; second car on pitch 19.00; electricity (5A) 15.00; animal 7.00.
-- Less 15% outside Jul/Aug. plus 7th night free.

Open:
15 May - 30 September.

Address:
Champs Romain, 24470 St Pardoux La Riviére

Tel.
53.56.94.64.
FAX: 53.56.38.70..

Reservations:
Write to site.

2402 Camping Les Granges, Grolejac, nr Sarlat

Well shaded site with pool close to Dordogne.

Les Granges is situated on undulating ground in woodland. Pitches are marked and numbered on level terraces which are mostly blessed with good shade from mature trees and shrubs; most have electricity. Sanitary blocks are of a high standard, with good hot showers and clean toilets. There are toilet and shower facilities for the disabled. The local doctor will call if needed. There is a moderate-sized swimming pool and larger shallow pool. Canoes and bicycles can be hired and there are table tennis, volleyball, minigolf and children's play facilities. Bar with terrace and a restaurant/snack bar which also provides takeaway food. Dancing and other entertainment are organised in high season. Certain basic items can be bought on site but there are shops and restaurants in the nearby town of Grolegac and the hypermarkets of Sarlat are not far. The site is popular with tour operators, but there is a sensible balance and most `animation' is organised by the site. Les Granges could provide a good base for touring the Dordogne area and the present French owners have created an ambience that will assist in ensuring a pleasant stay.

Directions: Site is signposted in the village of Grolejac on the D704 Sarlat-Gourdon road. From north, leave N20 at Souillac towards Sarlat, but later keep left twice towards Gourdon.

Charges 1993:
-- Per unit incl. 4 persons Ffr. 135.00; extra person 25.00 (child under 2 free); special pitches 25.00 extra; electricity 16.00.
-- 20% less on unit rates outside 15/6-1/9.

Open:
1 May - 30 September.

Address:
Grolejac, 24250 Domme.

Tel:
53.28.11.15.

Reservations:
Made for exact dates with deposit and fee.

2403 Camping Les Périères, Sarlat

Good quality small site with large pitches and swimming pool very close to town.

This little site is in a pleasant setting amid attractive trees on the edge of the town of Sarlat. It has some 100 individual pitches mainly on terraces on a semi-circle of a fairly steep hillside with shade in many parts. They are of very good size and all are equipped with electricity, water connections and drainaway. It becomes full from late June to late August, so reservation is advisable, but a proportion of the site is not reserved, so space could be found if you are early. The five sanitary blocks, of varying size, are of good quality and should be quite sufficient, providing individual basins with shelf and mirror (mostly in private cabins), and free hot water. On the more level ground there is a small swimming pool, open all season when conditions are favourable, a paddling pool and 2 tennis courts. Small shop. Pleasant bar and snack bar. Table tennis. Library, with board games. Washing machine and dryer. Football ground. Fitness track with exercise halts. Good quality bungalows to let. With much free ground available, the site has a spacious air and is quite free from overcrowding.

Directions: Site is east of the town on the D47 road towards Croix d'Alon.

Charges 1993:
-- Per unit incl. up to 3 persons Ffr. 126.00, high season, incl. 2 persons, low season 92.00; electricity 18.00; extra person 27.00; child (under 7 yrs) 16.00; local tax 1.00 or 0.50.

Open:
Easter - 30 September.

Address:
24200 Sarlat.

Tel:
53.59.05.84.
FAX: 53.28.57.51.

Reservations:
Made for min. 1 week with deposit.

Camping Les Périères

24200 SARLAT, DORDOGNE - PÉRIGORD

The 4-star site in a natural amphitheatre of woods and meadows.
A peaceful oasis in the heart of Black Périgord, yet only half a mile from the medieval town and gastronomic centre of Sarlat.

LARGE INDIVIDUAL PITCHES - EXCELLENT TOILET BLOCKS
SWIMMING POOL - TENNIS COURTS - VOLLEYBALL
TABLE TENNIS - LOUNGE BAR - SHOP - LIBRARY

Please show reception staff this Guide when you arrive at a site
- it helps them, us and eventually you too

2405 Castel Camping Les Hauts de Ratebout, Belvès, nr Sarlat

Good family site with swimming pool, on a hill away from habitations southwest of Sarlat.

Not a particularly large site, this one has some 200 separated pitches, varying in size from 80 - 130 sq.m. and on fairly flat or terraced ground without shade. It is in a fine, if slightly exposed, hill top situation with different aspects. Over 100 of the pitches have electricity and 35 are fully plumbed. On site is a swimming pool (200 sq.m.) not heated, a shallower one (100 sq.m.) and small children's pool. All services including the pools are available from 1 May - end of season. The four modern toilet blocks have British WCs, washbasins in private cabins with free hot water and free hot showers and facilities for the handicapped. Water taps abound. Self-service shop with limited hot takeaway service. A pleasant restaurant and bar area opens to the pool-side terrace. 2 tennis courts. General room with library, pool, football table, TV. Sports facilities include volleyball, table tennis, and tennis. Adventure playground. Multi-gym with various training equipment (on payment). Washing machine and dryer. Many organised activities in season, particularly sports for children. Used by tour operators. American motorhomes not accepted. More suitable for families with children under 16 years old.

Directions: From Belvès, just off the D710 60 km. south of Périgueux, proceed 2 km. on D710 then left on D54 at camp sign and follow through to site.

Charges 1994:
-- Per person Ffr 25.80 - 32.30; child (under 8 yrs) 18.20 - 22.70; pitch 37.00 - 46.20; electricity (6A) 16.00; extra car 10.00.

Open: Easter - 30 Sept.

Address: Ste. Foy de Belvès, 24170 Belvès.

Tel: 53.29.02.10. FAX: 53.29.08.28..

Reservations: Made for a few days or more, with deposit Ffr. 350 per week (or 50 per day) and fee (80).

2404 Castel Camping Le Moulin du Roch, Sarlat

Family managed site in remote situation midway between Sarlat and Les Eyzies.

Most of the 195 separated pitches at Moulin du Roch are in rows backing onto fences but there are also many levelled places in woodland with shade. The toilet blocks are of very good quality and a well equipped washing area even includes a dishwasher. On the site is a small/medium swimming pool, available from April if conditions permit, but not heated. There is a small shop and the site has recently completed a new large restaurant and excellent takeaway. Children's playground. Table tennis. Tennis. Bicycle hire. Canoeing nearby. Mobile homes to let for long stays. The site becomes full for most of July/Aug. and many of the pitches are taken by British tour operators or clubs. There are organised entertainments and sporting activities, including canoe trips, but they are run by the site (not tour operators). A friendly management makes visitors very welcome.

Directions: Site is 10 km. from Sarlat on road to Les Eyzies.

Charges 1993:
-- Per unit incl. up to 3 persons Ffr. 129.00; extra person 33.00; electricity 15.00. Less outside July/Aug.

Open: End-April - 25 Sept.

Address: Rte. de Eyzies, 24200 Sarlat.

Tel: 53.59.20.27.

Reservations: Accepted from 1/1 - 31/5 (min. 1 week July/Aug); deposit and fee (Ffr. 90).

2406 Camping Le Paradis, St. Léon-sur-Vézère, Montignac, nr Sarlat

Exceptionally attractive riverside site halfway between Les Eyzies and Montignac.

This site is well placed for exploring the Dordogne and its prehistoric grottos and other sites. Le Paradis is very well kept and is laid out with mature shrubs and bushes of different types. It has 200 individual pitches of good size on flat grass, divided by trees and shrubs, all with electricity, water and drainaway; some special pitches for motorhomes. The two toilet blocks are of very high quality, with 2 baby baths in each ladies'; free pre-set hot showers with pushbutton (water runs on). On site is a good swimming pool complex with one deep swimmers' pool (25 x 10 m.), another shallower one (17 x 7 m.), plus a paddling pool. Good sized self-service shop. Restaurant with choice of menu and also a comprehensive takeaway service. Canoeing on Vézère river from an attractive little beach constructed on the riverside; also organised trips. 2 tennis courts. BMX track. Washing machines and dryers. A good quota of British clients, many through tour operators, but organised games, competitions and evening events are run by the site, who try to maintain a French flavour. This is a site of real quality which we thoroughly recommend.

Directions: Site lies beside the D706 road 10 km. north of Les Eyzies near the village of St Léon-sur-Vézère.

Charges 1994:
-- Per person Ffr. 30,00; child under 4 yrs free; pitch 47.60; electricity (3A) 14.50.
-- Less 10% - 25% outside main season.

Open:
Easter/1 April - 22 Oct.

Address:
St. Léon-sur-Vézère, 24290 Montignac.

Tel:
53.50.72.64.
FAX: 53.50.75.90.

Reservations:
Made for any length with deposit and Ffr. 100 fee.

2407 Camping Lestaubière, Pont St Mamet, nr Bergerac

Small country site with swimming pool, midway between Bergerac and Périgueux.

Having direct access from the main N21 (though screened from it by woodland), one thinks first of this as a useful transit site but in fact most people stay for a while. It takes only 66 units, mostly on fairly flat, shaded woodland ground at the top of site, some on more sloping open meadow with views. Pitches are marked and all have electrical connections. A swimming pool and paddling pool encourage longer stays, as does the small lake with diving platform and beach. The two toilet blocks have British WCs, washbasins with free hot water (in private cabins in the larger block); they should be large enough. A large washing room houses ample dishwashing and laundry sinks - there are also baby baths. There is a general room with bar and separate room for young with amusement machines, reached via a pleasant shaded patio terrace under vines and chestnuts. Small shop. Occasional organized activities. Good provision of children's play equipment. Volleyball. Boules. Tennis, fishing and riding nearby. The site has many British and Dutch visitors and can become full in July/August, so reservation is advisable. Good English spoken.

Directions: Site is 1 km. north of Pont St. Mamet on N21.

Charges 1993:
Per person 21.50 Ffr; pitch 23.50; child (under 7) 13.00; electricity (3A) 13.00.

Open:
15 May - 7 Sept.

Address:
Pont St. Mamet, 24140 Douville.

Tel:
53.82.98.15.

Reservations:
Made for exact dates (min. 1 week) without deposit to guarantee admission.

If you write to sites fo information or reservations,

please mention this guide or use the forms on page 181

2411 Camping Aqua Viva, Carsac, nr Sarlat
Clean site with good pool complex in heart of the Perigord Noir.

The site is divided into two sections, separated by the access road. One side is very quiet and spacious, with pitches (some enormous) terraced in woodland. The other half contains pitches on flat grass and has an excellent main pool, children's pool, small lake (for inflatables and canoes) and high quality minigolf. Canoe lessons in the lake and guided trips on the Dordogne organised by the site as are other sporting activities. Each part of the site has a very modern and spotlessly clean toilet block, with disabled facilities, laundry and baby areas. The lake area also contains the reception, plus a small reasonably priced restaurant and a bar and terrace where evening entertainment is arranged in season. Small shop, and takeaway food available. The site is ideally situated for visits to Rocamadour and Padirac as well as the many places of interest of the Dordogne region. It is also close to Sarlat for markets and hypermarkets.

Directions: Site is 6 km. from Sarlat on D704 road from Sarlat to Souillac.

Charges 1994:
-- Per pitch Ffr 18.00 - 41.00; adult 15.00 - 29.00; child 7.00 - 21.00; electricity 3A 11.00, 6A 16.00, 10A 21.00.
Open:
Easter - 20 October.
Address:
Carsac, 24200 Sarlat.
Tel:
53.59.21.09.
FAX: 53.29.36.37.
Reservations:
Made with deposit (Ffr 35 per day) and fee (100).

2412 Camping La Palombière, Ste. Nathalène, nr Sarlat
Clean site with good recreational facilities east of Sarlat.

This is a spacious site in a peaceful valley with quiet, well shaded woodland pitches delineated by trees and bushes. Two very clean modern toilet blocks are provided with laundry, baby and disabled facilities. A large recreational area contains a children's play area, small football pitch, tennis and volleyball courts. Boules pitches are terraced at the edge of the field and a minigolf course is set on a higher level by the entrance The good sized main pool and children's pool are flanked by a raised terrace from which parents can keep an eye on youngsters. Above this again is a larger terrace serving the reception, bar and restaurant complex, from which a good range of meals is available. There is a well stocked shop, including meat, fresh milk and newspapers. From reception, bicycles can be hired, and canoe trips reserved. The site organises sports competitions and evening activities in season, including talent shows, a weekly disco, cabaret and even Giant Scrabble! This is an ideal site for families where children are at an age where they need a wide range of activities, but it nevertheless preserves a relaxed ambience and general tranquillity.

Directions: Take the D47 east from Sarlat towards St Nathalène. Site is signposted from the main road, just before the village.

Charges 1993:
-- Per pitch: simple Ffr 29.60 - 42.30, with electricity 43.60 - 56.30, with water and drainage also 47.60 - 60.30; adult 20.40 - 29.20; child (under 7 yrs) free -19.80.
-- Less 10% for retired people in mid/low seasons.
Open:
15 April - 30 Sept.
Address:
Ste. Nathalène, 24200 Sarlat.
Tel:
53.59.42.34.
FAX: 53.28.45.40.
Reservations:
Made with deposit and fee - contact site.

2413 Camping Les Grottes de Roffey, Ste. Nathalène, nr Sarlat
Well organised site with good pool, restaurant and shop.

This site is situated some 5 km. east of Sarlat. Clearly marked pitches are set on very well kept, grass terraces with good views across an attractive valley. Some have good shade, although others are more open and all have electricity. There are two toilet blocks with modern facilities which were clean when seen. A very good pool complex, with two deep pools, a fountain and a children's pool, is complemented by a concrete play space and children's play area. All these are close to the main reception, bar, restaurant (indoor and with terrace) and shop area, all located within converted farm buildings surrounding a courtyard. We were very impressed with the shop, well stocked with a variety of goods, and with a tempting home-made charcuterie section and plenty of ideas for the barbecue. The restaurant menus were imaginative and sensibly priced, and takeaway food is available. The site is conveniently located for Sarlat and all Dordogne attractions and is a pleasant place to stay in its own right. It caters well for families with younger children.

Directions: Site is 5 km. east of Sarlat on the D47 Sarlat - Souillac road.

Charges 1993:
-- Per pitch Ffr 41.00; adult 30.50; child (under 7) 22.00; electricity 14.00; local tax (15/6-1/9) 1.00.
-- Less 20% outside 15/6 - 31/8.
Open:
Easter - 30 September.
Address:
Ste. Nathalène 24200 Sarlat.
Tel:
53.59.15.61.
FAX: 53.59.19.27.
Reservations:
Made with deposit - contact site.

2414 Camping Bel Ombrage, St Cybranet, nr Cénac

Clean site with good pool near Dordogne.

Bel Ombrage sits in a pretty location by the little River Céou, with a beach onto a backwater which is safe and clean for bathing. There are 180 well shaded, flat grass pitches of good size, marked out by trees and bushes. Two very modern toilet blocks are kept clean, with laundry, disabled and baby facilities. The site boasts a very good pool complex, but lacks a bar or restaurant, though soft drinks and ice-creams are sold by the pool and a bread van calls each morning. It is a short walk to the village of St Cybranet, where there are restaurants and a well stocked store. Tennis courts are close by and canoeing and other excursions can be booked at reception. Bel Ombrage is situated very close to Domme and Castelnaud, and would make an ideal base for touring the Dordogne area.

Directions: Take the D57 from Vézac towards Cénac. After St Cybranet, the site is a short distance on the left.

Charges 1993:
-- Per pitch Ffr 36.00; adult 22.00; child 14.00; electricity 15.00.

Open:
1 June - 5 Sept.

Address:
24250 St Cybranet.

Tel:
53.28.34.14.

Reservations:
Write to site.

2410 Camping-Caravaning Le Moulinal, Biron

Spacious, attractive site with lake, developed around former watermill of Château Biron.

Not only does Le Moulinal provide a good base for exploring the southern Dordogne, but it has extensive wooded grounds to explore with picnic areas. There are 200 pitches of 100 sq.m. min, of which all have electricity. They are level, grassy and well drained with views over the lake. The sanitary facilities have been built to harmonise with the surroundings and provide mostly British toilets, washbasins, some in cabins, and hot showers. Good supply of hot water for washing up sinks and laundry 2 washing machines and dryer. Facilities for the handicapped and babies.

The 5-acre lake with sandy beach is suitable for swimming and boating (canoes available) and fishing. Shop. Bar/restaurant serving good meals (including 4 course menu enfant!) open mid-May - end Sept, plus a snack bar/takeaway on the other side of the lake. A rustic children's play area on grass overlooks the lake. Leisure facilities include tennis, volleyball, table tennis, archery, fishing, canoeing, handicrafts. Excursions organised on foot, on horseback or by bicycle and accompanied if wished and entertainment in high season. There is a new, large, heated swimming pool with jacuzzi and children's pool. Tents, chalets, bungalows and caravans for hire. Popular with tour operators. The site is now run as a `Club de Vacances' - all visitors must pay a small membership fee in return for access to a wide variety of activities.

Directions: Using the D104 Villéreal to Monpazier road, 9 km from Villéreal, take the D53 south to Biron (3 km). Continue to follow the D53 to Lacapelle Biron (4½ km - the D53 becomes the D150 on crossing the regional boundary before reaching Lacapelle Biron). Site is signposted to west from Lacapelle Biron on the D255. From D911 Fumel - Villeneuve road take D162 and after 6½ km, turn right at sign for Lacapelle Biron.

Charges 1994:
-- Per unit incl. 2 persons Ffr. 115.00; extra person (over 4 yrs) 32.00; child (under 4) 26.00; mandatory Club membership (all persons over 2 yrs) 4.00.
-- Less in low season.

Open:
2 April - 17 Sept.

Address:
24540 Biron.

Tel:
53.40.84.60.
FAX: 53.40.81.49.

Reservations:
Made with deposit (Ffr 250) and, in high season only, fee (150)

2408 Le Moulin de David, Gaugeac, Montpazier

Secluded valley site with pool, on south west of the Dordogne.

Owned and run by a French family who continually seek to improve it, this pleasant little site is one for those who enjoy peace, away from the hustle and bustle of larger sites closer to the main Dordogne attractions, yet it is sufficiently close for them to be accessible. Set in 14 ha. of wooded countryside, it has 100 all-electric pitches, split into 2 sections; 35 below the central reception complex, in a shaded situation, and 65 above on partly terraced ground with varying degrees of shade. Spacing is good and there is no crowding. The site has been attractively planted with a pleasing variety of shrubs and trees. The two sanitary blocks (one in each part of the site) are reasonably good, with showers, washbasins in cabins and toilets and a washroom for the disabled in the lower block doubles as a baby room. Dishwashing and laundry sinks are adequate and there is now a laundry room.

The reception block embraces a restaurant (doubles as games and TV room), bar with shaded patio and takeaway. Good shop. 2 swimming pools, one for small children and the other for adults and older children; also a concrete sun terrace. Between these and the upper site is a children's play area and a small lake. Some organised events and games for adults and children. Boules. Half-court tennis. Table tennis (but bring own bats). Volleyball. Library. Trampoline. Bicycle hire. Money exchange. Tents, mobile homes and caravans for hire; one tour operator has 20 pitches at present. Delightful wooded walk via long distance footpath (GR 36) to Biron Château, about 2-3 km distance. The bastide town of Montpazier is also walkable.

Directions: Site is just south off the Montpazier - Villeréal road (D2), about 2 km. west of Montpazier.

Charges 1994:
-- Per pitch Ffr. 39.00; person 29.00; child (under 2 yrs) free; electricity 3A 17.00, 5A 21.00.

Open:
Mid-May - end-Sept.

Address:
Gaugeac,
24540 Montpazier.

Tel:
53.22.65.25.

Reservations:
Advisable for Jul/Aug. with Ffr. 250 deposit plus fee (85).

4701 Moulin du Périé - see editorial report opposite
This site has asked to appear out of sequence because of the advertisement above.
It would otherwise have appeared on page 39 in Lot-et-Garonne.

2409 Camping Soleil Plage, Vitrac, nr Sarlat
Spacious site with enviable location beside the Dordogne.

The site is situated in one of the most attractive sections of the Dordogne Valley, right on the riverside. It is divided into two sections -one section of 56 pitches has its own toilet block and lies adjacent to the reception, bar, shop and restaurant complex, which is housed in a renovated Peregourdine farmhouse. It is also close to a small sandy river bank and canoe station, where canoes and kayaks can be hired for down-river trips or transport up-river for a paddle back. Near the reception area is a new swimming pool, paddling pool, tennis court and minigolf course, and a bar housing weekly discos in season, and other indoor events, although most activities take place on the restaurant forecourt.

The larger section of the site (124 pitches) is about 250 metres from the reception area, and offers river bathing from a sizeable pebble bank. All pitches are bounded by hedges and are of good size, and in this section there are a few giant pitches for large families. Open air table tennis tables, a volleyball court and a children's playground (overdue for renovation) occupy part of a large central recreation space. Sanitary facilities are provided by two blocks, one very modern and, in contrast, an old block which, for example, has men's partitioned basins in the open. Generally there are ample showers and washbasins in private cabins, but WCs are a bit thin on the ground. Water can be very hot in the dishwashing sinks in the old block. Takeaway. Washing machine. TV room. Volleyball. The site is becoming increasingly popular, though in late August it begins to empty. Reservations are advised for peak weeks.

Directions: Site is 8 km south of Sarlat. Take the D704 and it is signposted from Montfort castle. Coming from the west on the D703, take the first right turn 1 or 2 km. after the bridge at Vitrac-Port, and follow the signs.

Charges 1994:
Per person 28.50 Ffr; child (5-14 yrs) 20.00; pitch 42.00; local tax 1.00 (over 10s) in high season; electricity (3A) 15.00.
-- Less 20% outside 20/6 - 1/9.

Open:
1 April - 30 Sept. (full services 1/6-15/9)

Address:
Vitrac, 24200 Sarlat.

Tel:
53.28.33.33.
FAX: 53.29.36.87.

Reservations:
Made for exact dates: min. 1 week with deposit and fee; send for booking form.

4701 Moulin du Périé, Sauveterre-la-Lémance, Fumel
Immaculate, pretty little site tucked away in rolling wooded countryside.

Despite a largely Dutch and English clientele, and Dutch ownership, this site achieves its aim of preserving a French atmosphere, from the warm welcome of a drink in the bar on arrival to French cuisine in the courtyard restaurant. The site has some 125 pitches, well spaced and marked on flat grass. Most have good shade, though inevitably pitches on a newer section have less, while trees and shrubs are growing. Grass areas and access roads are kept immaculately clean, as are the three modern, well appointed toilet blocks, which also contain baby and disabled facilities. The attractive main buildings are converted from an old mill and its outhouses. Flanking the courtyard, as well as the restaurant (open air, but covered), are the bar/reception area in which people can meet and keep younger children under supervision (there is even a Lego pit). Small shop selling such essentials as bread, milk, gas, and various other groceries. Snacks and takeaway food are available at the bar. Good small supermarket in the village, with hypermarkets in Fumel. The site has a clean but rather small swimming pool, with a children's pool much the same size. A small lake next to the pool is used for inflatable boats and swimming. Next to this is a large games field for football, volleyball, etc. New 'boulodrome'. Two table tennis tables, a trampoline and a children's playground. The site organises a number of activities on and off site in season, including a weekly French meal and barbecues round the lake. No tour operators, but a few tents and a caravan are for hire. Many clients return again and again, so it is advisable to book early.

Directions: Sauveterre-la-Lémance lies by the Fumel - Périgueux (D710) road, midway between the Dordogne and Lot rivers. From the D710, cross the railway line, straight through the village and turn left (northeast) at the far end on to a minor road. Site is 2 km. up this road.

Charges 1994:
Per person Ffr 28.50; child (under 7 yrs) 14.00; pitch and car 41.00; extra car 7.00; animal 20.00; electricity (6A) 15.00.
-- Less 25-50% outside 15/6-31/8 for stays of over 7 days.

Open:
April - Sept

Address:
Sauveterre-la-Lémance, 47500 Fumel.

Tel:
53.40.67.26.
FAX: 53.40.62.46.

Reservations:
Advisable for Jul/Aug.

3301 Camping de la Dune, Pyla-sur-Mer, nr Arcachon

Site with good pool and other amenities separated from sea by well known giant dune.

La Dune is a good example of a busy French 3-star family site. It is an informal, friendly, lively site and although the amenities are not luxurious, they are comprehensive and serve their purpose well. From its situation at the foot of the enormous dune you can reach the beach either by climbing over the dune (a ladder goes up nearly to the top) or driving round, or you can use the free medium-size swimming pool at the far end of the site. The marked-out pitches, which vary somewhat in size, are on undulating ground, about half in a pinewood with some shade, and the remainder in sun (1,000 bushes for hedging were planted in 1992). Nearly half are caravan pitches with electricity, water and drainaway. There are now three new, well equipped sanitary blocks in addition to the existing one which has been refurbished with roomy showers and washbasins en-suite. They should be a good provision with WCs of different types, individual basins with many in private cabins (with H&C) and a good supply of free hot showers. Several small shops of different types. Pleasant little bar and restaurant with takeaway also (opens June, all other facilities open all season). Tennis. Minigolf. Riding. Open-air cinema opposite. Organised sports, tournaments etc. mid-June to end Aug. Children's playground. Mobile homes and chalets for hire.

Directions: Site entrance is off the D112 coast road about 6 km. south of Pilat-Plage.

Charges 1993:
-- Per unit incl. 2 persons: with tent Ffr 80.00 - 95.00; with caravan incl. electricity and water 90.00 - 115.00; extra person 20.00; extra child (under 7) 10.00; extra car 25.00; dog 5.00; local tax (over 18s) 1.10.
-- 1994 prices similar.

Open:
1 May - 4 Oct.

Address:
33260 Pyla-sur-Mer.

Tel:
56.22.72.17

Reservations:
Made for min. 1 week with 25% deposit and fee (Ffr. 110). .

● Safe bathing in camp swimming pool or from beach over the dune

● Close to Bassin d'Arcachon, ideal for sailing, and to the Atlantic Ocean, with vast beaches of fine sand

● Wide range of amenities available on site

● Caravan pitches with electricity, water and drainaway

CAMPING DE LA DUNE
33260 ROUTE DE BISCAROSSE
PYLA-SUR-MER
LA TESTE
Close to the famous Dune du Pilat, the highest in Europe, and to the forests of the Landes

3302 Camping de Fontaine-Vieille, Andernos-les-Bains, nr Arcachon

Large site on east side of Bassin d'Arcachon with swimming pool and frontage to Bassin.

Fontaine-Vieille is a large well established site with over 850 pitches on flat grassy ground, some with lovely views, in the residential area of the small town of Andernos. The site stretches along the edge of the Bassin d'Arcachon under light woodland. Pitches are individual ones marked by stones in the ground, 540 with electricity. The several sanitary blocks, of rather unusual design, provide an adequate number of hot showers (perhaps on the small side), washbasins, some in private cabins and a proportion of British WCs. All the blocks are being refurbished (on a rota basis) to a high standard in terms of fittings. Maintenance and cleaning when seen in July appeared to be very good.

A beach runs along the Bassin which can be used for boating when the tide is in. When it is out, it is sand and mud but they claim that bathing in the channels is still possible. On site there is also an unheated 15 x 12 m. swimming pool, open from late May, plus paddling pool (charged for - Ffr. 70 leisure card for entire stay). Self-service shop, bar with terrace and restaurant with takeaway also (all from first half of June - town shops, etc. near). 4 tennis courts. TV room. Children's play area. Cinema (English films). Washing machines. Boats, sailboards and bicycles for hire. Organised sports. As good a value site as you will find round the Bassin. No tour operators or mobile homes when seen. Two stations for camping cars.

Directions: Turn off D3 at south end of Andernos towards Bassin at camp sign.

Charges 1994:
-- Per unit with 2 persons Ffr. 56.00 - 75.00, acc. to season; extra person 12.00 -16.00; child (2-7 yrs) 10.00 - 12.00; extra tent or car 5.00 - 7.00; electricity 16.00 - 20.00; local tax 1.10.

Open:
15 May - 19 Sept

Address:
33510
Andernos-les-Bains.

Tel:
56.82.01.67

Reservations:
Made for any length with deposit and fee.

Thinking of camping or caravanning at home?
Remember the GOOD CAMPS GUIDE - BRITISH ISLES

3303 Airotel de l'Océan, Lacanau-Océan, nr Bordeaux
Pinewood site with swimming pools close to Atlantic beach.

This site has some 550 pitches, all under the tall trees of a pinewood and on very sandy soil - caravans often have to be installed by tractor. Plots are numbered and marked and some are now separated by newly planted hedges, mostly on a slight slope in either direction. There are 200 electrical connections available. The 6 toilet blocks are in modern style with washbasins in private cabins with free hot water and free controllable hot showers with 2 taps; the hot water supply is claimed to be particularly good here. Toilets are in 4 separate blocks; 5 continental WCs to every 1 British. The total provision and maintenance are probably adequate, if somewhat hard pressed in high season. Facilities for the disabled. The sandy beach (partly naturist) is 800 m. away, the first half easy but the second part quite heavy going over the dunes. On site are two swimming pools both of 100 sq.m., not heated. Supermarket, general shop and bar/restaurant (1/6 - 15/9). Takeaway. Tennis. Table tennis. Children's playground. TV room. Amusement machines. 7 washing machines. Large caravans and bungalows for hire. Special barbecue area. Lacanau-Océan has many weekend visitors from Bordeaux.

Directions: Site is on the north side of Lacanau-Océan; follow signs in town.

Charges 1993:
-- Per unit with up to 3 persons: tent Ffr. 110.00, caravan or trailer tent 120.00; electricity 20.00; small tent pitch with 1 person 80.00; extra person 25.00; extra car or tent 20.00; m/cycle or dog 15.00; local tax 1.10 per person (over 10 years).
-- Less 30% in low season.
Open:
1 May - 30 Sept.
Address:
33680 Lacanau-Océan.
Tel:
56.03.24.45.
FAX: 57.70.01.87.
Reservations:
Made Sat. to Sat. only with large deposit (Ffr. 500) and booking fee (120).

3305 Camping Les Ourmes, Hourtin
Conveniently situated site close to lake, providing good value.

Situated only 500 m. from the largest fresh water lake in France, only 10 minutes drive from the beach and with its own pool, this is essentially a holiday site. Pitches, marked but in most cases not actually separated, are situated amongst tall pine trees giving good shade. There are 300 pitches in total, of which some have electricity. There is a medium sized swimming pool with paved sunbathing area and separate large `leisure area' including a children's play area, volleyball and basketball courts and table tennis tables (under cover). There is an evening entertainment programme, TV room, games room, bar/snack bar (serving snacks and takeaway meals) and a shop. Sanitary facilities in three purpose built blocks are of a good standard with free hot showers (with hooks, shelf but no separated dressing area), some washbasins in cabins and British type WCs. This site had a busy, cosmopolitan feel, with visitors of many different nationalities when we visited. Although not the most luxurious site in the area, it seems to offer good value. Watersports on lake.

Directions: Follow Route du Lac from the town centre and site is signposted.

Charges 1994:
-- Per unit incl. 2 persons Ffr. 82.00; extra person (over 2 yrs) 14.00; extra small tent or extra car 10.00; electricity 6A 18.00; local tax (over 10) 1.10.
Open:
1 April - 30 Sept.
Address:
Av. du Lac, 33990 Hourtin.
Tel:
56.09.12.76.
FAX: 56.09.23.90.
Reservations:
Write to site for details.

3304 Camping-Caravaning Int. Les Viviers, Claouey, nr Arcachon

Large site on the peninsular of Cap Ferret, with frontage to the Bassin d'Arcachon.

Les Viviers is a pleasant pinewood site covering a large area, divided by sea water channels and lakes which have been developed to form a positive feature of the site. Sluice gates allow the water level to be maintained so that bathing from the sandy beach, fishing and use of non-powered boats is possible within the site (swimming instructor/lifeguard).

There are 1,100 numbered pitches, some in more open situation than others, level and grassy (sandy), with pinewood shade and electrical connections in all parts. There are twelve toilet blocks, the largest four of which have recently been completely and stylishly rebuilt to a high standard and the others refurbished. They have British WCs, washbasins with shelf and mirror (some in cabins) and have free hot water in these and the showers and sinks. A commercial area near the entrance provides shops, restaurant, bar, takeaway and other facilities (probably from early June - early Sept.), with a little train (Petit TGV), a feature of the site, running in the high season. General room. Cinema. Disco. Minigolf. Children's play area. Sauna, solarium. Sports organiser. Bicycle hire. Motorcaravan service point. Washing machines and dryers. The Atlantic beaches are only ten minutes run away so, with the Bassin d'Arcachon (tidal), there are good facilities for all watersports activities.

Directions: Site entrance is on D106 road 1 km. south of Claouey.

Charges 1994:
-- Per unit, with up to 3 persons Ffr. 75.00 - 139.00 with tent, 80.00 - 149.00 with caravan, if booked in advance; extra person (over 2 yrs) 21.00; local tax (over 7 yrs) 1.10; extra car or boat 22.00; dog 13.00; electricity (6A) 21.00.

Open:
1 May - 30 Sept.

Address:
Claouey,
33950 Lège-Cap Ferret.

Tel:
56.60.70.04.
FAX: 56.60.76.14.

Reservations:
Made for min.
1 week, w/end
- w/end, with
deposit and fee.

3308 Camping de la Barbanne, St. Emilion, nr Libourne

Satifactory, friendly site in fine wine region 40 km. east of Bordeaux, with swimming pool.

La Barbanne takes some 160 units on flat grass - older parts have tarred access roads, a degree of shade, electricity and generally pleasant surroundings; newer parts are on a rather dusty field with no electricity, although shade is developing as the trees which have been planted grow. Campers find their own space (pitches are not marked yet), so there could be a rather undignified scramble on occasion to find something in the old part. The site has a good, larger new toilet block in modern style with all British WCs, 6 of the washbasins in private cabins and all with free hot water, and fully controllable hot showers at one end of the newer meadow. The old block with half continental WCs and no private washing cabins is less satisfactory. Small, unheated swimming pool is on site. Grill room and bar July/Aug. to eat there or take away. 2 tennis courts. Volleyball. Table tennis. Bicycle hire. Minigolf. Fishing on site. Some mobile homes for hire.

Directions: Site is 3 km. north of St Emilion on the road to Lussac. St Emilion itself bars caravans so approach the site by taking the D243 from Libourne or from Castillon on the D936 via D130/D243.

Charges 1994:
-- Per adult Ffr. 20.00; child (under 7) 11.00; pitch 24.00; electricity (6A) 15.00.

Open:
1 April - 30 September.

Address:
33330 St. Emilion.

Tel:
57.24.75.80.

Reservations:
Made for min. 4 days without deposit.

3306 Camping Palace, Soulac-sur-Mer, nr Royan

Large uncrowded site close to beach, south of Royan.

This big, flat site has good-sized individual pitches regularly laid out. Those for tents are on very sandy ground, but those for caravans are on hardstandings, all amongst tall pines providing good shade with electricity available. Reservations are made for all and would be needed to make sure of finding a place in the main season. There are eight small, separate toilet blocks with facilities in private cabins and a wait could be expected at peak times. They have British WCs and the washbasins are gradually being converted from cold to hot water; free hot showers are preset and chain-operated and water does not run on. English spoken. It is a more formal site than no. 3307. A wide beach is 400 m. from the site gates and bathing, said not to be dangerous in normal conditions, is controlled by the site's lifeguards. However, the site now has its own smallish swimming pool with lifeguards, which is attractively set in a part grass, part tiled area with its own facilities, etc. Self-service shop, butcher, fish and general shops (mostly 1/6-15/9). Restaurant (May-15/9). Bar with dancing on Sats. until 12. Tennis. Supervised children's playground with paddling pool. Programme of sports, entertainments and excursions for adults and children from 15/6. Washing machines. Treatment room; doctor will call.

Directions: Site is 1 km. south of Soulac and well signposted. The shortest and simplest way is via the ferry which runs from Royan across the Gironde estuary to the Pointe de Grave, but this is quite unreasonably expensive with a caravan. Alternatively make the trip via Bordeaux.

Charges 1993:
-- Per person (over 3 yrs) Ffr. 27.00 plus local tax (over 10 yrs) 1.20; caravan pitch incl. water/electricity 67.00; tent pitch 50.00.

Open:
Easter - 30 Sept.

Address:
B.P. 33,
Bd. Marsan de Montbrun,
33780 Soulac-sur-Mer.

Tel:
56.09.80.22.
FAX: 56.09.84.23.

Reservations:
Made for min. 1 week with deposit.

On the Côte d'Argent, Gironde.
Sea, Sun and Woodland.

CAMPING PALACE
★ ★ ★ ★
33780 SOULAC sur MER Tel: (56) 09.80.22

Supermarket, Restaurant and Bar
Large Pitches
Supervised Children's Amusements
Evening Entertainments

Reservations Advisable – write for a booking form

Please make us aware of your experiences at these or other sites.
See Readers' Reports on page 181

3307 Camping-Caravaning L'Amelie Plage, Soulac-sur-Mer
Relaxed, wooded site south of Royan with direct access to the beach.

Amelie is a large family site in pine woods bordering a wide sandy beach where bathing is supervised only in season, but is said not to be dangerous. A popular site with continentals, there are no British tour operators. It is divided into two sections providing a total of 527 pitches of about 100 sq.m. The main section with the shop and bar provides a wide choice of pitches due to the undulating nature of the site. Some are on level ground, others on terraces and all are well shaded and fairly accessible (access roads are windy and narrow in some places). The newer section, bordering the beach, has more sun and rather more sandy pitches. The five toilet blocks are of reasonable standard but could be under pressure at peak times. British seatless toilets, rather less in total compared to showers and basins. The cabins with basins are rather small but adequate, chain operated warm showers. Well stocked self service shop. Pizzeria/snackbar/restaurant with takeaway. Entertainment in season. Children's play area. Table tennis. Boules. Barbecue area. Telephones. Well equipped laundry van near reception. Riding and tennis nearby. Caravans for hire.

Directions: Site is 4½ km from Soulac-sur-Mer in village of L'Amelie Plage, signed from the D101. Short stretch of poorly made up road before reception.

Charges 1993:
-- Per unit incl. 1 or 2 persons Ffr 69.50; extra person 13.00; extra tent or car 10.00; dog 5.00; visitor 10.00; electricity (4A) 17.50, (6A) 20.00, (10A) 23.00; local tax 1.10 (over 10s).
-- Less outside 15/6-5/9.

Open:
Easter - Oct.

Address:
33780 Soulac-sur-Mer.

Tel:
56.09.87.27/56.09.85.26.
FAX: 56.73.64.26.

Reservations:
Necessary in high season and made with deposit (Ffr. 340) and fee (60).

4001 Airotel Le Boudigau, Labenne-Océan, nr Bayonne
Pinewood site close to beach 12 km. north of Bayonne.

Between the Landes and the Basque country, this site is well placed for some interesting excursions as well as being close to a wide sandy beach. This is 500 m. on foot from one side of the site and rather longer by car (car park available) and includes an area for naturists. The site has a good swimming pool (16 x 8 m.) The 320 numbered pitches are all covered by pines and of very fair size with young shrubs planted to define pitch area. Although the terrain is basically sandy, most pitches have to have a hard core, flat or slightly sloping. About half have electricity. Sanitary installations consist of two identical blocks for basins and toilets, in standard modern style, with a further small unit at one end of the site. About 3 British to 1 continental WCs, wash- basins in good cabins with free hot water; 40 hot, pre-set showers (no shelf) in a separate block. At entrance and open to all are a well stocked supermarket, snack bar/restaurant (open 15/6), separate bar and soundproofed disco. Cinema weekly. Washing machines and dryers. TV room. Table tennis. Minigolf. Amusement machines. Children's play area. Entertainment in season. Folk music. Bicycle hire. Mobile homes, caravans and bungalows to let. Used by a tour operator.

Directions: Turn off N10 at Labenne for Labenne-Océan and site is on right in village. From the north, join N10 via St. Geours de Maremne.

Charges 1994:
-- Per person Ffr 15.00; pitch 24.00 - 64.00, acc. to season; local tax: adult 1.10, child (10-18 yrs) 0.55; animal 10.00; electricity (3A) 16.00.

Open:
late May - late Sept.

Address:
40530 Labenne-Océan.

Tel:
59.45.42.07.
FAX: 59.45.77.76.

Reservations:
Made for any length with deposit (25%) and booking fee (Ffr. 130).

4002 Camping Les Chênes, Dax

Well kept and attractive site on outskirts of busy spa town.

Dax is not a place that springs at once to mind as a holiday town but, as well as being a spa, it promotes a very comprehensive cultural programme of events such as concerts, special shows, 'courses landaises', corridas etc. during the season. This site is very pleasantly situated on the edge of town amid parkland and close to the river; walks available - or a fitness track with exercise points.

A number of the 250 pitches are occupied by French seasonal caravans or persons taking a thermal course but they say they should always be able to find you a space somewhere. One part has tall trees, the rest is open. The pitches are of two types: good-sized 'boxes' with surrounding hedges which include electricity, and others on open ground where electricity is also available. The central toilet block is of good quality and should be large enough, with one British to two continental WCs, washbasins all in cubicles with curtain, having shelf, mirror and free hot water and a good supply of pre-set, free hot showers with pushbutton or chain. Facilities for the disabled. Many electrical connections. Shop and hot takeaway food (1 May-30 Sept.). Good restaurant under same ownership adjacent with one cheap menu each day. TV room. Caravans, mobile homes and studio for 4 persons to rent. This is a very reliable site, particularly suitable for adults (or those with older and more independent youngsters). A 'centre thermal' is to be constructed at the site for 1994.

Directions: Site is west of town on south side of river, signposted after main river bridge and at many junctions in town (Bois de Boulogne).

Charges guide:
-- Per pitch incl 1 or 2 persons and electricity Ffr. 75.00, pitch with water and drainage also 87.00; extra person 16.00; child (under 7) 8.00; animal 6.00; local tax 1.10.
-- Less in low season.

Open:
1 April - 31 Oct.

Tel:
58.90.05.53.

Reservations:
Not made.

see advertisement with
Eurosol on page 36

4005 Camping Le Col Vert, Vielle-Saint-Girons, nr Castets

Site with long frontage to a good lake for water sports.

This extensive site stretches right along the Lac de Léon for 1 km. on a narrow frontage which makes it particularly suitable for those who want to practise water sports such as sailing and windsurfing. Bathing is also possible; the lake bed shelves gently making it easy for children and the camp has a supervised beach, sailboarding courses are arranged and there are some boats and boards for hire. The site has now added a heated swimming pool (also supervised) with sunbathing area.

The 500 pitches are all flat and covered by light pinewood, most with good shade. They are of around 100 sq.m., only partly separated, some 50 with water and electricity. The four toilet blocks, of different types and ages but nearly all renovated to the same standards, are good average rather than luxurious, but the total supply is good. They have mostly British WCs, washbasins in private cabins or cubicles with free hot water and free hot showers (now in all blocks) with pre-set hot water (found on the cool side) with pushbutton. There are washing-up sinks mainly with cold water but with hot tap to draw from. There is a range of facilities on site including shops, sports area with tennis and volleyball, a fitness centre and workshops, and sauna and solarium. A terraced bar/restaurant is by the lake (open to all). Simple hot takeaway food service. TV room. Table tennis. Amusement·machines. Washing machines (4), dryer and dishwasher. Children's playground. Minigolf. 2 jogging tracks. Riding nearby. Much 'animation' in season: children's games, tournaments, etc. by day and dancing or shows evenings. Deposit boxes. Chalets for hire.

Directions: Roads to lake and site lead off the D652 St. Girons - Léon road.

Charges 1994:
-- Per pitch incl. 2 persons Ffr 125.00 - 175.00, acc. to area and unit; extra person 30.00; child (under 7 yrs) 25.00; local tax (July/Aug. only) 1.10, child 0.55; car 11.00; electricity (6A) 18.00, (10A) 30.00.
-- Less 10% - 50% (excl. electricity) outside 10/7 - 21/8.
-- Outside 2/7 - 27/8, pay 2 weeks and get 3rd free.

Open:
Easter - mid-Nov.

Address:
Lac de Léon,
40560 Vielle-Saint-Girons.

Tel:
58.42.94.06.

Reservations:
Made for any length with £27 deposit and £20 fee per week booked.

see advertisement in
previous colour section

4003 Les Pins du Soleil, St. Paul lès Dax, nr Dax

Family orientated site with swimming pool close to spa town of Dax.

This site will appeal to families, particularly those with younger children who prefer to be some way back from the coast within easy reach of shops, cultural activities, etc. and well placed for touring the area. Dax is a busy spa town with many attractions - Les Pins du Soleil is actually at St. Paul lès Dax, some 3 km. from Dax itself. The site has 140 good sized pitches of which 100 have electricity and drainage. Although new, the site benefits from being developed in light woodland so there is a fair amount of shade from the many small trees.

An attractive, medium sized swimming pool has a surrounding sunbathing area. The modern sanitary facilities include free hot showers with dressing area, washbasins with H&C, British style WCs and facilities for the handicapped. Children's playground. Volleyball. Table tennis. Laundry facilities. Bus to thermal baths. Caravans and bungalows to let. There is a takeaway, small supermarket and a bar on site, but no restaurant (there are many in Dax).

Directions: Approaching from west on N124, avoid bypass and follow signs for Dax and St. Paul. Almost immediately turn right onto D954 and site is a little further along on the left. It is also well signposted from the town centre.

Charges 1994:
-- Per pitch incl. 2 persons without electricity Ffr. 72.00, with electricity (4A), water and drainage 105.00; extra person 18.00; child (under 7 yrs) 10.00; animal 6.00; extra car 8.00; local tax 1.10, child (4-10 yrs) 0.55.

Open:
6 April - 30 October.

Address:
40990 St. Paul lès Dax.

Tel:
58.91.37.91.

Reservations:
Are made with deposit (25% of charges), fee (Ffr. 60) and compulsory insurance (18 per week).

4004 Camping La Paillotte, Azur, nr Soustons

Good lakeside site with an individual atmosphere.

La Paillotte, in the Landes area of southwest France, is a site with a character of its own. The camp buildings (reception, shop, restaurant, even sanitary blocks) are all Tahitian in style, circular and constructed from local woods with the typical straw roof (and layer of waterproof material underneath). Some are now being replaced but still in character. It lies right by the edge of the Soustons lake, 1½ km. from Azur village, with its own sandy beach. This is particularly suitable for young children because the lake is shallow and slopes extremely gradually. For boating the site has a small private harbour where your own non-powered boat of shallow draught can be kept. Sailing, windsurfing (with lessons) and rowing boats and pedaloes for hire. The Atlantic beaches with their breakers are 10 km. Alternatively the site has two swimming pools.

All pitches at La Paillotte are marked-out individual ones and usually shady. New shrubs and trees have been planted. Pitches vary in price according to size, position and whether they are equipped with electricity, water, etc. No dogs are accepted. The circular rustic-style sanitary blocks are rather different from the usual camp site installations. They have British WCs or free hot showers in the central enclosed positions, then individual washbasins with free hot water in partly enclosed positions. On the outside are some washing-up sinks with hot water, plenty of places to hang things and flat surfaces. Separate children's block. They seem quite large enough. Self-service shop. Good restaurant, partly self-service. Takeaway. Bar. Organised sports, games and activities for children and adults. TV room. Table tennis. Amusement room with juke box. Library. Treatment room. Bicycle hire. Mobile homes to let. La Paillotte is an unusual site with its own atmosphere which appeals to many regular clients. Reservation for main season is most advisable. Used by tour operators.

Directions: Coming from north along N10, turn west on D150 at Magescq. From south go via Soustons.

Charges guide:
-- Per unit incl. 2 persons: standard pitch 91.00, with electricity 108.00, with water and electricity 126.00, near lake 147.00 - 165.00; extra person (over 2 yrs) 26.00; extra car 10.00; Local tax (over 10) in July/Aug 1.10.
-- Less 30% 1-27/6 or 20% 28/6-4/7 and 29/8-15/9.

Open:
1 June - 15 Sept. with all services

Address:
Azur, 40140 Soustons.

Tel:
58.48.12.12.
FAX: 58.48.10.73.

Reservations:
Made for Sat. to Sat. only, with deposit and fee.

see advertisement in previous colour section

4006 Camping Eurosol, St. Girons-Plage, Castets, nr Dax
Well shaded site with swimming pool just back from sea.

Eurosol is 500 m. from a sandy beach with supervised bathing and there are also two swimming pools on site. On undulating ground in a pinewood with numerous tall trees, pitches are marked at the corners but have nothing to separate them and so there is little privacy. On flatter ground are some special caravan pitches with their own water and electrical points. On the site generally, about 500 of the 742 pitches are accessible for caravans (with electricity), so in high season space may be more easily obtainable for tents. Reservation is therefore advisable for caravans especially as only half the site is reserved. There are 4 main toilet blocks plus two smaller units. They have British seatless WCs, washbasins in cabins with free hot water, pre-set free hot showers with pushbutton which runs on a bit and hot water to the sinks. Maintenance variable. Self-service shop. Large bar. Snack bar with hot takeaway food in high season. Tennis. Games room with table tennis. Minigolf. Comprehensive recreation programme in July/Aug. with several events each day for children and adults both daytime and evening. Bureau de change. Deposit boxes. Mobile homes for hire.

Directions: To reach site, turn off D42 road at St. Girons towards St. Girons-Plage, and site is on left before coming to beach.

4002 Camping Les Chênes - see page 34

Charges 1993:
-- Per unit incl. 2 persons Ffr 105.00, with electricity 130.00, with water and drainage also 135.00; with 3/4 pers. respectively 155.00, 180.00, 185.00; 5 persons 175.00, 200.00, 205.00; extra person 20.00; local tax 1.10 (child 0.50).
-- Less 20% outside 1/7-25/8.

Open:
1 June - 15 Sept.

Address:
40560 St. Girons-Plage or to address in advertisement when closed.

Tel:
58.47.90.14.
FAX: 58.47.76.74.

Reservations:
Made, normally for min. 1 week with deposit (Ffr. 300) and fee (100); perhaps Sun. to Sun. only in peak 3 weeks.

4007 Camping Lous Seurrots, Contis-Plage, nr Mimizan

Large and shady site close to beach to south of Mimizan.

This site is very close to the sea with a frontage overlooking an estuary, but a walk or drive of about 500 m. to the sandy Atlantic beach. The camp has been extended and now has some 700 pitches, mostly in a pinewood on sandy, undulating ground, numbered and roughly marked out and the majority with good shade. Electrical connections are available over 80% of the area. Sanitary installations consist of 8 rather elderly blocks (with free hot water) spread throughout the site. Some blocks have all British WCs, others nearly all continental; washbasins partly in private cabins but mostly in groups of 5 to 8; controllable hot showers with 2 taps. They appear to comprise an adequate, if fairly basic provision with good maintenance when visited. Reservations are made for high season. Self-service shop. Bar/restaurant with takeaway food also. 2 tennis courts. Washing machines. No British tour operators. There is an attractive, sandy, beach-like area beside the river used for barbeques and picnics which is directly accessible from the site.

Directions: Turn off D652 on D41 to Contis-Plage and site is on left as you reach it.

Charges guide:
-- Per person Ffr. 19.00; child (under 7) 10.00; car 6.00; pitch 23.00; electricity 15.00; dog 5.00; local tax 1.30.
-- Discounts in April (30%), 1/5 - 15/6 (10%) and Sept (10%).
Open:
Easter/1 April - 30 Sept.
Address:
Contis Plage,
40170 St. Julien en Born.
Tel:
58.42.77.97.
FAX: 58.42.86.65.
Reservations:
Are made and must be confirmed in writing with deposit (Ffr. 350).

4009 Camping Lou Broustaricq, Sanguinet, nr Arcachon

Spacious municipal site close to lake to south of Arcachon for families.

This is a good municipal site with some 555 individual pitches on flat ground in light woodland, partly shaded by high trees. Caravan pitches are 110 sq.m. and all have hardstanding, electricity and water, pitches for tents an average of 100 sq.m. A path of about 200 m. leads from the camp to the big lake (no cars this way, but access for cars with boats 2 km.) and it is about 20 km. to Arcachon or Pilat-Plage. The site has 7 toilet blocks with sexes mixed. They have seatless and continental WCs, washbasins in private cabins, free hot water in showers and sinks and a bathroom for the handicapped. They should be a good provision. This is a very reliable site, where there is always a chance of finding space, which has now added an attractive swimming pool complex with sunbathing area. 2 good tennis courts. Minigolf. Table tennis. Children's playground. Commercial centre by entrance includes supermarket and other shops, snack bar and hot takeaway food service, mostly opening mid-June. Mobile homes to rent. It is used by tour operators.

Directions: To reach site, turn to northwest off D46 at camp sign northeast of Sanguinet.

Charges guide:
-- Prices for 27/6-5/9, otherwise in brackets. Per tent incl. 1 or 2 persons Ffr.74.00 (51.50), with 3 or 4 persons 108.00 (68.00); caravan incl. electricity and 1-2 persons 108.00 (56.50), 3-4 persons 136.00 (74.50); motorcaravan with up to 4 persons 98.00 (1-2 persons 56.50, 3-4 persons 74.50); extra person 16.00; animal 8.50.
Open:
All year.
Address:
40460 Sanguinet.
Tel:
58.78.62.62.
FAX: 58.78.66.33.
Reservations:
Made for any length with sizeable booking fee.

Please show reception staff this Guide when you arrive at a site

- it helps them, us and eventually you too

4008 Camping Caravaning Eurolac, Aureilhan, nr Mimizan

Attractively laid out, lakeside site with good sized pitches and pools, 9 km. from sea.

In a peaceful situation by a lake (with a minor road to cross), Eurolac is largely used by families but offers a good choice of activities - bathing or boating in the lake (with sailing school in season), windsurfing (boards for hire), a good riding school on site and organised events for young and old. The Atlantic beaches are 9 km. (for surfing). Butterfly shaped swimming pools were built in 1991.

The terrain is flat, grassy and park-like and divided into 475 numbered pitches of good size with shade from some mature trees, 280 of which have electricity and water connections. The five sanitary blocks give a very reasonable provision, and the newest ones are of particularly good quality with mostly British seatless WCs. Individual basins with shelf and mirror in private cabins. Free hot water in basins and showers, and can be drawn from tap for washing-up. Showers are chain-operated, and water does not run on. During the main season there is `animation', with various activities and events being organised for both adults and children. Shop (20/6-10/9), bar/restaurant (April - early Sept.) and takeaway. General room with TV, bar and some special evenings; dancing twice weekly in season. Jacuzzi. Tennis courts. Games room. Table tennis. Volleyball. Basketball. Minigolf. Children's playground. Creche. Bicycle hire. Treatment room. Washing machines. Chalets, caravans and bungalows to let. Motorcaravan station. No pets taken July/Aug. Some tour operators (tents and static vans). A very popular site, the facilities could become stretched in high season. Good English is spoken.

Directions: Turn north off D626 at camp sign 3 km. east of Mimizan-Bourg.

Charges 1994:
-- Per unit incl. 2 persons Ffr 49.00 - 105.00, with electricity 59.00 - 122.00; extra person 20.00; extra car 10.00; boat 15.00.

Open:
12 May - 30 September.

Address:
Aureilhan,
40200 Mimizan.

Tel:
58.09.02.87.
FAX: 58.09.41.89.

Reservations:
Any period with 30% deposit and Ffr. 105 fee.

see advertisement in
next colour section

N4012 Domaine Naturiste Arnaoutchot, Vielle-Saint-Girons

Large naturist site with extensive facilities and direct access to beach.

Although `Arna' is a large site, its layout in the form of a number of sections, each with its own character, makes it quite relaxing. These sections amongst the trees and bushes of the Landes provide a variety of reasonably sized pitches, most with electricity, although the hilly terrain means that only a limited number are flat enough for camping cars.

The sanitary facilities include not only the usual naturist site type of blocks with individual British type WCs and communal hot showers, but also a number of tiny blocks with one hot shower, WC and washbasin each in an individual cabin. When seen (June) they were very clean despite our stay coinciding with a period of torrential rain! The facilities, situated centrally, are extensive and of excellent quality. They include a heated, indoor swimming pool, outdoor pool (open 7/6-26/9), sauna, a bar/restaurant, a large supermarket and a range of other shops, mainly built of timber in an attractive style (June - mid-Sept). The site has the advantage of direct access to a large, sandy (mainly naturist) beach, although access from some parts of the site may involve a walk of perhaps 600 - 700 m. The `Arna Club' provides more than 30 activities and workshops (in the main season) including riding, archery, golf, tennis, petanque, swimming, rambling, cycling, sailing school, excursions and special activities for children. TV, video and games rooms. Cinema. Library. Hairdresser. Laundry facilities. Chalets, mobile homes and tents for hire.

Directions: Signposted off the D42 road at Vielle-Saint-Girons.

Charges 1994:
-- Per pitch incl. 2 persons Ffr 66.00 - 132.00, acc. to season; extra person (over 3 yrs) 16.00 - 32.00; extra car 5.50 - 11.00; animal 6.50 - 13.00; leisure club free - 4.50; electricity (3A) 18.00, (6A) 30.00; local tax in high season 1.10.

Open:
11 April - 31 Oct.

Address:
40560 Vielle-Saint-Girons.

Tel:
58.48.52.87.

Reservations:
Made with deposit of £25 and £15 fee.

4701 Moulin de Périé, Sauveterre-la-Lémance, Fumel
This site has asked to be featured out of order - see editorial report and advertisement on pages 26/27.

4702 Camping Les Ormes, Villeréal, nr Villeneuve-sur-Lot
Country site with various amenities, some 35 km. southeast of Bergerac.

This is a smallish site in a quiet country situation where the Dutch owners have developed a number of amenities and which seems to appeal to many British campers and caravanners. The 140 pitches, 110 with electricity, are in various situations. The majority are of standard size on terraces or gently sloping ground in an unshaded field with hedge and tree separations. Some 40 very large pitches are in well shaded woodland, and yet others are unmarked in a remote field. A good toilet block in the main field includes a baby washing room and plentiful washing-up and clothes sinks. Both this and the original central block in the wood, have British WCs, washbasins in cabins with free hot water, shelf and mirror, free hot showers with screening and seat; pre-set water with pushbutton which runs on for a bit. Unit for disabled. Hot water also free for sinks. There is a small lake on site with a good sandy beach which can be used for bathing or boating with inflatables etc; also for fishing (stocked by camp). A small beach bar is open in season and there is also a swimming pool (200 sq.m.). Self-service shop, bar, restaurant, to eat there or takeaway (all perhaps from late May). Tennis. Table tennis. Room for young. TV room. Domestic and wild animals kept. Washing machine. Organised games for children in season. Horse riding. Villeréal, a little town with some atmosphere, is 3 km. away and Montpazier and Monbazillac under 20. Chalets for hire.

Directions: Site is signposted from Villeréal itself on the D676 from Monflanquin and the D255 from Devillac.

Charges 1994:
-- Per person Ffr 23.00; child (under 7) 11.50; pitch 30.00, larger pitch 34.00; electricity 14.00.
-- 30% less outside 20/6-10/9.

Open:
1 April - 30 Sept

Address:
47210
St. Etienne-de-Villeréal.

Tel:
53.36.60.26.

Reservations:
Made for any length with deposit (Ffr. 350).

4703 Castel Camping Château de Fonrives, Rives, Villeréal

Neat, orderly site with swimming pool, in southwest of the Dordogne.

This is one of those very pleasant Dordogne sites set in pretty part-farmed, part-wooded countryside. The park is a mixture of hazelnut orchards, woodland with lake, château (mostly 16th century) and camping areas. Barns adjacent to the château have been tastefully converted - the restaurant particularly - to provide for the reception, the bar, B&B rooms, shop and games areas. The swimming pool is on the south side of this. When visited there were 100 fair sized pitches (average 120 sq.m, all with electricity) but the site reports that there are 100 new ones, all with water and electricity. Those near the woodland receive moderate shade, but elsewhere there is little to be gained from hedges and young trees. All pitches have a rubbish bin, with bottle bins also in places. Some 'wild' camping is possible in one or two areas. The original sanitary block is clean and adequate with free hot water, pushbutton showers and washbasins in well appointed private cabins. The site reports that there are now two additional blocks. The lake has a small beach and can be used for swimming, fishing or boating. Small field set aside by the pool for volleyball and football. Children's play area. Reading room. Minigolf. Plenty of organised activities in season. Some tour operators. Mobile homes and tents for hire.

Charges 1994:
-- Per adult Ffr 28.00; child (under 7 yrs) 17.00; pitch 45.00; electricity 18.00 - 25.00; dog 10.00.
-- Less 20% in May, June and Sept.

Open:
15 May - 30 Sept.

Address:
Rives, 47210 Villeréal.

Tel:
53.36.63.38.

Reservations:
Advisable for Jul/Aug.

Directions: Site is 2 km. NW of Villeréal, on the Bergerac road (D14/D207).

6402 Camping-Caravaning Ametza, Hendaye Plage

Large, spacious site, near the beach and the border with Spain.

Only fully open in the main season, this neat, well laid out site is on sloping terrain, terraced where necessary, giving views of both the sea and the inland Basque countryside. The 320 pitches are on grass, with shade and are well marked, some with hedging. There is a large pool with shower facilities and sun bathing area and a tennis court. It is within walking distance of the beach (700 m). When seen there were no tour operators but some mobile homes. Two well maintained toilet blocks, one of which is new, provide a mixture of seatless British and continental toilets, adequate pre-set hot water, with push button system for showers, not all of which had dividers and shelves and basins in cabins with mirror, shelf, hooks and plug socket. Facilities for the disabled are provided in the new block. Small shop. Bar/restaurant with takeaway dishes. Children's play area. Some organized entertainment. Washing machines.

Charges 1993:
-- Per unit incl. 2 persons Ffr. 84.00; extra person 18.00; child (under 7) 10.00; extra car 6.00; electricity 14.00; 3 services 26.00; local tax 1.00.

Open:
15 June - 15 September.

Address:
64700 Hendaye Plage.

Tel:
59.20.07.05.

Reservations:
Recommended for July/Aug. and made with deposit and Ffr. 24.00 cancellation insurance.

Directions: From Bayonne, use RN10 and D912 Corniche road to Hendaye Plage. Turn left in direction of Hendaye town before beach. Site is immediately on left over railway. From autoroute, take St. Jean-de-Luz (sud) exit.

6401 Europ Camping, St. Jean-Pied-de-Port

Neat, purpose designed site in the foothills of the Pyrénées near the border.

Opened in 1987 with well designed facilities, including a swimming pool, Europ is a quiet, tranquil site, attractively situated with views of mountains and vineyards. It is 2 km. from St. Jean-Pied-de-Port and 20 km. from the Forest of Iraty. The owner has a 4-wheel drive jeep for hire to explore the mountains or the Basque coast close at hand. Family run, the owners offer a friendly welcome. The site is maturing and all 94 pitches (100 sq.m.) are clearly marked and equipped with water, electricity and drainage. The swimming pool is of a reasonable size (20 x 8 m) with a smaller children's pool (4 x 4 m), at present with gravelled surround, and a sauna. The one large, mixed toilet block has pre-set hot water and a good supply of hooks and shelves in the showers, individual washcabins with mirrors and plug sockets, British WCs and separate facilities for the disabled. Covered clothes and washing up sinks and two washing machines and one dryer. Bar and restaurant (all season). Takeaway. Small shop. Children's play area. Volleyball. Petanque. Sauna. Barbecue areas. Car wash area. Telephone. Riding and tennis near. Used by tour operators.

Charges 1993:
-- Per adult Ffr 28.00; child (under 7) 14.00; pitch 39.00; extra car 19.00; dog 10.00; electricity 19.00.

Open:
Easter - end-Oct

Address:
Ascarat, 64220 St. Jean-Pied-de-Port.

Tel:
59.37.12.78 or 59.37.16.29. FAX: 59.37.29.82.

Reservations:
Made in writing with 30% deposit.

Directions: Site is 1 km. northwest of St. Jean-Pied-de-Port in the hamlet of Ascarat and is signposted from the D198 Bayonne road.

6403 Camping Municipal Ur-Alde, St. Palais

Satisfactory site in southwest France, near Pyrénées and Basque country.

Ur-Alde is a flat site by a river and adjoining a sports complex with swimming pool and tennis courts. There are about 50 individual pitches on one side heavily shaded by tall poplars, 25 large special caravan pitches on the other with electricity, water and drainaway, separated by hedges, and some open meadows, not divided up, for the overflow. The toilet block is a good one, with free hot water. No shop. General room with beer/soft drinks bar. Playground. Washing machines. Barbeque.

Charges guide:
-- Prices for July/Aug. otherwise in brackets.
-- Per unit incl. 3 persons: caravan pitch with all services 65.00 Ffr. (45.50), otherwise 60.00 (42.00); tent 40.00 (38.00); extra person 12.00; child 6.00.

Open:
at least 15 June - 15 Sept.

Reservations:
Not made and site can become full 10/7-16/8.

Note: When this site is closed there is a more basic municipal site at Sauveterre-de-Bearne, which is open all year. Camping Municipal du Gave is beside the river, 12 km. north on the D933.

Directions: Site is on eastern edge of town towards Mauléon.

6404 Camping Zelaïa, Ascain, nr St. Jean-de-Luz

Pleasant little site inland from St. Jean-de-Luz.

This is a well kept little site, quietly situated in the Basque country and by the foothills of the Pyrénées, about 10 km. from the sea at St. Jean-de-Luz. There are 170 average-sized, individual pitches with good shade of which 120 have electricity. Two modern, well maintained toilet blocks serve the site; sexes are mixed but there are a few private cabins with bidets for women. There are washbasins with shelf, mirror and cold water, good fully controllable free hot showers, tap to draw off hot water by sinks and British and continental toilets. Own sewage disposal plant. Two washing machines. Only open for a short season, the site can become full at busy times. It has two swimming pools (17 x 8 and 4 x 4 m.). Self-service shop and cooked dishes July/Aug. only. Games room. Volleyball. Children's playground. Some organised activities in season.

Charges guide:
-- Per unit incl. 2 persons 66.00 Ffr.; extra person 15.10; child (under 7 yrs) 9.00; extra car 10.00; m/cycle 5.50; electricity 13.00.

Open:
15 June - 15 Sept.

Address:
64310 Ascain.

Tel:
59.54.02.36, or when closed 59.29.60.09.

Reservations:
Made for any length.

Directions: Site is 3 km. west of Ascain on D4.

6405 Airotel International d'Erromardie, St. Jean-de-Luz
Good seaside site close to some well known Basque resorts.

Airotel Internationsl
d'Erromardie

(St Jean-de Luz)

*General view of camp and
beach*

Sites right by the sea in this region are not all that numerous but this is a good one with only the site access road to cross to reach a beach of fine shingle. It is said to be safe for bathing (some submerged rocks at low tide) although, as usual around here, it is supervised by lifeguards. The beach is public and can be busy at weekends. The site is mainly flat, grassy, and consists of several different parts separated by hedges with little shade. All pitches are now individual ones, with electricity, which mainly adjoin access roads and back onto hedges, etc. so the site does not become overcrowded. The two large sanitary blocks are very satisfactory with washing facilities in private cabins. The newer block, of particularly good quality, has free hot water in all facilities. British WCs. Washbasins with mirrors and shelves in private cabins. Free hot showers, some pre-set with pushbutton, and free hot water for some basins and sinks. Swimming pool. Shop adjoining (from 1/6). Takeaway. Golf near. Caravans and a number of mobile homes for hire. St. Jean-de-Luz, an attractive, lively little seaside resort with plenty of history and character, is a short drive. The more select and sedate Biarritz is about 15 km. as is the Spanish frontier at Hendaye and Behobia. San Sebastian, parts of the Pyrénées, and many charming old Basque villages in the interior can be reached easily on day trips.

Directions: Turn off main N10 north of St. Jean-de-Luz towards sea by sign to `Campings' and `Plage d'Erromardie', then 1 km. to site. From autoroute A63, take exit for St. Jean-de-Luz Nord.

Charges 1993:
-- Prices outside 10/7-28/8 in brackets.
-- Per pitch incl. 2 persons Ffr 100.00 (58.00), incl. electricity 110.00 (72.00), with water also 120.00 (82.00); extra person 20.00 (15.00) (under 5 yrs free); local tax (over 10s) 1.00; extra car 15.00; dog 5.00.

Open:
15 May - 25 Sept.

Address:
64500 St. Jean-de-Luz.

Tel:
59.26.07.74.

Reservations:
Made for foreigners with substantial deposit and small booking fee for periods of at least a week.

6408 Camping Tamaris-Plage, St. Jean-de-Luz

Pleasant, well tended site with individual pitches, close to a beach.

Well outside the town but just across the road from a sandy beach, this well kept, neat, little site has 52 numbered pitches, all with electricity. They are of very good size, but not separated, on slightly sloping ground with some shade. It becomes full for nearly all July and August with families on long stays, so reservation then is advisable. The single new toilet block is of superb quality and unusual design and should be ample provision for the site. It has free hot water in the washbasins and showers (some in private cabins), dishwashing sinks with hot and cold water and facilities for the handicapped. A multi-purpose gym is installed in adjoining buildings (reduced membership for campers) with a sauna and sunbed. Shop (in season) and self-service restaurant with takeaway (both late May - early Sept). General room with TV. Washing machine. Minigolf. Children's playground. 10 bungalows to let.

Directions: Proceed south on N10 and 1½ km. after Guethary take first road on right (before access to the motorway and Mammoth centre commercial) and follow camp signs.

Charges 1993:
-- Per caravan or motorcaravan (100 sq.m. pitch) with electricity, incl. 2 persons Ffr 140.00; tent pitch (80 sq.m.) incl. 2 persons 110.00; extra person (ovr 2 yrs) 25.00; extra car 15.00; local tax 1.50 (over 10 yrs).
-- Less 15% outside 15/7-31/8.

Open:
1 April - 30 Sept.

Address:
Acotz,
64500 St. Jean-de-Luz.

Tel:
59.26.55.90.

Reservations:
Made for longer stays with Ffr. 100 fee; write to site

6406 Camping du Pavillon Royal, Bidart, nr Biarritz

Comfortable, popular camp by a sandy beach with excellent toilet blocks and pool.

Le Pavillon Royal has an excellent situation on raised terrain overlooking the sea, and with good views along the coast to the south and to the north coast of Spain beyond. Beneath the camp - and only a very short walk down - stretches a wide sandy beach. This is the Atlantic with its breakers and a central marked-out section of the beach is supervised by lifeguards. There is also a section with rocks and pools. If the sea is rough, there is a swimming pool (20 x 10 m.) on the camp. The site is divided up into 335 separate pitches, many with electricity, all marked out and many larger than before and levelled. They include some special ones for caravans with electricity, water and drainaway. Much of the camp is in full sun - shade in one part only. Roads are asphalted. No dogs are taken. All sanitary blocks are of the highest quality with mainly British WCs, washbasins in cabins with shelf and mirror, and free hot water in basins, and fully controllable showers, sinks and baby baths; good units for disabled all thoroughly cleaned twice daily. Washing facilities closed at night except for night units. Well stocked shop and restaurant with takeaway food also (open all season). General room. TV room. Games room with table tennis, also usable for films etc. Children's playground. Washing machines and dryers. Sauna. Reservation in high season is advisable.

Directions: Do not go into Bidart, as the camp is on the Biarritz side. Coming from north, keep on main N10 by-passing Biarritz, and then turn sharp back right on last possible road leading to Biarritz. After 600 m. turn left at camp sign (easy to miss). From A63 motorway take C4 exit.

Charges 1993:
-- Per unit incl. 2 persons and electricity Ffr 115.00 - 135.00, with water also 136.00 - 160.00; extra person (over 4 yrs) 17.00 - 20.00; extra car 25.00.

Open:
mid-May - 25 Sept

Address:
64210 Bidart.

Tel:
59.23.00.54.
FAX: 59.23.44.47.

Reservations:
Made for exact dates with deposit and fee.

see advertisement opposite

6407 Castel Camping Le Ruisseau, Bidart, nr Biarritz

Pleasant, busy site with swimming pool, just back from sea, with reasonable charges.

This site, just behind the coast, is about 2 km. from Bidart and 2½ km. from a sandy beach but it does have three swimming pools on the terrain: two (15 x 7 and 12 x 6 m.), both heated, on the main camp and one (18 x 10 m.), with slide, on the newer area opposite. There is also a little lake, where boating is possible, in the area at the bottom of the site which has a very pleasant open aspect and now includes a large play area. Pitches on the main camp are individual, marked-out and of a good size, either on flat terraces or on a slight slope. The terrain is wooded so the great majority of them have some shade. There are 300 here with a further 100 on a second area where shade has developed and which has its own good toilet block. Electrical connections nearly everywhere. The sanitary facilities (unisex) consist of two main blocks and some extra smaller units. They have British and some continental WCs, washbasins in private cabins with free hot water, free hot showers, nearly all pre-set, and are regularly refurbished and maintained. Shop. Large self-service restaurant with takeaway food also, and separate bar with terraces, and TV. 2 tennis courts (free outside July/Aug). Volleyball. Table tennis. Riding from site. TV room. Games room. Minigolf. Small practice golf course. Sauna. Solarium. Children's playground. Washing machine. `Animation' during main season: organised sports during day and evening entertainment twice weekly in season. Bicycle hire. Surf boards to rent. The site is popular with tour operators.

Directions: Site lies east of Bidart on a minor road towards Arbonne. From autoroute take Biarritz exit, turn towards St. Jean-de-Luz on N10, take first left at traffic lights and follow camp signs. When travelling south on N10 the turning is the first after passing the autoroute entry point.

Charges 1994:
-- Per unit incl. 2 persons Ffr 91.00; extra adult 23.00; child (under 7) 11.00; electricity 17.00; dog 6.00; local tax (over 10) 1.50.
-- Less 20% in May, June and Sept.

Open:
25 May - 30 Sept. with all amenities.

Address:
64210 Bidart.

Tel:
59.41.94.50.

Reservations:
Made for exact dates, for min. a week or so in main season, with deposit (Ffr 350), fee (62) and cancellation insurance (18). Total Ffr. 430.

6409 Camping La Chêneraie, Bayonne

Good class site with swimming pool in pleasant situation 8 km. from sea.

A site of good quality in a pleasant setting, La Chêneraie is only 8 km. from the coast at Anglet where there is a long beach and big car park. It also has a medium sized free swimming pool on the site, open July/Aug. and longer if the weather is good, which makes it comfortable base for a holiday in this attractive region. Bayonne and Biarritz are near at hand.

There are distant mountain views from the site which consists of meadows, generally well shaded and divided partly into individual pitches and with some special caravan plots with electricity, water and drainage. In the sloping part of the site, terraces have been created to give level pitches. A wooded area, not used for camping, is available for strolls. The sanitary installations consist of one very large central block of good quality with British toilets and free hot water in washbasins (in private cabins) and in fully controllable hot showers, and 3 smaller units in other parts. Baby baths. Facilities for the handicapped. Shop. General kiosk. Restaurant, with all day snacks service and takeaway. Swimming pool (shop, restaurant and pool mid June - mid Sept.). Good tennis (free outside July/Aug). Small pool for fishing, boating with inflatables, etc. Table tennis. Children's playground. TV room. First aid room. Washing machine and dryer. Fully equipped tents for hire. A good site to know which may have room if you arrive by early afternoon. Popular with tour operators.

Directions: Site is 4 km. northeast of Bayonne just off the main N117 road to Pau. From new autoroute A63 take exit C6 marked `Bayonne St. Esprit'.

Charges 1994:
-- Per person 20.00 Ffr; child (under 7) 12.00, local tax (over 10s) 1.00; pitch 45.00; electricity 18.00.
-- Less 20% outside 1/6-15/9.

Open:
Easter -30 Sept.

Address:
64100 Bayonne.

Tel:
59.55.01.31.
FAX: 59.55.11.17.

Reservations:
Made for min. 1 week with deposit (Ffr. 400) and fee (100).

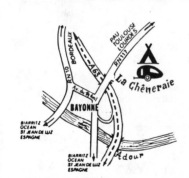

AUVERGNE - Allier

AUVERGNE
Allier - Puy-de-Dôme - Cantal - Haute-Loire

Green, spacious, fresh, clean and beautiful are words which readily come to mind when describing the Auvergne. Definitely a region for those who like nature and the outdoor life, the scenery, plants and wildlife are all remarkable. Walking is perhaps the best way to enjoy the delights of the Auvergne, as the region is criss-crossed with footpaths of varying degrees of difficulty. There are numerous lakes, river gorges and two National Parks to explore. In particular the areas around the Plomb du Cantal and the Puy de Sancy are stunning in their beauty. There are many towns worth exploring - amongst my favourites are rugged St. Flour, classy Vichy and medieval Salers - but best of all is the **fresh air**.

0301 Camping de la Filature, Ebreuil
Small peaceful riverside site with a difference.

Situated near the spa town of Vichy and bordering the Massif Central area, this site provides the opportunity to explore this lesser known and unspoilt area of France known as the Auvergne. Originally developed around a spinning mill (even today the hot water is provided by log burning - note the chimney), the site has an individuality not normally evident in French sites. This is being perpetuated by its new English owners with their artistic flair.

Beside the River Sioule, there are 50 spacious, grassy pitches with some shade from mature fruit trees, all with electricity (3 or 6A). At the time of our visit a rare orchid had been discovered by the river bank and indeed the whole area is a naturalist's paradise. Sanitary facilities, converted from the original buildings, are all individual, opening into an alley way with gaily painted arches. They are not in the same category as some of the new modern units, not very smart, but well cleaned, retiled and they do provide free hot water, French and British toilets, 6 showers and a bathroom, washcabins and hairdrying. River bathing is said to be possible but it may be a little shallow at the height of summer. Fishing facilities (drying room, permits, tackle, etc). Bicycle hire - many tracks for mountain biking near. Riding, canoeing and tennis near. Washing machine and ironing facilities. Bread to order. Takeaway food - traditional French cooking or straight forward English. A site speciality is selling local wine. Minigolf. Table football. Children's play area. Table tennis. Barbecue facilities. Rooms and 3 mobile homes for hire. A few tour operator pitches.

Directions: Site is signposted at exit 12 of the new A71 autoroute to Clermont Ferrand in the direction of Ebreuil. Site lies to west of Ebreuil beside the river.

Charges 1993:
-- Per unit incl. 2 persons Ffr 58.00; extra person (over 10 yrs) 16.00, (under 10 yrs) 10.00; electricity 3A 8.00, 6A 16.00.

Open:
1 April - 30 Sept.

Address:
03450 Ebreuil.

Tel:
70.90.72.01.
FAX: 70.90.74.48.

Reservations:
Made with deposit (Ffr 200 per week of stay or full amount if stay costs less).

DON'T WAIT TO DIE TO COME TO HEAVEN, COME TO THE CAMPING DE LA FILATURE - IN THE AUVERGNE.

Specialities:

- HOT hot water, even in low season.
- CLEAN facilities, even in high season.
- Take-away food and pizza like Mamma makes.
- Spacious plots beside one of the cleanest rivers in Europe; one of France's finest trout rivers.

For information in the U.K., ring Stamford (0780) 55857

Camping de la Filature
03450 Ebreuil
Tel: (010 33) 70 90 72 01
FAX: (010 33) 70 90 79 48

0302 Castel Camping-Caravaning Château de Chazeuil, Varennes sur Allier
Useful night-stop in central France, adjacent to main road.

Although adjacent to the main N7, this site is attractively situated in a large park and traffic noise should be no problem. The site is established around the château with a range of good quality amenities including a new sanitary block with modern fittings and facilities, with provision for the handicapped. A swimming pool is open mid-June to mid-September. Pitches are marked and 60 have electricity (4-10A), with many mature trees providing shade. Reading room. Children's play area. Fitness track (2 km.) in wood. Table tennis. This site should provide a pleasantly relaxing night-stop or a base to explore the Bourbonnais region.

Directions: Site is situated on the eastern side of the main N7, 25 km south of Moulins, almost opposite the D46 turning for St Pourcain.

Charges 1994:
-- Per person Ffr 25.00; child (under 7) 15.00; pitch 20.00; car 18.00; m/cycle 8.00; electricity 18.00.

Open:
1 May - 30 Sept.

Address:
03150 Varennes sur Allier.

Tel:
70.45.00.10.

Reservations:
Made for min. 3 days with Ffr. 300 deposit.

0303 Camping Les Acacias au Bord du Lac, Bellerive, Vichy
Well tended site quite close to town with swimming pool adjacent.

Quietly situated, although on the edge of the town and with few on-site activities, this small site has a well kept and peaceful look and very helpful owners. There are 90 individual pitches with electricity, of good size and separated from each other by neat full hedges. Of these 60% have TV (satellite) and water connections also. The site, which extends to the edge of the river, is in two parts separated by an access road. With a sanitary block (recently renovated) in each part, there should be an ample coverage. They have British seatless and continental toilets, basins in private cabins with free hot water, and a good supply of free hot showers with immediate hot water. No shop but supermarket and restaurants close. TV room with BBC by satellite. Table tennis. Laundry facilities. Vichy itself is a well kept town with select parts, comprehensive sporting facilities and a wide range of entertainment in season. Municipal swimming pool complex, with large open-air and heated covered pool, is a short walk. Small pool with tiled surrounds has been installed on site.

Directions: Site is on the south side of town in the suburb of Bellerive just south of the river; cross river by Pont Bellerive bridge (site is not signed from other bridges), turn left, and follow camp signs.

Charges 1994:
-- Per person Ffr. 20.00 - 25.00; child (under 7 yrs) 10.00 - 13.00; pitch 22.00 - 30.00; car 10.00 - 14.00; electricity (5A) 13.00.

Open:
25 March - 20 Sept.

Address:
03700 Bellerive sur Allier.

Tel:
70.32.36.22 (winter: 70.32.58.48).

Reservations:
Site is full for most of July/Aug but reservations made without deposit.

0304 Camping Champ de la Chapelle, Braize
Very quiet, rural site with large pitches in the 10,500 hectare Forest of Troncais.

This small site is the perfect answer for those who want to get away from it all. With only 80 pitches set in 5.6 hectares, they are large (up to 250 sq.m.) with plenty of shade and open space. The policy is to keep the site small, quiet and unsophisticated. The reward is the wealth of wild life that abounds here - you may see red squirrels, deer, bee-eaters or hoopoes. Of the 80 pitches, 62 have electricity (16A) and water. Only 7 static pitches and no tour operators. The sanitary block is new and well appointed with British toilets. Washbasins are in private cabins, showers are pre-set, pushbutton type. Good dishwashing facilities. Washing machine and dryer. Small snacks kiosk. Bread sometimes available but no shop - supermarket 5 km. Children's play area, volleyball, flipball and petanque. Mountain bike hire. There are are many lakes in the area - one at 5 km. offers fishing, bathing, pedaloes, canoes, sail-boarding, minigolf, volleyball, tennis and, in high season, organised rambles. Horse riding, archery near. The whole area is a paradise for nature lovers, cyclists and walkers. Immediately adjacent to the camp is the Auberge 'Le Rond du Chevreuil'.

Directions: From the N144 Bourges - Montlucon road take the D978A eastward and then the D28 to Braize from where the site is signposted.

Charges 1993:
-- Per unit incl. 2 persons Ffr. 52.00, with electricity, water and 3 persons 74.00; extra person over 5 yrs 10.00, under 5 yrs 5.00.

Open:
Whitsun - 15 Sept.

Address:
03360 Braize.

Tel:
70.06.15.45.

Reservations:
Made for any period with deposit (Ffr. 300) and fee (60).

6302 L'Etang de Flechat, Orcival, nr Clermont-Ferrand

Remote, rural site, yet close enough to some major attractions, with lake bathing.

L'Etang de Flechat takes some finding but a friendly welcome awaits. Set in hilly country, just southwest of the Puy de Dôme itself, it provides a good base for exploring this region, both countryside and town. The 75 pitches are arranged either on hillside terraces or around the lake margins. Most are of good size and shadiness; some 48 have electricity and, although not numbered, are well separated. The one modern toilet block is adequate but not exceptional and includes a laundry room, general TV room and phone kiosk. Free hot water.

The medium sized lake is available for bathing, fishing and boating (pedaloes for hire) and there is a beach with play area next to it so parents can supervise children while using the beach. Drinks terrace off the bar, snack bar (basic menu and lake trout) and takeaway, and reception room overhang the water's edge. Small shops (limited hours only). Children's playground. Table tennis. Some organised activities. One or two caravans and mobile homes plus a chalet for hire. A pleasant, quiet, if somewhat unspectacular site.

Directions:: Site is about 2 km. WNW of Orcival on an unmarked road linking the D555(D27E) Gioux-Orcival road and D74 east out of Rochefort-Montagne.

Charges 1993:
-- Per unit incl. 2 persons Ffr 60.00; extra person 15.00; child (under 5 yrs) 7.00; electricity 15.00; pet 6.00; local tax (adults) 1.00.

Open:
1 May - 15 Sept.

Address:
Orcival, 63210 Rochfort-Montagne.

Tel:
73.65.82.96.
(winter: 50.66.11.02 or 50.60.38.76.)

Reservations:
Advisable at peak season.

6303 Hotel de Plein Air L'Europe, Murol

Spacious site with pool high in the Auvergne.

The site is located a few minutes from the centre of the village, and just a 15 minute walk over the hill to the delightful Lac Chambon, with sandy beach and watersports. It has a good sized swimming pool, with paddling pool, and a tennis court. There is a sizeable football field and volleyball court at one end of the site, close to one of the three modern toilet blocks, which were very clean. There are just over two hundred good sized, grassy pitches, marked out by trees and bushes, with plenty of shade. Nourishment is supported by a small shop selling basics, some local specialities, and bread in the morning. The takeaway food service also operates from the shop, which abutts a bar/restaurant with poolside terrace. The site is ideally situated for visits to the southern Auvergne, being only a short drive from St Nectaire, the Puy de Sancy, Le Mont Dore, or the pretty spa town of La Bourbolle - you could of course hike, since this is famous walking country, and a number of excursions are organised by the site. Local markets at Murol (Wednesday), Chambon (Friday) and Saint-Nectaire (Sunday).

Directions: Take exit 6 from the A75 motorway and drive through St Nectaire and on to Murol. The left turn towards the site is signposted in the village.

Charges 1993:
-- Per pitch Ffr. 95.00; electricity 16.00.

Open:
25 May - 8 Sept.

Address:
63790 Murol.

Tel:
73.88.60.46. or 73.61.61.18 (low season).

Reservations:
Made for min. 1 week with 25% deposit.

All the sites in this guide are regularly inspected by our team of experienced site assessors

1501 Castel Camping Le Belvédère du Pont de Lanau, Lanau, nr St Flour

Peaceful, terraced site with fine views in picturesque Auvergne south of St. Flour.

Situated in a pleasant mix of high country, lakes and deep valleys, La Belvédère used to be difficult to reach but recent road improvements make this peaceful site much more accessible. The region has plenty to offer the discerning visitor and a stay is worthwhile. The 150 or so pitches are all on flat terraces on a quite steep hillside with good views. They vary in size and most are well shaded. The highest ones are only for tents, leaving about 80 (some higher ones with difficult access) for caravans; these all have electrical connections, 36 with water also. Four new pitches of 150 sq.m. have been added by extending the terraces. These have little shade but do have their own private sanitation. The two original toilet blocks and a third new one have a mixture of WC types; washbasins in cubicles or cabins with free hot water, mirror and shelf, a good quota of fully controllable hot showers and baby baths. There is a swimming pool (14 x 6 m.) plus a children's pool (8 x 4). In addition to the up-and-down walking on the site itself, many good walks are available from the camp and numerous excursion possibilities. A nearby lake can be used for sailing, windsurfing and fishing. Self-service shop. Restaurant/bar/pizzeria, with limited food available each day and takeaway. Large new children's playground. Animation in high season. Table tennis. Sauna. Mobile homes, studios and rooms to let. Friendly reception. Tour operators take about 20% of the pitches.

Directions: Site is on D921 south of St. Flour, about halfway between Neuvéglise and Chaudes-Aigues.

Charges 1994:
-- Per unit incl. 2 persons: simple Ffr. 100.00, with electricity 115.00, with 3 services 125.00, pitch with barbecue 145.00, large (150 sq.m.) with view and private sanitation 180.00; extra person (over 2 yrs) 25.00.
-- Less 20% in June and Sept.

Open:
25 May - 6 Sept.

Address:
15260 Lanau.

Tel:
71.23.50.50.
FAX: 71.23.58.93.

Reservations:
Made for min. 1 week with deposit (Ffr. 900), fee (100) and cancellation insurance.

BRITTANY
Ille-et-Vilaine - Côtes d'Armor - Finistère - Morbihan

Brittany is an ideal holiday destination for anyone, but perhaps especially for families. Its coastline has everything - small sheltered coves with rock pools, majestic cliffs and headlands, vast expanses of sandy beaches and intriguing off-shore islands. Brittany is most easily reached via Roscoff or St.Malo, but is also within a days comfortable drive from Cherbourg, Caen or Le Havre. Beautiful as the coastline is, the interior should not be forgotten, particularly the little visited Parc Regional d'Armorique with its startlingly impressive scenery and slow measured lifestyle, and a visit to Le Mont St. Michel is really a `must'. Bretons are very proud of their heritage, and there are ample opportunities to delve into Brittany's fascinating history. Many Bretons consider themselves to have much in common with the Welsh, Irish and Cornish; the region has an unique quality.

2201 Camping Les Capucines, St. Michel-en-Grève, nr Lannion
Small site with good pitches not far from beach.

Quietly situated 1 km. from the village of St. Michel with its good beach, this attractive site has 80 pitches of good size on flat or slightly sloping ground. All are well marked out by separations of hedges, etc. and 45 have electricity, water and drainaway. The two toilet blocks, one modern, give a good supply, with British WCs, washbasins with free hot water mainly in private cabins set in flat surfaces with good hooks, controllable free hot showers and facilities for babies and the disabled. There is a swimming pool (14 x 6 m.) on site, solar heated and open from June. No shop but essentials available on site and baker calls. Takeaway. Bar. Washing machine. Tennis. Table tennis. Minigolf. Bicycle hire. Children's playground. General room.

Directions: Turn off main D786 road northeast of St. Michel where signposted and 1 km. to site.

Charges 1994:
-- Per person Ffr 23.50 (plus local tax July/Aug); child (under 7) 15.00; tent 35.00; caravan 50.00; electricity (2A) 8.00.
-- less 10% outside high season except electricity.
Open:
4 June - 5 Sept.
Address:
St. Michel-en-Grève, 22300 Lannion.
Tel:
96.35.72.28.
Reservations:
Any length with deposit (Ffr. 200) and fee (30).

2202 Camping Armor Loisirs, Trébeurden, nr Lannion
Quieter, small site with neat individual pitches, quite close to the sea.

Armor Loisirs is neatly laid out and well maintained, with 122 individual pitches of 100 sq.m. marked out by quite high hedges, which give a fair amount of privacy; 72 pitches are fully serviced. The main toilet block is only adequate and is really in need of refurbishment; it has British toilets, washbasins in cubicles and showers with free hot water. With a very small block in another part, the provision should suffice (toilets are shortest). A simple, family site, British owned and run, it has a relaxed and friendly atmosphere. There is some evening entertainment in season. Children's play area and games room. The nearest beach is 700 m. Bar. Takeaway counter. Restaurant area. No shop but milk and bread kept. Laundry facilities. No tour operators.

Directions: Site is south of Trébeurden, towards Pors Mabo. Take D65 from Lannion and, on entering Trébeurden, turn left at Bar le Molène. Follow signs to camp, forking right, then left.

Charges 1993:
-- Per person 17.00 Ffr; child (under 7) 9.00; pitch for tent 14.00; pitch for caravan 16.00; electricity 14.00; car 9.00.
Open:
23 May - 6 Sept.
Address:
Route de Pors Mabo, 22560 Trébeurden.
Tel:
96.23.52.31.
Reservations:
Advisable for peak weeks with Ffr. 350 deposit (or £35 cheque).

2203 Camping Nautic International, Caurel, Mur-de-Bretagne, nr Pontivy

Small, friendly, lakeside site in central Brittany with facilities for watersports.

Nautic is attractively situated on the north shore of the long, sinuous Lac de Guerledan which is used for all sorts of watersports. There are pleasant walks around the shores and through Breton countryside and forests. The site is terraced down to the shore of the lake and provides 100 quite large pitches - average 100 sq.m. and all with electricity - in beautiful peaceful surroundings. In addition to a range of boating activities on the lake (small boats may be launched from the site), there is an imaginatively designed swimming pool (25 x 6m.) and smaller pool (6 x 6m.), heated by a wood burning stove (open from June). The toilet facilities, in one block, have been modernised, and provide mostly British toilets, hot showers, some individual wash cabins, one toilet for the disabled and facilities for babies with a playpen. Shop. Takeaway food and bar in July/August. TV room. Sauna and fitness room. Children's play area. Fishing. Tennis. Table tennis. Archery (July/Aug). Volleyball. Watersports and riding near. Used by one British tour operator.

Directions: Turn off the N164 between Mur-de-Bretagne and Gouarec to village of Caurel. Follow camp signs from there.

Charges 1993:
-- Per person Ffr. 22.00; child (under 7) 16.00; local tax - July/Aug.(over 10 yrs) 1.00; pitch 24.00; car 10.00; electricity 14.00.

Open:
May - Sept.

Address:
Route de Beau-Rivage, 22530 Caurel.

Tel:
96.28.57.94.

Reservations:
Write to site

2204 Camping Le Chatelet, St. Cast-le-Guildo, nr St. Malo

Pleasant site with views over the bay and steep path down to beach.

Le Chatelet is pleasantly and quietly situated with views over the estuary from many pitches. It is well laid out, mainly in terraces with 190 individual pitches of good size marked out by hedge separators; all have electric points and 6 water and drainage also. The two toilet blocks, one above the other but with access at different levels, have British and continental WCs, plentiful washbasins in private cabins and preset free hot water in both these and the showers. There are also small units for night use at extremities of the site.

A little lake on site, with some pitches around it, can be used for fishing and a heated swimming pool, with children's pool have been added to the amenities. Large shop. Bar lounge and general room with TV, pool table; dancing weekly in June, July and Aug. Hot food service to take away or eat on spot (June onwards). Games room with table tennis, amusement machines. Organized games and activities for all the family in season. A path leads down direct to a beach from camp, about 150 m. but including steps. St. Cast, 1 km. away to the centre, has a very long beach with many opportunities for sailboarding and other watersports. Used by a tour operator. Mobile homes for hire.

Directions: Best approach is to turn off D786 road at Matignon towards St. Cast; just inside St. Cast limits turn left at sign for `campings' and follow camp signs on C90.

Charges 1994:
-- Per person Ffr 19.00 - 25.00; child (under 7) 10.00 - 14.00; pitch (100 sq.m.) 67.00 - 90.00; tent pitch 52.00 - 70.00; electricity (3A) 15.00 - (10A) 18.00.

Open:
2 April - 24 Sept.

Address:
Rue des Nouettes 22380 St. Cast de Guildo.

Tel:
96.41.96.33.
FAX: 96.41.97.99.

Reservations:
For July/Aug - made (min. 1 week) with deposit (Ffr. 200) and booking fee (120).

Please show reception staff this Guide when you arrive at a site - it helps them, us and eventually you too

2209 Camping Château de Galinée, St. Cast le Guildo

Well kept family run site 5 km. from St. Cast.

This site is in a parkland setting on level grass with numerous and varied mature trees. It has 272 pitches, all with electricity (6A), water and drainage and separated by many newly planted shrubs and bushes. The top section is mostly for mobile homes which are for hire. The main tiled, modern sanitary block has free hot water to the pre-set showers and the washbasins in private cabins, British WCs and a good unit for the disabled. A smaller separate block has toilets only. Dishwashing is under cover and there is a laundry room. Attractive, heated swimming and paddling pools with a sun terrace, are located behind the bar and restaurant, which also has an excellent takeaway menu. Further facilities include a shop, 3 tennis courts, bicycle hire, children's play area and field for ball games. Entertainment is organised during peak season featuring traditional Breton music (twice weekly) and discos. Gate locked 22.00-07.00hrs.

Directions: From the D168 Ploubalay-Plancoet road turn onto D786 towards St. Cast. Site is very well signed on left about 5 km. before Matignon.

Charges 1994:
-- Per pitch incl. water and drainage Ffr 35.00 - 45.00; adult 18.00 - 22.00; child (under 7) 7.00 - 10.00; extra car 5.00; electricity (6A) 15.00.

Open:
Easter or 1 May -15 Oct.

Address:
22380 St. Cast le Guildo.

Tel:
96.41.10.56.
FAX: 96.41.03.72.

Reservations:
Made with deposit Ffr 200 and fee 100 (min. 1 week July/Aug).

2205 Camping Le Vieux Moulin, Erquy, nr St Brieuc

Family run site with individual pitches and reasonable prices, 1 km. from sea.

About 1 km. from a beach of sand and shingle, this site is probably the best along this stretch of coast. It has recently been extended to provide a total of 250 pitches, about 150 of which have electricity. They are of good size, in square boxes, with trees giving shade in many places. The newer pitches are arranged around a pond. The sanitary facilities are being extended and improved also, so should be adequate. There are 3 blocks of good quality with mostly British toilets and plenty of individual basins (with preset warm water and some in private cabins) and free hot showers. Facilities are provided for the disabled and for babies. A smart new crêperie with takeaway food completes the new developments. Solar heated swimming pool and childs' pool (from 1/6). Tennis. Shop. Bar lounge (discos in high season). Gym. Children's playground. TV room. Games room with table tennis. Washing machines and dryer. The site becomes full, busy and possibly noisy late at night in July and August.

Directions: Site is some 2 km. east of Erquy. Take the minor road towards Les Hôpitaux and site is signposted from the junction of D786 and D34.

Charges 1994:
-- Per person 23.00 Ffr; child (under 7) 18.00; car 17.00; pitch 35.00; electricity 18.00.

Open:
1 April - 30 Sept.

Address:
22430 Erquy.

Tel:
96.72.34.23
(winter: 96.72.12.50).

Reservations:
Made for a min. of 1 week.

2206 Camping de la Hallerais, Taden, nr Dinan

Well regulated, municipal site in attractive part of northern Brittany.

As well as being an attractive old town itself, Dinan is quite a short run from the resorts of the Cote d'Emeraude. The Hallerais site, just outside Dinan, beyond the little harbour on the Rance estuary, is a municipal site but a good one. The site slopes down towards the river, where one can walk. The 250 pitches, all but 20 with electricity, water and drainaway, are mainly on shallow terraces, with trees and hedges giving a park-like atmosphere. The three toilet blocks are of very good quality, and are well heated in cool seasons. British toilets. Individual basins in washrooms, and in good private cabins with shower, shelf, mirror and light. Free hot water everywhere. Self-service shop (July/Aug.) with takeaway. Tennis courts. Fishing. Games and TV rooms. Children's playground. Washing machines. Mobile homes for hire.

Directions: Taden is situated northeast of Dinan; on leaving Dinan on D766, turn right to Taden and camp before reaching big bridge and N176 junction. From N176 take Taden/Dinan exit.

Charges guide:
-- Per person 15.20 Ffr; child (under 7) 7.70; car 3.45; pitch 18.20; electricity 11.85; local tax 2.20 per pitch.

Open:
15 March - 31 Oct.

Address:
Taden, 22100 Dinan.

Tel:
96.39.15.93

Reservations:
Made for min. 1 week with deposit of Ffr 100.

2207 Castel Camping Manoir de Cleuziou, Louargat, nr Guingamp

Quiet site, rurally situated in grounds of Breton manor house.

Located 20 km. from the north Brittany coast, this site is in the grounds of the attractive, rather imposing, 16th/18th century Manoir de Cleuziou which is now used as an hotel and restaurant. The site offers a solar heated pool and terrace by the house and a small bar, but will probably suit those who like a quieter site. There are 200 large and well tended pitches, all with electricity and water, separated by hedges, shrubs and roses, on two flat, grassy fields. Sanitary facilities consist of 2 blocks (one in each field) with good, free hot showers and washbasins in cabins (unisex), plus several small, neat toilet blocks, located within easy reach of all pitches. There are further facilities at the pool, together with washing machines and dryers. There is a small shop in high season only (bread and milk may be ordered at other times) and takeaway food to order. Campers may use the hotel restaurant but it is reported to be quite expensive. Tennis. Children's play area. Mobile homes to rent. One British tour operator.

Directions: From N12-E50 take exit for Louargat. Site is signposted in town centre on Route de Tegrom. After 1 km. turn right, then 1½ km. to site.

Charges guide:
-- Per unit incl. 2 persons Ffr 80.00 - 85.00, incl. 3 persons 95.00 - 100.00; extra person 23.00; child 11.50; electricity 15.00; extra car 10.00; dog 4.00.

Open:
April - 31 Oct.

Address:
St. Eloi, 22540 Lourgat.

Tel:
96.43.14.90.
FAX: 96.43.52.59.

Reservations:
Made with deposit (Ffr 400) and fee (100).

2210 Camping L'Abri Cotier, Etables-sur-Mer

Small, tranquil, family run site 500 m. from sandy beach.

This site is arranged in two sections, separated by a small country lane. Pitches are marked out on level grass, divided by mature trees and shrubs. Some are in a charming ancient walled area with a quaint, old-world atmosphere. The second section has an orchard setting. The proud owners have created and nurtured a friendly atmosphere. In total there are 130 pitches, 100 with electrical connections (2/4 or 6/10A); 4 holiday caravans are available for hire. Excellent sanitary facilities in good modern blocks which are heated in low season, comprise British WCs, free pre-set hot showers, washbasins both open and in private cabins, all spotlessly clean when we visited. Washing up under cover and a small laundry room. 2 units for the disabled with shower, basin and toilet. Baby bath and shower.

The site boasts a new heated swimming pool with children's pool and outdoor jacuzzi. An attractive bar is adjoined by a shaded terraced area, with a children's play area close by, set under a weeping willow tree. There is a well stocked shop with fresh produce, and a takeaway service. Other facilities include a games room with billiards, darts, pinball, table tennis and animation is organised during peak season. Bicycle hire. Barbecues permitted. Gates locked at 23.00 hrs.

Directions: Follow D786 north from St Brieux; site is well signed before St Quay Portrieux.

Charges 1993:
-- Per unit Ffr 28.00; person 18.00; child (under 7 yrs) 12.00; electricity 4A 14.00, 6A 17.00; extra car, boat or small tent 10.00.

Open:
1 April - 30 Sept.

Address:
Ville Rouxel, 22680 Etables sur Mer.

Tel:
96.70.61.57.
FAX: 96.70.65.23.

Reservations:
Made with deposit (Ffr 100 for 1 week, 200 for 2); sterling cheque acceptable (£15 or £25).

BRITTANY - Côtes d'Armor

2208 Castel Camping Le Ranolien, Ploumenac'h, nr Perros Guirec

Good quality site in outstanding location on the `Côtes de Granit Rose'.

Le Ranolien has been attractively developed around a former Breton farm - everything here is either made from, on or around the often massive pink rocks. The original buildings are sympathetically converted into site facilities and there is an imaginative swimming pool complex with terraces, and with water cascading over the boulders. The site is on the coast, with beaches and coves within easy walking distance and there are spectacular views from many pitches. The 550 pitches are of a variety of sizes and types, mostly large and flat - some are formally arranged in rows with hedge separators, but most are either on open ground or under trees, amongst large boulders. Electricity is available on 350 and there are some special pitches for motorhomes with water and drainage also. The main toilet block, heated in cool weather, is of very good quality and is supplemented by several other more open blocks around the site. The facilities include washbasins in cabins, mostly British WCs and good showers; hot water everywhere is free. Dishwashing facilities are mostly in the open. A large, busy site, with several tour operators present, there is a range of good facilities open over a long season, including a restaurant, crêperie, attractive bar and a supermarket and gift shop. Minigolf. Tennis. Table tennis. Games room. Small children's play area. Laundry facilities. Mobile homes for hire. Reservation is necessary for high season, but outside July and August one should usually find a quiet corner.

Directions: From Lannion take D788 to Perros Guirec and on towards Ploumenac'h. Site is signposted 2 km. east of Ploumenac'h.

Charges 1993:
-- Per pitch incl. 2 persons Ffr 100.00 (75.00), incl. 3 persons 100.00 (75.00 ·outside 1/5 - 26/9); extra person 30.00; child 15.00; electricity 18.00; water 10.00; drainage 5.00; extra car 12.00; dog 5.00.

Open:
2 Feb - 15 Nov.

Address:
Ploumenac'h,
22700 Perros Guirec.

Tel:
96.91.43.58.
FAX: 96.91.41.90.

Reservations:
Made with deposit (Ffr 400) and fee (100).

2211 Camping Fleur de Bretagne, Kerandouaron, Rostrenen

Small, peaceful, family run site centrally situated for north and south Brittany ports.

Neil and Barbara Eardley only opened this natural, informal 12 acre site in June 1992. It offers 100 unmarked pitches, 31 with 4 or 10A electricity, in attractive terraced fields of varying sizes, separated by hedgerows. A small lake situated alongside a wooded area at the lower end of the site is available for trout fishing (rods available for hire). The traditional old farmhouse has been converted to house a very reasonably priced restaurant and bar with terrace and beer garden, takeaway and games room for pool and table tennis.

Two tiled sanitary blocks have British toilets and free hot water to pre-set showers, with large dressing area, and the washbasins (some in private cabins). Hair dryers are provided and there are 2 units for the disabled with toilet, basin and shower. Small laundry and under cover washing up. An unheated open air swimming pool has a small sun terrace. Good size children's playing field with swings and volleyball net. Bread, milk, water and wine are available and also home-made honey. The town is just 1½ km. away. Barbecues allowed. No noise after 22.00 hrs. Ten tour operator tents are sited to blend into the surroundings.

Directions: Rostrenen is on the N164; the site is south on the D764 (Pontivy) road, signed on left after approx 1 km.

Charges 1993:
-- Per pitch Ffr 25.00; adult 14.00; child (4-13 yrs) 8.00; car 6.00; m/cycle 3.00; electricity 12.00; local tax 1.00.

Open:
March - October.

Address:
Kerandouaron,
22110 Rostrenen.

Tel:
96.29.16.45.

Reservations:
Write or phone.

2913 Camping des Abers, Landeda

Attractively situated site in western Brittany.

This 12 acre site is beautifully situated almost at the tip of the Ste. Marguerite peninsular, on the south shore of L'Aber Wrac'h. There are 200 pitches spread over some ten quite distinct areas, partly shaded and sheltered by mature trees. These areas have been landscaped and terraced, where appropriate, on different levels to avoid any regimentation or crowding. All are easily accessed by good internal roads, water, drainage and electrical points are available, with some special pitches for motorcaravans.

There are three modern toilet blocks placed at strategic points. They are all clean and bright with cubicled washbasins, good showers (on payment), dishwashing sinks and fully equipped laundry. Facilities for the disabled are limited at present but planned for improvement. Mini-market and van with organic vegetables calls daily. The site itself offers a good selection of takeaway dishes or there is an excellent restaurant almost next door. There is a splendid beach reached direct from the site with good bathing (at high tide) or fishing, sailing and watersports and miles of superb coastal walks. Outdoor table tennis, a good adventure playground, TV room and a new indoor games room. Live music twice weekly in high season. Fishing, watersports, tennis and riding close. 4 mobile homes for rent. Gates locked 22.30 - 07.00 hrs.

Directions: Cross Aber Wrac'h by D13 or D113, then from Lannilis follow signs for Ste. Marguerite and `camping'.

Charges 1994:
-- Per person Ffr. 16.00; child (1-7 yrs) 8.00; pitch 22.00; car 6.00; electricity 11.00; dog 5.00.

Open:
15 May - 15 Sept.

Address:
29214 Landeda.

Tel:
98.04.93.35.

Reservations:
Write to site.

Le "CAMPING DES ABERS"
★ ★ ★

Situated in an exceptional tourist region with marvellous views of the sea 10 terraced acres equipped with all necessary facilities, next to safe sandy beach.

Sailing ~ Sea Angling ~ Walking
Swimming ~ Windsurfing ~ Horse Riding

2900 Camping Les Mouettes, Carantec, nr Roscoff

Sheltered site in attractive bay, near to Roscoff ferry port.

Les Mouettes is less than 15 km. from the ferry port so is ideal for a short stay when heading to or from home. However the area has plenty to offer for longer holidays for those who do not wish to drive far, with beautiful bays and many places of interest within easy reach. The site is comfortable and peaceful in a wooded setting with many attractive trees and shrubs, and there is access to a small beach at the front of the site. The 273 pitches, mostly of good size, are arranged in named groups, with electrical connections throughout (6A). The 4 sanitary blocks (unisex) are clean with free hot water to all facilities, offering washbasins in cabins, mainly British toilets and a good supply of showers with hooks and shelves, all arranged in long rows. Good baby bathrooms and facilities for the disabled available.

The centrally located bar has a terrace overlooking the heated swimming pool, water slide pool and children's pool, and discos and other entertainment are organised in the main season. Takeaway meals are served and there is a good shop. Volleyball. Minigolf. Table tennis. Games/TV rooms. Archery (July/Aug.) Children's play area. Small fenced fishing lake. Bureau de change. Laundry facilities. Site owned mobile homes located together at the top of the site. Used by British tour operators.

Directions: From the D58 Roscoff - Morlaix road, turn to Carantec. Site is 1 km. before the town, signed to the left.

Charges 1993:
-- Per pitch Ffr 64.00; person 24.00; child (under 15 yrs) 15.00; local tax 1.00; electricity 16.00; water/drainage 5.00; dog 12.00.
-- Less outside 1/7-31/8.

Open:
1 May - 30 Sept.

Address:
29660 Carantec.

Tel:
98.67.02.46.
FAX: 98.78.31.46.

Reservations:
Write to site with deposit (Ffr. 200) and fee (120).

2906 Camping Caravaning Le Pil Koad, Poullan-sur-Mer, nr Douarnenez

Family run, small site just back from the sea in Finistère.

Pil Koad provides 200 pitches on fairly flat ground, marked out by low separating hedges and of quite good, though varying, size. Nearly all have electrical connections (10A). Trees provide shade in some areas. There are two toilet blocks, in modern style with British WCs (and a few continental) and washbasins partly in private cabins but mostly not. Free, preset hot water in these and in the hot showers, which have pushbuttons. The site is 6 km. from Douarnenez and 5 km. from the nearest sandy beach. There is a heated swimming pool and paddling pool by the bar area, a tennis court and a large new room for entertainment. Small shop (20/5-15/9). Bar. Simple takeaway at times; meals in village. Table tennis. Minigolf. Volleyball. Children's playground. Laundry facilities. Bicycle hire. Mobile homes and chalets to rent. Used by British tour operators.

Directions: Site is 500 m. from centre of Poullan on road towards Douarnenez. From Douarnenez take circular bypass route towards Audierne; if you see road for Poullan sign at roundabout, take it, otherwise there is camping sign at turning to Poullan from D765 road.

Charges 1993:
-- Per person 25.00 Ffr; child (2-7 yrs) 15.00; pitch incl. car 55.00; electricity (10A) 22.00.
-- Less 15-20% outside 22/6-1/9.

Open:
1 May - 30 Sept.

Address:
Poullan,
29100 Douarnenez.

Tel:
98.74.26.39.
FAX: 98.74.55.97.

Reservations:
Made with deposit (Ffr. 300) and fee (120) for min. 1 week.

Please make us aware of your experiences at these or other sites

- See Readers Reports on page 182

2901 Castel Camping Ty Nadan, Arzano, nr Quimperlé
Country site beside the River Ellé, with swimming pool.

Ty Nadan is situated deep in the countryside in the grounds of a country house, some 18 km. from the sea. It has 200 individual pitches (150 with electricity) of good size on fairly flat grass, on the banks of the river. Two toilet blocks are of an unusual design with access from different levels. They are of fair quality with mixed British and continental WCs, and free hot water in the washbasins (in private cabins), sinks and showers (with pushbutton). Access for the disabled may be a little difficult, although there are facilities. Dishwashing facilities are in the ladies' block (!) There are plenty of activities for young people here. On the main part of the site are a heated 17 x 8 m. swimming pool (caps compulsory), tennis courts and a restaurant, takeaway and bar. Across the road, by the attractive house and garden, is a minigolf course, and in converted Breton outbuildings, a TV room and delightful crêperie. Shop. Billiard room. Table tennis. Trampolines. Bicycles, skateboards, roller skates, boats for hire. Canoeing on river. Riding. Small roller-skating rink. Minigolf. Washing machine. Organised activities, many for children, during season, particularly sports, excursions, etc. Chalets for hire. Popular with tour operators.

Directions: Make for Arzano which is northeast of Quimperlé on Pontivy road and turn off D22 just west of village at camp sign.

Charges 1994:
-- Per person 25.00 Ffr; child (under 7) 16.00; pitch 49.00; extra car 10.00; electricity (6A) 13.00; water/drainage 13.00.
-- Less 5-20% outside July/Aug.

Open:
16 April - 10 Sept.

Address:
Rte d'Arzano, 29310 Locunolé.

Tel:
98.71.75.47.
FAX: 98.71.77.31.

Reservations:
Made for exact dates with deposit and fee (Ffr. 100).

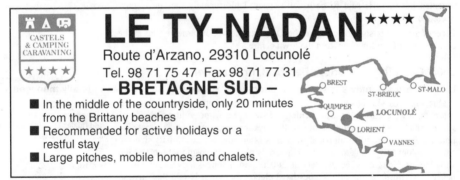

CASTELS & CAMPING CARAVANING
★★★★

LE TY-NADAN★★★★
Route d'Arzano, 29310 Locunolé
Tel. 98 71 75 47 Fax 98 71 77 31
– BRETAGNE SUD –
■ In the middle of the countryside, only 20 minutes from the Brittany beaches
■ Recommended for active holidays or a restful stay
■ Large pitches, mobile homes and chalets.

BREST
ST-BRIEUC
ST-MALO
QUIMPER
LOCUNOLÉ
LORIENT
VANNES

2902 Camping Int. du Saint-Laurent, La Forêt-Fouesnant, nr Concarneau
Shady, attractively situated seaside site with various amenities.

St. Laurent is a well-established site, situated by the sea on a sheltered wooded slope at the mouth of an estuary, with some attractive views. There is direct access to two small strips of beach and a jetty, but at low tide the sea recedes from the estuary leaving a large expanse of wet sand and rocks. The best beach is about 800 m. Pitches are on level terraces, under tall trees divided into individual numbered plots, not over large. Many electrical connections. The sanitary installations are in three tiled blocks of satisfactory quality with free hot showers, British and continental WCs; washbasins (shelf and mirror) some in private cabins. Interesting sea water pools (now good for crabbing!) have been replaced with a conventional swimming pool, children's pool and whirlpool. Torches needed. Supermarket and bar/restaurant (mid-June - early Sept). Takeaway (July/Aug. only). Sports field with volleyball, basketball. Children's playground. Tennis. Table tennis. Golf 1 km. Washing machines. Exchange facilities. 40% of the pitches are occupied by British tour operators.

Directions: Approach from Quimperlé either via N783 (Concarneau) or via Rosporden and D70; from Quimper via N783. Follow signs for Fouesnant but turn left to Kerleven and camp before town.

Charges 1993:
-- Per person 22.00 Ffr; child (under 7) 11.00; local tax 1.00 for over 16s in July/Aug.; pitch with electricity and water 65.00; vehicle 11.00.
-- Less 30-50% outside 26/6-20/8.

Open:
1 April - 30 Sept.

Address:
La Forêt-Fouesnant, Concarneau

Tel:
98.56.97.65.

Reservations:
Not made.

2903 Camping du Letty, Bénodet, nr Quimper

Family run site with high quality amenities and access to small beach.

Du Letty is personally run by the owner and is a select site built around a former farm, with excellent facilities. On the edge of the popular resort of Benodet, it is not far on foot to the main beaches, but there is direct access from the site to an attractive small beach at the mouth of the river (safe bathing depends on the tides). There are over 500 pitches here, although the site does not appear large as they are arranged in small groups enclosed by neat, high hedges and trees. There is plenty of well kept, grassy space and almost all pitches have electrical connections, water and drainage.

Sanitary facilities are in 7 blocks around the site and are all of very good quality with modern fittings. They offer mixed WCs, washbasins in large cabins and controllable hot showers on payment (4fr). Baby bathrooms (3) are provided and in one block, facilities for the disabled. There is no swimming pool here, but the site does provide an extensively equipped fitness room, sauna, solarium, jacuzzi and tennis courts. A beautifully furnished library/reading room, a hairdressing room, laundry, games room with billiards, and attractive bar are also located in the converted farm buildings. Snack bar and takeaway. Entertainment is organized in high season. Children's play area. The owner only allows a few tour operator pitches. Reservations are not accepted but there is said to be usually space. Unfortunately the site is only open over a short season.

Directions: Site is signposted from the D44 Benodet - Concarneau road at the eastern edge of the town, or from the town centre.

Charges 1993:
-- Per adult Ffr. 20.00; child (under 7 yrs) 10.00; pitch 33.00; car 10.00; m/cycle 8.00; electricity (1,2,5 or 10A) 10.00 - 26.00; local tax 1.00.

Open:
15 June - 6 Sept

Tel:
98.57.04.69.

Reservations:
Not made.

2904 Camping Le Vorlen, Beg Meil, nr Quimper

Large informal family site with swimming pool, adjacent to sandy beach - family managed.

This spacious site is set on 24 acres of level ground in a rural setting and caters for a wide variety of tastes with good sized pitches providing a choice of sun or shade within a number of small 'bays' or meadows, which create an impression of tranquillity unusual in such a large site. Because of its size the site is seldom fully booked. The atmosphere is pleasantly cosmopolitan and the situation provides easy access (about 200 m.) to a long sandy south facing beach. Two thirds of the 600 pitches have electricity, and it is said that anyone wanting a pitch with electricity will not be disappointed. There are two modern toilet blocks with ample showers, free hot water, individual wash cabins, British toilets, and numerous sinks for washing up. In the two original blocks, in the older part of the site near the main entrance, the showers and basins have been modernised and enlarged and baby baths provided (one unit for the handicapped). They have British style WCs, all with external entry. A swimming pool (200 sq.m. - open 25/6-1/9 only) and paddling pool have been built at the newer, opposite end of the site from reception and shade is developing around them. Mini market and takeaway (25/6-1/9). Launderette. Children's play area. Bar in season just outside site entrance with some regional music. English spoken in high season only. 45 holiday caravans for hire.

Directions: Follow signs to Beg Meil village; site is signposted from there.

Charges 1993:
-- Per person Ffr. 20.00; child (under 7) 12.00; pitch 38.00; vehicle 8.00; electricity 12.00.
-- Less 20% outside 25/6-1/9.

Open:
1 May - 20 Sept.

Address:
29170 Fouesnant, Beg Meil.

Tel:
98.94.97.36.
FAX: 98.94.97.23.

Reservations:
Write with deposit of Ffr. 120 (Eurocheque).

see advertisement
opposite

2905 Castel Camping L'Orangerie de la Lanniron, Quimper
Quiet site in the grounds of a riverside estate, 15 km. from the sea.

This is a peaceful site in an attractive country estate setting on the banks of the Odet river. It is just to the south of Quimper and about 15 km. from the sea and beaches at Bénodet. The original outbuildings have been attractively converted around a walled courtyard which now includes a heated swimming pool (144 sq.m.) with children's pool and a small play area. There are 199 grassy pitches on fairly flat ground laid out in rows alongside access roads; most with electricity and 45 with all three services. Some of the pitches are on a newer area further from reception (a reader reports that these are not so well tended). The original sanitary block, along one side of the courtyard, is good, with free hot water in all services. A second modern block serves the newer pitches at the other side of the site. They have British toilets, individual basins in private cabins with mirrors, shelf and light and free warm water in all basins, showers, sinks. Shop. Bar with snacks and takeaway and restaurant (both 15/6-31/8). General reading room. Games rooms. Billiards room. Tennis court. Minigolf. Table tennis. Fishing. Golf practice. Archery. Bicycle hire. Children's playground. Large room for organised activities. TV/video room with satellite. Washing and drying machines. The busy town of Quimper, which has some attractive old areas, is under 3 km. and a `Rallye' hypermarket is close by. Site is used by tour operators.

Directions: Site is south of town which has a ring road system. Follow either the general `Camping' signs or, closer to site, signs with 'Camping Lanniron' name; if neither is indicated, follow `Bénodet/Quimper Sud'.

Charges 1994:
-- Per person 23.00 Ffr; child (2-7 yrs) 12.00; car 15.00; normal pitch (100 sq.m.) 40.00, special pitch (140 sq.m. with water and electricity) 73.00, (140 sq.m. with electricity, water and drainage) 78.00; electricity (10A) 19.00.
-- Less 20% outside Jul/Aug.

Open:
1 May - 15 Sept.

Address:
Château de Lanniron, 29000 Quimper.

Tel:
98.90.62.02.
FAX: 98.90.84.31.

Reservations:
Made for min. of about a week with deposit (Ffr. 200) and fee (80).

2907 Camping International de Kervel, Plonévez, nr Douarnenez
Pleasant spacious site close to sea near Douarnenez.

This site lies about 700 m. from the sandy Kervel beach and Douarnenez with its harbour is about 10 km. About 250 numbered pitches of good size are on flat or very slightly sloping grass, mainly in small groups of 6 or so, in enclosures with plenty of grassy space and surrounded by tall hedges. Each group has its own rotary dryer, and all pitches are equipped with electricity, some with water and drainaway also. Many pitches are occupied by British tour operators but the design of the site gives reasonable privacy. Sanitary installations consist of two modern blocks, the newer a particularly large one with facilities for the disabled and for babies. Mostly British WCs, washbasins with shelf and free hot water, mainly in private cabins; hot showers. Water points around. The amenities include a heated swimming pool with water slides and children's pool. Well stocked shop (late May-Aug.) Spacious bar. Takeaway. Tennis court (free). Minigolf. Games room with table tennis, bar billiards, pin-tables. Children's playground. Washing machine and dryer. Bicycle hire.

Directions: Turn off D107 towards Kervel 8 km. east of Douarnenez and west of Locronan and follow signs to camp.

Charges 1994:
-- Per person 25.00 Ffr; child (1-10 yrs) 15.00; local tax 1.00; car and pitch 70.00; electricity (3A) 13.00; water 20.00; dog 10.00; extra car 10.00.
-- Less 30% in low season.

Open:
1 May - 14 Sept.

Address:
29550 Plonévez-Porzay.

Tel:
98.92.51.54.
FAX: 98.92.54.96.

Reservations:
Made with deposit (Ffr 300) and fee (120); probably min. 1 week.

2908 Camping Le Panoramic, Telgruc-sur-Mer, nr Châteaulin
Family site in west Brittany, quite close to a good beach.

This medium sized site, situated on quite a steep hillside with fine views along the coast, is well tended and personally run by the owner. The 220 pitches are arranged on flat terraces, mostly in small groups with hedges and 20 pitches have services for motorhomes. A good sandy beach is around 700 m. downhill by road, a bit less on foot. The main site has a well kept toilet block (some up-and-down walking). Another very good one is open for the main season in an annexe across the road where there is a heated swimming pool, child's pool and whirlpool. Mainly seatless WCs, some continental, washbasins in cubicles with free hot water and showers. Facilities for the disabled and baby baths. Hot water for clothes and dish washing. Small shop, bar and takeaway food in season only. Sports ground with tennis, volleyball. Children's playground. New games room and children's club in season. Washing machines and dryers. Bicycle hire. Barbecue area. Mobile homes for hire. Used by British tour operators.

Directions: From Telgruc town centre, take road with signs to camp and Trez-Bollec-Plage and continue to site on right.

Charges 1994:
-- Per person 23.00 Ffr; child (under 7) 12.00; pitch 45.00; car 10.00; electricity (6A) 20.00, (10A) 28.00; water 15.00.

Open:
15 May - 15 Sept.

Address:
29146 Telgruc-sur-Mer.

Tel:
98.27.78.41.
FAX: 98.27.36.10.

Reservations:
Made for any period with deposit.

2910 Camping du Manoir de Pen-ar-Steir, La Forêt-Fouesnant, nr Concarneau
Charming, small site for a quiet stay, with few on-site amenities.

Manoir de Pen-ar-Steir will appeal to those who prefer a quiet place without lots of amenities and entertainment. It is arranged on terraces up the steep sides of a valley in the grounds of an old Breton house wih a picturesque, garden-like quality, with lots of well tended trees and flowers, including a pond and stream. There are some steep slopes to reach most of the pitches, but they are all on flat, grassy, terraces with hedges around them; all have electrical connections. There are 2 sanitary blocks of an older style but of reasonable standard with mixed British and continental toilets and cabins with basin and shower, with hooks and mirror, plus washbasins in rows. The provision should be adequate. There are also a few excellent, modern facilities in a small block behind the house. Washing machines and dryer. Tennis court, minigolf and children's playground on site but no bar, restaurant or shop (baker 50 m.), but the town and nearby resorts are easily reached. Some mobile homes and one British tour operator. The ability to speak French at this site may be useful.

Directions: Site is on NE edge of La Forêt-Fouesnant, on D44 to Quimper.

Charges 1993:
-- Per adult Ffr 22.00; child (under 7 yrs) 13.00; pitch/car 38.00; electricity 12.00; dog 4.00.

Open:
All year.

Address:
29133 La Forêt-Fouesnant.

Tel:
98.56.97.75.
FAX: 98.51.40.34.

Reservations:
Write to site for details.

2909 Camping Le Raguénèz Plage, Névez, nr Pont-Aven

Well regulated, attractive site in small seaside village, with beach access.

This site is personally run by the owner who takes great pride in her site. She has planted many attractive shrubs and trees and all is kept very clean and neat. A sandy beach can be reached by footpath from the site (300 m.) and there is a sailing school and small fishing port adjacent to the site. The 287 pitches all have electrical connections and are of good size, on flat grass, arranged in rows on either side of asphalt access roads, separated by hedges and trees. The sanitary facilities are in 3 well designed blocks of different size and are of very good quality. They provide British WCs, pre-set hot showers, washbasins in private cabins, plus free hairdryers and include good baby bathrooms and excellent facilities for the disabled. Hot water is free throughout. The site has no pool but a sauna is available, plus table tennis, volleyball and a games room and animation is offered for children. A small bar and restaurant (open from 1/6) have an outside terrace, again with lots of flowers; breakfast is served here. Takeaway. Small shop (supermarket 5 km.). Good children's play areas. Reading, TV rooms and films. Sauna. Laundry. Exchange facilities. Fishing and watersports near. Used by British tour operators. Mobile homes for hire.

Directions: From the D783 Concarneau - Pont-Aven road go south to Névez. Site is signposted from there, 5 km. on Raguénès-Plage road.

Charges 1994:
-- Per unit incl. 2 persons Ffr. 96.00; extra adult 23.00; child (under 7 yrs) 12.00; electricity (2A) 15.00, (6A) 20.00
-- Less 20% outside July/Aug.

Open:
Easter - 30 Nov.

Address:
Rue des Iles, 29920 Névez.

Tel:
98.06.80.69.
FAX: 98.06.89.05.

Reservations:
Recommended in high season; min. 7 days July/Aug. Write to site with deposit (Ffr. 300).

2911 Grand Camping de la Plage, Le Guilvenec, nr Pont l'Abbé

Friendly site, ideal for families, with access to good sandy beach.

Grand Camping is located on the edge of a long sandy beach between the fishing town of Le Guilvenec and the watersports beaches of Penmarc'h on the southwest tip of Brittany. This spacious site is surrounded by tall trees, which provide shelter, and is made up of several flat, sandy meadows. The 410 pitches are arranged on either side of sandy access roads, mostly not separated but all numbered. There is not much shade. Electricity available on most pitches (2, 5 or 10A). Motorcaravan service point opposite the entrance to the site.

The 5 excellent sanitary blocks are of differing designs, but all provide modern, bright facilities including large, free, controllable showers, washbasins in cabins, British WCs and good facilities for children. Toilet for the disabled. As well as the obvious attractions of the beach, the site offers a heated swimming pool and childs' pool, tennis courts and many other leisure facilities including volleyball, minigolf, golf practice, badminton, petanque, table tennis, giant chess/drafts, a sauna and bicycle hire. Fishing, watersports, riding near. Children's play area. TV room. There is a bright, airy and well furnished bar, with a crêperie and terrace overlooking the pool. Takeaway. Laundry facilities. Exchange facilities. Barbecues permitted. Entertainment is organised in season for adults and children. There is plenty to occupy one at this friendly site but the bustling fishing harbour at Le Guilvenec and the watersports of Penmarc'h and Pointe de la Torche are within easy travelling distance. Gates locked 22.30 - 06.30 hrs. Used by 2 British tour operators.

Directions: From Pont l'Abbé, take the D785 road to Penmarc'h. Site is signposted from there or from the D57 to Le Guilvenec, on the coast road between the two towns.

Charges 1994:
-- Per adult Ffr 25.00; child (under 7 yrs) 15.00; pitch incl. car 60.00; electricity 2A 10.00, 5A 16.00; local tax 1.00.
-- Less 20% outside July/August.

Open:
Easter - 15 Sept.

Address:
Rue de Men-Meur, BP.9, 29730 Le Guilvenec.

Tel:
98.58.61.90;
when closed: 98.58.14.14.
FAX: 98.58.89.06.

Reservations:
Recommended and accepted until 15/6 with deposit (Ffr. 300) and fee (120).

BRITTANY - Finistère / Ile et Vilaine

2912 Camping Manoir de Kerlut, Plobannalec, nr Pont l'Abbé
New, developing site in grounds of manor house on river estuary.

Manoir de Kerlut is situated on the banks of a river estuary, 2 km. from the beaches of Lesconil and not far from the fishing and watersports opportunities of the southwest coast of Brittany. There are pleasant walks in the park and along the river bank. A new site (1990), with strikingly modern buildings, it has been constructed on flat grass near the house. It provides 240 pitches, all with electricity (5/6A), many with water and drainage and hardstandings available on 10 or so pitches. One area is very open with hedges only just planted, the other is amongst mature bushes and some trees which provide shade. Generally, however, the site has a rather open feeling that only time will alter. Large modern bar with entertainment in season, and two heated swimming pools with children's pool. Well stocked small shop. Takeaway. Sauna, solarium and small gym. Tennis. Volleyball. Badminton. Petanque. Children's play area. Games room. Bicycle hire. Exchange facility. Laundry. Two very good sanitary blocks provide hot showers, washbasins in cabins and British WCs. Facilities for babies and the disabled. Hot water is free. Mobile homes to rent. Very popular with British tour operators. Traditional evenings in the château in 1994.

Directions: From Pont l'Abbé, on the D785, take the D102 road to Lesconil. Site is signposted to the left, shortly after the village of Plobannalec.

Charges 1994:
-- Per person 25.00; child (under 7 yrs) 10.00; pitch incl. car 60.00; electricity 2A 10.00, 5A 16.00.
-- Less 20% outside July/August.

Open:
15 May - 15 Sept.

Address:
29740 Plobannalec-Lesconil.

Tel:
98.82.23.89
FAX: 98.58.89.06.

Reservations:
Write to site with deposit (Ffr. 300) and fee (120).

> see advertisement in
> next colour section

3501 Camping de la Ville Mauny, Dinard, nr St. Malo
Modern, family run site, 2 km. from town and beaches.

12 beaches of fine sand within radius of 3 miles. About 2 miles from Dinard, with all the amenities of a first class resort: beaches, olympic seawater pool, casino, 18 hole golf course, shopping, seafood restaurants, etc. Mobile Homes for hire by the week, all with flush toilet, nearly all with shower and hot water. Prices from about 800 frs. off-season for 6 persons all-inclusive to about 1700 in July/August. Sauna, Heated Swimming Pool, Tennis.

Write to camp at 35800 Dinard or 'phone (from UK) 010.33.99.46.94.73

This site is personally run with a friendly atmosphere. Situated quietly, away from main roads, it is a good base for the Dinard and St. Malo area, being only 2 km. from the nearest sandy beach and 2 km. from the town centre. It offers 200 individual pitches of good size on flat grass, with trees and hedges, though an extension is planned. Electricity in all parts, and some 30 pitches with water also. The two modern sanitary blocks are of good quality with British WCs, washbasins in private cabins with free hot water, and free showers with pre-set hot water (pushbutton). Baby baths. Hot water also for sinks. One block can be heated. Tennis facilities and a heated swimming pool, with children's pool (open from June) are provided. Good children's playground with inflatable 'bouncy castle'. Shop. Lounge bar. self-service restaurant and takeaway. TV room. Games room with table tennis. Washing machines and dryers. Activities for children and adults in season. Some 50 pitches are occupied by large privately owned permanent caravans, some of which are let by the site.

Directions: Site is in southern outskirts of Dinard, signed from D603 road to St. Briac. From St. Malo and Dinard, take D168 to St. Brieuc, then right on D603 towards St. Briac and Lancieux, and at once right and left following camp signs.

Charges 1994:
-- Per person Ffr 22.00; child (under 7)11.00; local tax 2.00; tent or caravan 45.00; motor-caravan 55.00; car or m/cycle 9.00; electricity 15.00 (3A) - 28.00 (10A); water connection 12.00.
-- Less 20% April/May; 10% June/Sept/Oct.

Open:
15 April - 15 October.

Address:
35800 Dinard.

Tel:
99.46.94.73.
FAX: 99.88.14.68.

Reservations:
Min. 5 nights (1 wk in high season) with 25% deposit.

3504 Camping Le P'tit Bois, St. Jouan des Guérêts, nr St. Malo

Busy, well kept site near ferry port and yachting centre of St. Malo.

This flat, grassy, family orientated site is situated on the outskirts of St. Malo, ideal for one night stops or for longer stays in this interesting area. Le P'tit Bois is very neat and clean, with 160 pitches, nearly all with electricity (5A), divided by hedges into groups and separated by shrubs and flowers. Some are under trees giving shade. There is one main sanitary block, a little open in cool weather, but providing good quality facilities with British WCs, washbasins all in cabins with mirrors, shelves and lights and modern, preset showers. Laundry facilities are available (in the ladies' block). Free hot water throughout. There is a bright restaurant, with takeaway food and swimming pools with terrace and water slide. Good children's playground and games room. Small shop. Minigolf. Tennis. Volleyball. Bicycle hire. Service point for motorcaravans. Many British tour operators here and site-owned mobile homes, but this does mean that the facilities are open over a long season.

Directions: St. Jouan is west off the St. Malo - Rennes road (N137) just outside St. Malo. Site is signposted from the N137.

Charges 1994:
-- Per person Ffr 25.00; child (under 7yrs) 18.00; pitch 60.00; extra car 10.00; electricity 18.00.
-- Less 20% in May, June and Sept.
Open:
1 May - 15 Sept.
Address:
35430 St. Jouan-des-Guérêts, St. Malo.
Tel:
99.81.48.36.
FAX: 99.81.74.14.
Reservations:
Made on receipt of 30% of total cost (no fee).

3502 Castel Camping des Ormes, Epiniac, nr Dol-de-Bretagne

Impressive site on an estate of wooded parklands and lakes, with 18 hole golf course.

This site is in the northern part of Brittany, about 30 km. from the old town of St Malo, in the grounds of the Château des Ormes. It has a pleasant atmosphere, busy in high season but peaceful at other times, with a range of facilities. The 450 pitches are divided into a series of different sections, each with its own distinctive character and offering a choice of terrain - flat or gently sloping, wooded or open. There are elctrical connections (3/6A) on 200 pitches.

Two swimming pools and a children's pool overlook a small lake with pedalos and canoes for hire. The pools are sheltered by the bar and restaurant buildings, parts of which are developed from the original, 600 year old watermill. A particular feature is an 18 hole golf course; also a golf practice range and a beginners 5 hole course. Shop. Takeaway. Games room. Bar and disco, recently refurbished. Minigolf. Bicycle hire. 3 tennis courts. Fishing. Horse riding on site. Sanitary installations are of a good standard, providing British style WCs, washbasins in private cubicles, pre-set hot water in showers and sinks, at no charge. Ample facilities for the disabled. The site reports the addition of a motel adjacent. A popular site with British visitors.

Directions: Access road leads off the main N795 about 7 km. south of Dol-de-Bretagne at Le Pont Melin.

Charges 1994:
-- Per person 26.00 Ffr; child (under 7) 13.00; pitch 65.00; electricity (3A) 13.00, (6A) 15.00; water and drainage 5.00.
-- Less 10% outside July/Aug.
Open:
20 May - 10 Sept.
Address:
35120 Dol-de-Bretagne.
Tel:
99.73.49.59.
FAX: 99.73.49.55.
Reservations:
Made for minimum of 1 week - details from site.

3503 Camping Municipal de Paron, Fougères

Satisfactory, well kept site on some main through routes.

Paron is a neat, little, municipal site which makes a good staging point on the routes from St. Malo, Cherbourg, Le Havre etc. It is modern and has a well kept air. The 90 pitches are all individually marked and of good size, some being separated by rows of bushes and trees. They are on flat grass with several hardstandings. The good sanitary block has British WCs, washbasins, partly in private cabins, and large showers with hot water between the hours: 7-10 am, 12-2 and 7-10 pm.. No shop (baker 500 m.) Tennis and minigolf nearby. American motorhomes not accepted. The site has had good reports from readers and is well worth consideration. Office open 9-11 am and 5-8 pm.

Directions: Site is 300 m. east of eastern bypass on D17 to La Chapelle-Janson. Easiest approach is from bypass; some signs from town centre but easy to miss.

Charges 1993:
-- Per adult Ffr. 8.00 - 11.50; child (under 7 yrs) 4,00 - 6.00; pitch 9.50 - 13.50; car 5.50 - 8.00; m/cycle 3.50 - 5.00; electricity 13.00 - 27.00, acc. to amps and season.

Open:
1 April - 30 September.

Address:
35300 Fougères.

Reservations:
Write to site.

5602 Camping de la Plage, La Trinité-sur-Mer, nr Carnac

Site close to beach with individual pitches and satisfactory installations.

CAMPING-CARAVANING DE LA PLAGE ★ ★ ★ ★
56470 LA TRINITÉ-SUR-MER   Tel: 97 55.73.28

YOU DO NOT HAVE TO DRIVE OUT TO THIS BEACH THERE IS DIRECT ACCESS TO IT FROM OUR CAMP

The area of Carnac and La Trinité is a popular one with holidaymakers. The two sites at the sea front of La Trinité, La Plage and La Baie, are both owned by the same family and have the great asset of direct access to a good sandy beach. There are also shops and a site-owned bar very close, and it is not too far to walk to La Trinité village. The available area at both sites has been fully utilised for camping with narrow access roads which may become congested in high season (American morohtomes not accepted). However the 200 pitches at La Plage are separated by hedges and bushes giving some privacy and shade. Nearly all have electricity, water and drainaway. The two sanitary blocks are satisfactory with mostly British toilets, washbasins in cubicles or cabins with free hot water, and free pre-set hot showers. They should be an adequate provision. Washing machine and dryer. Freezer service. The site has a mature feel, with a small swimming pool and slide and a good children's playground to add to the attractions of the beach. 2 tennis courts. Volleyball. Table tennis. Minigolf. TV room and large screen for videos. Sailboards and bicycles for hire. Organised activities and entertainment in July/Aug. Shop 150 m.

Directions: Site is signposted from the D186 coast road running from La Trinité to Carnac-Plage but entrance easy to miss. Site access can be congested.

Charges 1994:
-- (Probable) Per person Ffr. 21.00; child (under 18) 15.00; local tax 1.00 for over 18s July/Aug; pitch 95.00 (49.00 ouside 15/6 - 31/8); electricity 15.00.

Open:
21 May - 15 Sept.

Address:
56470 La Trinité-sur-Mer.

Tel:
97.55.73.28.

Reservations:
Made (from Jan.) for at least a few days, with exact dates; deposit (Ffr. 400) and fee (100).

CAMPING CARAVANING EUROLAC★★★★
40200 AUREILHAN

13 hectares of paradise on the lake of Aureilhan – Sailing – Relaxation – Sport – Swimming pool and Paddling pool
All of 4 star quality • Open 12/5 – 30/9 • Bungalows, Chalets and Mobile Homes for hire
Special Tariffs during the low season. • For further details and reservations: Telephone 58 09 02 87 or Fax 58 09 41 89

Manoir
de Kerlut

★ ★ ★ ★ Camp Site
in Southern Brittany

le Magazine

There is something about France that strikes a chord in all of us. No other country inspires such passionate interest, perhaps because France and things French have always stood as the epitome of style, beauty and high culture. It was these passions that led to the creation of Le Magazine and devoted Francophiles have helped it to grow and prosper ever since.

Le Magazine brings the best of France to readers six times a year. With high quality editorial from award winning contributors from the quality press covering subjects as diverse as the arts, business, travel, food and wine, fashion and real estate, it can truly claim to be the most comprehensive magazine for France.

The Magazine is divided into three main sections, French Lifestyle, French Holidays and French Property. It is available in the UK through W H Smiths and John Menzies and leading newsagents, or to subscribe, fill in the form below or call Freephone 0800 833257.

5605 Camping Kervilor, La Trinité-sur-Mer, nr Carnac

Quieter, more spacious site, slightly inland from busy resort.

Kervilor may be a good alternative for those who find the beachside sites in La Trinité too busy and lively. In a village on the outskirts of the town, it has 200 pitches on flat grass and is attractively landscaped with trees (silver birches) and flowers. The pitches, 150 with electricity (3 or 6A), are in groups divided by hedges, and are separated by shrubs and trees. Sanitary facilities are provided by two modern blocks of good standard with further facilities in an older, less smart block by the entrance. They offer controllable, free hot showers, washbasins, many in cabins, and British WCs (with some continental for men). Centrally placed is a bar with a terrace overlooking a medium-sized swimming pool, with children's pool and a solarium. At one end is a play area with children's play equipment on sand and with minigolf, pétanque, tennis, volleyball and table tennis outside and under cover. Mobile homes for hire. Small shop for basics and takeaway food in season, but the facilities of the town are not far away by car (1½ km.). The sandy beach is 2 km.

Directions: Site is north of La Trinité-sur-Mer and is signposted in the town centre. From Auray take the D186 Quiberon road; turn left at camp sign at Kergrok on D186 to La Trinité-sur-Mer, and left again at outskirts of town.

Charges 1994:
-- (Probable) Per person Ffr 20.00; child (under 7 yrs) 13.00; tourist tax (over 10 yrs) 1.00; car and pitch 60.00; electricity 10.00 (3A) - 13.00 (6A).
-- Less 25% outside high season.

Open:
18 May - 15 Sept.

Address:
56470 La Trinité-sur-Mer.

Tel:
97.55.76.75.
(winter: 97.55.76.94).
FAX: 97.55.87.26.

Reservations:
Made with 25% of total cost and fee (Ffr. 120).

5604 Camping de Penboch, Arradon, nr Vannes

Quietly situated site on the Golfe du Morbihan with good facilities.

Penboch is situated 200 m. by footpath from the shores of the Golfe du Morbihan where there is plenty to do, including watersports, fishing and boat trips to the islands. There are also old towns, with weekly markets near. The site is in a peaceful, rural area and is divided into two parts - one in woodland, the other main part, across a minor road on more open ground with hedges and young trees. The site is well kept and offers 175 pitches on flat grass, mostly divided into groups; electricity is available on most pitches (6/10A) and there are plenty of water points. Three sanitary blocks, the largest on the main part of the site, offer good showers with free hot water, washbasins in cabins and British WCs. There is a friendly bar with snacks and takeaway and basic food supplies are kept (all in season only). A heated swimming pool with water slide and children's pool (15/5-15/9) are in the centre of the site and a good children's playground is provided with interesting play equipment. Games room. Washing machines and dryers. Amrican motorhomes accepted in low season. Popular with tour operators and site owned mobile homes and bungalows for rent.

Directions: From N165 at Auray or Vannes, take D101 road along northern shores of Golfe du Morbihan. Take turn to Arradon, and site is signed.

Charges 1993:
-- Per person Ffr 19.00; child (under 7 yrs) 13.00; pitch 56.00; electricity (6A) 14.00, (10A) 16.00; water/drainage 10.00; local tax (over 18 yrs) 1.00.
-- Less in low seasons.

Open:
20 April - 20 Sept.

Address:
56610 Arradon.

Tel:
97.44.71.29.
FAX: 97.44.79.10.

Reservations:
Made for min. 12 days for 7/7 - 18/8.

5601 Castel Camping La Grande Métairie, Carnac

Good quality site in southern Brittany with many facilities.

La Grande Métairie is quietly situated, a little back from the sea, close to some impressive rows of the famous 'menhirs' (giant prehistoric stones). It has much to offer on site and is lively and busy over a long season. There is a feeling of spaciousness with a wide entrance and access road, with over 350 good individual pitches (with electricity - 30 m. cables needed in parts), surrounded by hedges and trees. Paddocks with ponds are home for ducks, goats and ponies to watch and feed and there is a large playing field with football posts. A heated swimming pool of 200 sq.m. is supplemented by another of around 100 sq.m. and two children's pools. Entertainment area including an outside amphitheatre for musical evenings and barbecues. The three large toilet blocks are good, with free hot water everywhere; British toilets; washbasins with shelf and mirror in private cabins; free preset, warm showers, operated by chain (no run-on).

Other amenities include a shop, boutique, restaurant, a good takeaway and a bar lounge and adjoining TV room and games room; occasional dances, etc. (Pitches near these facilities may be noisy late at night). Pony rides from site. Horse riding and golf near. Tennis. Minigolf. Children's playground. BMX track. Bicycle hire. Table tennis. Fishing (on permit). Organised events daytime and evening. Mobile homes for hire. The nearest beach is about 3 km. by road, so one would normally go by car. The site, although large and not cheap, is well known and popular so reservation from late June is necessary. Limited services before 28 May. American motorhomes accepted up to 30 ft. It has a large British contingent with about 40% of the pitches taken by tour operators and many British touring caravanners and campers.

Directions: From N165 take Quiberon/Carnac exit onto the D768. After 5 km. turn left on D781 to Carnac. Follow camp signs, turn left at traffic lights to site.

Charges 1994:
-- Per person Ffr. 24.00; local tax (over 15) 2.00 15/6-15/9; child (under 7) 15.00; pitch incl. car 100.00, with electricity 112.00; extra car 10.00.
-- Less 30% 28/5-30/6 and Sept, 50% before 28/5.

Open:
2 April - 17 Sept. all services from 28 May.

Address:
B.P. 85, 56340 Carnac-Cedex.

Tel:
97.52.24.01.

Reservations:
Made (min. 1 week) with deposit (Ffr. 300 per week booked) and fee (120).

BURGUNDY
Côte d'Or - Sâone-et-Loire - Nièvre - Yonne

Within easy reach of the Channel ports, there is more to Burgundy than just wine - it's warm, it's beautiful, it's interesting and it's the rich heartland of France. It has a prosperous feel about it and has been coveted as a place to settle since Roman times. Recent prosperity has been based on its most famous product - wine, but there is more to the region than this. It is criss-crossed by navigable waterways, it has the beautiful Parc regional de Morvan, and there are intriguing old towns with fascinating buildings, châteaux and shrines. It has some of the most striking religious architecture in Europe at Cluny, Vezelay and Fontenay, and wonderful food.

2101 Camping Municipal, Châtillon-sur-Seine

Very useful night halt on the way south, with modest charges, by swimming pools.

One of those well kept little municipal sites that one finds from time to time, this one has 60 pitches, mainly individual ones with separators between them on fairly flat grass, 48 with electricity. Mature trees provide shelter. The main toilet block, at one end of site, is satisfactory with plentiful washbasins in cubicles with free hot water and pre-set free showers; also a small central unit. Facilities for the disabled. Adjoining the site is the municipal swimming pool complex with both indoor and outdoor pools (on payment), and minigolf. No shop, but town is close. Snack bar in July/Aug. The site, which has much transit trade, can become full by evening in season.

Directions: On northeast outskirts of town, site is signposted from centre.

Charges 1994:
-- Per person Ffr. 11.00; child (under 7) 6.00; car 6.00; m/cycle 4.00; pitch 7.00; electricity 10.00 (2A) or 20.00 (4A).

Open:
Easter - 15 Sept

Address:
Esplanade Saint-Vorles, 21400 Châtillon s. Seine.

Tel:
80.91.03.05.

Reservations:
Not officially made, but if you write shortly before your visit, they will reserve until 7 p.m.

2102 Camping Municipal Les Cent Vignes, Beaune

Well tended municipal site in the Burgundy wine region.

This is a well kept site with 120 individual pitches of good size, separated from each other by hedges high enough to keep a fair amount of privacy. Rather over half of the pitches are on grass, ostensibly for tents, and the remainder on hardstandings with electricity for caravans. The two sanitary blocks are well constructed modern ones which should be large enough. Continental toilets except for one British per sex in each block. Washbasins now nearly all in private cabins with shelf and light. Free hot water for these, and for the pre-set showers (controlled by chain and water does not run on long) and the sinks. Shop, restaurant with takeaway. Children's playground. Washing machines. A popular site, within walking distance of the town centre, Les Cent Vignes becomes full from mid-June - early Sept. but with many short-stay campers there are departures each day and reservations can be made. Beaune is of course in the Burgundy wine producing area, and several `caves' in the town can be visited.

Directions: Take Dijon road from the Beaune ring road. After 400 m. turn left on D18 towards Savigny but keep left at first junction to site entrance.

Charges 1993:
-- Per person Ffr. 12.00; child (2-7 yrs) 6.00; local tax 2.00; pitch 18.00; electricity (6A) 17.00.

Open:
1 March - 31 Oct.

Address:
10 Rue Auguste Dubois, 21200 Beaune.

Tel:
80.22.03.91.

Reservations:
Made without deposit.

5801 Camping Les Bains, St. Honoré-les-Bains

Attractive `green' family-run site with pool, close to small spa-town.

With 120 large (100 sq.m.) separated pitches, (100 with 2 or 6A electricity) and many trees, this is an attractive site, well situated for exploring the Morvan area. There are opportunities for horse-riding, fishing etc. or for `taking the waters' which are said to be very good for asthma sufferers. The site has its own swimming pool which has been enlarged, with a separate aqua slide, a children's play area, and two small streams for children to fish in, one of which is warm from the thermal springs. There is a traditional family bar (with Hungarian pianist playing a variety of music) and takeaway food. Table tennis. Minigolf. Entertainment for children in July. Plans for a half court. Archery twice weekly in season. The sanitary facilities comprise three separate blocks, the most recently built having the latest modern facilities including British WCs, washbasins in separate cabins and ample hot showers with dividers. Maintenance in high season may be variable. There are dishwashing sinks (with hot water), a baby bath, facilities for the disabled and laundry facilities. Modern gites on site for hire all year.

Directions: From the north approach via the D985 from Auxerre, through Clamecy to St. Honoré-les-Bains, from where the site is signposted.

Charges 1994:
-- Per unit in July/Aug. incl. 3 persons Ffr. 90.00, otherwise per person 20.00; child (under 7 yrs) 12.00; local tax 1.50; pitch and vehicle 27.00; extra car 7.00; electricity (6A) 15.00.

Open:
1 May - 30 Sept.

Address:
B.P. 17, 15 Av. Jean Mermoz, 58360 St. Honoré-les-Bains.

Tel:
86.30.73.44.
FAX: 86.30.61.88.

Reservations:
Write to site with deposit (Ffr. 330) and fee (70).

8901

Sous-Rôche
Avallon

*The site's
peaceful setting*

5803 Castel Camping Manoir de Bezolle, St. Péreuse-en-Morvan

Well situated site for exploring the Morvan Natural Park and the Nivernais area.

This site has been attractively landscaped to provide a number of different areas and terraces, giving some pleasant views over the surrounding countryside. Clearly separated pitches are on level grass with some terracing and a choice of shade or otherwise. The majority have electricity (4A or more). Several features are worthy of special mention including a large, new swimming pool and a smaller one (1/6-30/9), lakes, a special restaurant with varied menu and also a bar providing good value snack meals, and a collection of unusual animals. These include deer, peacocks and angora goats - which provide mohair used to make designer clothing displayed and sold locally. The goats, particularly the young ones (clearly under the patronage of a large male known as 'His Excellency'!), are kept with the deer in a fenced field providing much entertainment especially for younger children.

The site is undergoing a 3 year updating programme including a new drainage system and roads. Two sanitary blocks, one new and purpose built, the other adapted in an older building but with modern fittings, provide hot, pre-set showers, washbasins in private cabins (cold water), seatless WCs, provision for the handicapped and a baby bath. Shop. Horse riding. Minigolf. Tennis. Games room. Bicycle hire for children. Table tennis. Fishing. Laundry facilities. Mobile homes for hire. The site is popular with British tour operators. Full services 15/6-15/9.

Directions: Site is situated midway between Châtillon-en-Bazois and Château-Chinon, just north of the D978 by the small village of St. Péreuse-en-Morvan.

Charges 1993:
-- Prices outside 15/6-31/8 in brackets.
-- Per pitch incl. 2 persons Ffr. 100.00 (74.00); extra person 24.00 (18.00); child (under 7 yrs) 20.00 (13.00); electricity (4A) 20.00, extra 2A 6.00; water connection 12.00; animal 9.00; extra car 10.00; local tax 1.00.

Open:
15 March - 30 September.

Address:
58110 Saint Péreuse en Morvan.

Tel:
86.84.42.55.
FAX: 86.84.43.77.

Reservations:
Made with deposit (Ffr. 300) and fee (100) for min. 1 week in high season.

8901 Camping de Sous-Rôche, Avallon

Simple but attractive site with reasonable charges in the Burgundy region.

This municipal camp is in a low-lying, sheltered, part wooded situation, 2 km. from the centre of Avallon. There is quite a choice of pitches on the pleasant grassy terrain - on shady terraces, on flat open ground, or by a stream. There are 60 electrical connections (4A) in several sections. It may be very busy and reservations could be advisable for peak times. The single toilet block is in the process of being modernised and now includes seatless WCs, including one with basin and ramp for the disabled, individual washbasins with mirrors and four in private cabins, showers with dividers and hooks, traditional sinks for clothes and washing up sinks, all with free hot water. Shop, takeaway food (July/Aug) and cooking facilities. Children's playground (on gravel). Information reading room with public telephone. It is a very useful night stop on the way to or from Lyon and the south, but worth a longer stay. Avallon is a picturesque town and is a good centre for visiting the wild valleys and lakes of the Morvan mountains. Charges are modest.

Directions: From centre of Avallon take N944 to south towards Lormes. After 2 km. turn left at camp sign.

Charges 1993:
-- Per person Ffr 15.00; child (under 7) 7.50; car 10.00; pitch 10.00; electricity 15.00.

Open:
15 March - 15 Oct.

Address:
Service Camping, Mairie, 89200 Avallon.

Reservations:
Are made, write to the Mairie.

7101 Camping Municipal, Mâcon
Pleasant night stop site with cared-for air.

The Mâcon municipal site presents a neat, cared-for appearance to those seeking a good night stop. It consists of a large expanse of well tended grass divided into several areas by tarred access roads. Pitches are not all marked out but, in view of the site's size, it should not often become too crowded. Three well equipped but basic sanitary blocks, one recently refurbished, should be quite adequate. Facilities include British toilets for ladies, mostly continental for men, partitioned basins with mirror and shelves (private cabins for ladies). Free hot showers, chain-operated and flow stops when released. Free hot water in basins of only one block in low season. Facilities for the disabled have been added. Modern buildings house a shop (May-Sept.), restaurant (all season) with takeaway, bar, and a room for general use. Children's playground. Footpaths. Swimming pool quite near. Charges are modest.

Directions: Site is on the northern outskirts of Mâcon on the main N6.

Charges 1993:
-- Per adult 14.40 Ffr; child (under 7) 7.20; car 7.80; m/cycle 3.90; caravan or tent 10.00; motorcaravan 15.50; electricity (5A) 11.60 (16/5-30/9) or 17.00 (1/10-15/5).
-- 1994 probably plus 5%.
Open:
15 March - 31 Oct.
Reservations:
Not made.

7102 Le Village des Meuniers, Dompierre-les-Ormes, nr Macon
Potentially superb municipal site in southern Burgundy.

Although opened in 1993, this site was by no means complete when we visited in early July. We were, however, able to make an initial (and very favourable) assessment. Judging by the commitment expressed by the local mayor and his assistant, and the amount of resources being allocated, this should be a superb site by the start of the 1994 season. The 80 attractively terraced pitches, on level newly sown grass, are large, have electricity, and enjoy some lovely views of the surrounding countryside - the Beaujolais, the Maconnais, the Charollais and the Clunysois. The site is ½ km from Dompierre Les Ormes, a small village of 850 people, with all services (banks, shops, etc). Sanitary facilities are in an unusual purpose designed hexagonal block, with the most up-to-date fittings, all of a very high standard, although we had to use the excellent facilities for the disabled as the shower heads had not been fitted to the others. Similarly, the bar, shop, takeaway, etc. were still to be fitted out. There are plans for 3 swimming pools, minigolf and other recreational activities, all scheduled for completion before 1994. The site has wooden gites, operated by Gites de France, and if the finishing touches still needed on the site are of the same quality as those in the gites, then this site will rate as one of the very best (if not the very best) municipals we have ever seen. This is an area well worth visiting, with attractive scenery, interesting history, excellent wines and good food.

Directions: Town is 35 km. east of Macon. Follow N79/E62 (Charolles/Paray/Digoin) road and turn south onto D41 to Dompierre-les-Ormes (3 km.) Site is clearly signed through village.

Charges 1993:
-- Per adult Ffr. 15.00; child 10.00; pitch 15.00.
Open:
15 June - 30 Sept.
Address:
71970 Dompierre-les-Ormes.
Tel:
Site: 85.50.29.43.
FAX: 85.50.28.25.
Reservations:
Contact site.

CHAMPAGNE-ARDENNE

Ardennes - Marne - Haute-Marne - Aube

This is a region relatively close to the Channel ports, and often rapidly driven-through in the quest to put 'more miles on the clock'. This is a pity because this region has much to offer the visitor. It is a region of forests, meadowlands and nature reserves; of lakes and rivers catering for all kinds of watersports; of history, with Rheims, Troyes and Langres all worth a closer look; of 'haute cuisine' with an impressive world-wide reputation, and of course the jewel in the crown - Champagne itself.

5102 Camping Municipal, Châlons-sur-Marne

Good staging point between Reims and Vitry-le-Francois.

This pleasant, well kept municipal site makes an excellent stopover on the new autoroute (A26) from Calais/Boulogne to Germany, Switzerland or southern France. Sited on flat ground on the river plain, 130 pitches are mainly in rows between access roads, with hardstandings for caravans and grass for tents. There is sparse shade in parts, electrical connections (5A) are available and 40 pitches have water connected. Some long-term French caravans, but also much transit trade and the site says it does not turn people away. The two main sanitary blocks have been renovated and are well equipped with free hot showers, washbasins in cubicles and have facilities for the disabled. A third, small new block for ladies contains a washing machine. One block can be heated. No shop, nearest 150 m. Basic snacks and takeaway in season. Children's playground. Tennis. Table tennis. Volleyball. Boules. TV room. Fishing and boating in pool. 'Snack van' in high season. Telephones (carte). A very clean, orderly and quiet site which makes an excellent overnight stop or short stay.

Directions: Site is south of Châlons; the easiest way to find it is from the N44. If using the autoroute use the La Veuve exit from the A4, connecting with the N44. Site is signposted from the town but the route is a little tortuous. Watch carefully for all signs.

Charges 1993:
-- Per person 21.00 Ffr; child (under 7) 7.00; pitch 19.00; car 12.00; electricity 16.00.

Open:
Week before Easter - Oct.

Address:
51000 Châlons-sur-Marne.

Tel:
26.68.38.00.

Reservations:
Write to site.

CÔTE d'AZUR
Alpes-Maritimes

Quite simply the Côte d'Azur is the French Riviera - arguably the most famous beach resort area in Europe, perhaps in the world, with resorts such as Cannes, Nice and Monte Carlo, it has an enviable climate, with summer temperatures averaging 24°C in July and August, and winter temperatures averaging 11°C in January - March. Although its main claim to fame is its seaside resorts and beaches (which naturally become very crowded during the summer season) there are many worthwhile excursions inland, to places such as Grasse (of perfume fame) and Sospel.

0601 Domaine Sainte Madeleine, Sospel

Peaceful site, with swimming pool, in spectacular mountain scenery.

Situated a few miles inland from Menton, and very near the Italian border, the approach to this site is not for the faint-hearted although, to be fair, the road is actually not as bad as it looks and the site itself makes the effort worthwhile. Although terraced, manoeuvering within the site presents no problem and the pitches, whilst not marked, offer sufficient space on fairly level well drained grass, with electrical connections to 70 of the 90 pitches and some shade. There is a 140 sq.m. swimming pool (heated in spring and autumn). The single sanitary block, of excellent quality, has seatless toilets, washbasins in private cabins, and good hot showers, although (unusually for France) these are on payment (Ffr 3.00). Laundry facilities with two washing machines. Although there are no catering facilities on the site, the attractive small town of Sospel is only a short, fairly easy drive and here can be found a quite wide variety of restaurants, bars, cafés and shops. Caravans and chalets for hire. Car wash area.

Charges 1994:
-- Per unit, incl. 2 persons Ffr. 70.00; extra adult 16.00; child 10.00; electricity 10.00.
Open:
All year.
Address:
06380 Sospel.
Tel:
93.04.10.48.
Reservations:
Write to site with Ffr. 200 deposit.

Directions: Site is on the D2566, some 4 km. beyond (ie. north of) Sospel. The D2566 can be reached from either the A8 autoroute via the Menton exit, or from the N7 at Menton.

0602 Caravan Inn, Opio, nr Grasse

Good quality site for caravans only, with large plots and swimming pools.

Near the hills around Grasse and 18 km. inland from the sea at Cannes, Caravan Inn has 120 plots which are appreciably larger than one usually finds on touring sites. They are mostly about 150-180 sq.m. and partly terraced, all with electricity and with water laid on, with much shade available. Half are kept for permanent caravans, the other half for tourists - caravans and motor caravans are taken, but not tents. The site has an attractive bar/restaurant with a terrace, providing good value waiter service and takeaway meals. There are two swimming pools (unheated) one for adults and one for children, (open at least 1/6-20/9) with a small charge. Shop. Restaurant. Tennis. Volleyball. Table tennis. Golf and riding nearby. Children's playground. TV on request in bar for big events. The four toilet blocks, though not large, are of good quality and between them give a good coverage to the site. One can be heated. British toilets, individual basins in cubicles with mirror, shelves, and free hot water in basins, sinks, showers and ladies' baths. English spoken. Gas barbeques only.

Charges 1993:
-- Per unit incl. 4 persons and electricity (2A) July/Aug Ffr 143.50 - 179.20 acc. to pitch type; other times incl. 2 persons 74.30 - 84.90; extra person 15.75, or child (under 6 yrs) 7.90; extra small tent 8.50 - 14.30; electricity 4A 11.45, 10A 14.30.
Open:
Easter - 30 Sept.
Address:
18 Rte de Cannes, 06860 Opio.
Tel:
93.77.32.00.
Reservations:
Made with 25% deposit and fee (Ffr 100), full payment on arrival; Sat. to Sat. only in July/Aug.

Directions: Turn off A85 9 km. east of Grasse onto D7 and D3 and continue to site. Site is on the D3 road (Châteauneuf de Grasse - Valbonne), signposted from Châteauneuf.

0605 Camping La Vieille Ferme, Villeneuve Loubet Plage, nr Antibes

Family owned site with good facilities, open all year, in popular resort area.

La Vieille Ferme has been developed and improved over the years and now provides over 100 level, grass pitches with some shade. These range from a special 'camping car' pitch, tarmaced and with water, drainage and electricity laid on, other special pitches with all facilities neatly hedged (some for winter camping), to simple terraced pitches for small tents. The toilet facilities in 4 units, provide British toilets, washbasins with pre-mixed hot water in a general wash room or in private cabins, and well equipped showers. One unit can be heated for winter use and there are facilities for the handicapped.

There is a shop in main season but a drinks, sweets and ices machine is situated in the TV room for all year use and essentials are kept in the office. The swimming pool (20 x 10 m.) can be covered for use in the winter. Table tennis. Boules. Refrigerator hire. Laundry facilities. Safety deposit and exchange facilities. The site is making every effort to provide facilities all year round within commercial viability and special rates are available for long stay winter visitors. A long pebbly beach is a 1 km. walk away or drive via a railway underpass (caravanettes take care). Parking is usually possible even in high season. English is spoken at reception. Chalets to let.

Directions: From west take Antibes exit from Esterel autoroute and turn left towards Nice when meeting N7 outside Antibes. After 3½ km. on N7 turn left for site. From east take N2 towards Antibes and turn right after Villeneuve Loubet Plage. The turning off the N7, though signposted, is not easy to see particularly at busy times but is between an antique shop and park. Site is 150 m. on right.

Charges 1994:
-- Prices outside 4/7 - 31/8 in brackets.
-- Per pitch incl. up to 3 persons (2 persons in low season): tent Ffr 97.00 (78.00); caravan pitch with electricity 130.00 (78.00); pitch with all services 142.00 (86.00); extra person 23.00 (18.00); child (under 5) 18.00 (12.50); extra car 20.00 (13.00); electricity 13.00 (2A) - 21.00 (10A); local tax 1.00.
-- Less 10% - 20% for longer stays in low season.

Open:
All year

Address:
Bvd. des Groules, 06270 Villeneuve Loubet Plage.

Tel:
93.33.41.44.
FAX: 93.33.37.28.

Reservations:
Advisable over a long season and made with substantial deposit and fee (Sat.-Sat. only in July/Aug. and at Easter).

0603 Domaine de la Bergerie, Vence, nr Nice

Large but quiet family type site attractively situated in hills behind Riviera.

La Bergerie is a family owned and run site, situated in the hills about 3 km. from Vence and 10 km. from the sea at the nearest point, at Cagnes sur Mer. It is a very extensive site, part grassy and part lightly wooded, in a quiet and rather secluded situation about 300 m. above sea level. Most parts have shade. However, even if it is less crowded than the coastal sites, it is difficult enough to find a pitch here in high season. There are 42 special pitches with water, drainage and electricity. The original sanitary facilities have now been supplemented by a large new, tiled block of a good standard with hot water throughout and the largest number of facilities (toilets, basins and showers) for the handicapped we have seen in France. Good provision also for children. British toilets, with some continental toilets in the older block. There are no letting units on the site, no tour operators or organized activities but there is an attractive small bar/restaurant, takeaway and shop (1/5-30/9). Children's playground and paddling pool. Table tennis. 10 shaded boules pitches, lit at night with competitions in season. Winter caravan storage.

Directions: Site is west of Vence; follow camp sign out of town (right and left turn) and, after 2 km. left at crossroads to site. Approaching from coast take Vence bypass which avoids town centre. From the autoroute take the Cagnes exit in the direction of Vence and follow camp signs.

Charges 1993:
-- Per unit with up to 3 persons Ffr 71.00; with electricity 86.00; special pitch with 3 services 101.50; extra person 17.00; child (under 5) 11.00; extra car 11.00; local tax (over 18s) 1.00.
-- Rates available from site for seasonal pitches.

Open:
15 March - 31 Oct.

Address:
Rte de la Sine,
06140 Vence.

Tel:
93.58.09.36.

Reservations:
Made only for the special pitches.

0604 Le Grand Saule, Cannes-La Bocca

Agreeable, small site with swimming pool, within Cannes limits.

This little site is in a pleasant setting, and although only 200 m. from a busy through road, the intervening wooded area seems to give it sufficient screening to make the camp itself quite peaceful. It is only 1½ km. from the beach at La Bocca and 4 km. from Cannes town centre, so it's position is unusually handy for one of the show places of the Riviera. A bus stop is close to the entrance gate. There is a small swimming pool of irregular shape on site, beside an attractive terrace bar and small restaurant (all services open all season).

The camping and caravanning side holds only 55 units (of any type), the majority being individual ones of quite good size in boxes with separating hedges etc. and with electricity, water points and drainaway. Other pitches are not fully marked out but have electricity and water not far away. Many have some degree of shade. There are also 25 small apartments to let for self-catering. The small toilet block, though kept busy, is well kept and clean, with British WCs, free fully controllable hot showers, washbasins with cold water (some in private cabins) and with hot water in clothes/dishes sinks and a washing machine. No shop - many very close. Tennis club adjoining, open to clients. Table tennis. Children's frames. Sauna. With its situation, the site is naturally not cheap.

Directions: From A8 autoroute take the Cannes-Ouest exit, turn towards Cannes, passing airport, left into Ave. de Coubertin, then into Ave. Jourdan, cross under autoroute, then 300 m. to camp on right. Le Grand Saule is signposted from most main junctions in La Bocca.

Charges 1994:
-- Per unit incl. 2 persons Ffr 87.00 - 124.00, 3 persons 124.00 - 163.00; car 18.00; electricity 18.00.

Open:
Easter - mid-Oct.

Address:
24-25 Bd. Jean Moulin,
06110 Le Cannet-Cannes.

Tel:
93.90.55.10.
FAX: 93.47.24.55.

Reservations:
Recommended and made from any day with refundable deposit equivalent to 1 weeks stay.

DAUPHINY ALPES

Isère

With its lively forward-looking University City of Grenoble as its centre, this region is a delight for all lovers of mountain scenery. The views are spectacular everywhere; well-engineered roads linking the pretty and welcoming villages, enable you to drive right into the heart of the mountains. The range of outdoor activities is impressive and includes climbing, caving, riding, fishing, walking and cycling as well as many others. For the rather less active (or the active in need of fortification) a visit to the Chartreuse distillery at Voiron is to be recommended.

3801 Le Coin Tranquille, Les Abrets

Family run site with swimming pool and restaurant, in peaceful surroundings.

Set in peaceful surroundings in the Dauphiny countryside, this is a pleasant and friendly site with some 185 pitches, all with electrical connections and separated by hedging. There is a fair amount of shade. Amenities include an 80 sq.m. swimming pool, plus paddling pool, and a restaurant (open all year) which is also used by locals and has an extensive, reasonably priced menu. Les Abrets is in the Bas-Dauphine region, well situated in relation to the Chartreuse Massif, the two Savoy regions and the Alps.

There are three fairly small sanitary blocks providing a range of facilities including both British and continental type WCs, hot showers and wash-basins (cold water only) in private cabins, and dishwashing facilities. Construction of a further, really first class block has been completed and this includes private wash cabins with hot and cold water, showers and special facilities for children and for the disabled. Shop. Takeaway. Laundry with ironing facilities. Two children's play areas, on grass. TV/video room. Live entertainment during the season. There is a games room downstairs and a quiet lounge.

Directions: Site is situated northeast of the town of Les Abrets. From the town take the N6 towards Chambery, turning left after about 2 km, from where the site is signposted.

Charges 1994:
-- Per pitch incl. 2 persons Ffr 102.00; extra adult 28.00; child 14.00; electricity 2A 8.00, 3A 12.00.
-- Less outside July/Aug.

Open:
1 April - 31 Oct.

Address:
38490 Les Abrets en Dauphine.

Tel:
76.32.13.48.
FAX: 76.37.40.67.

Reservations:
Write to site with deposit (Ffr. 600) and fee (50).

3802 Camping Municipal Porte de la Chartreuse, Voiron

Neat, modern little municipal site, quite satisfactory for overnight or a short stay.

With less than 100 pitches, most wih electricity, on flat grassy strips divided by access roads, the site becomes full each evening in high season, but they try to find room for all, which may mean squeezing a little close during this period. The two toilet blocks are both small but maybe just large enough; toilets of mixed type, washbasins in private cabins, hot showers on payment. One block can be heated. No shop on site; others at 500 m. Some mobile traders call. Games room. Children's playground.

Directions: Site is in northern part of the town beside the A48 road to Bourg and Lyon (perhaps some road noise).

Charges 1993:
-- Per adult 17.00; child (under 15 yrs) 10.00; pitch 15.00; caravan 15.00; motorcaravan 19.00; tent 8,00; electricity 15.00.

Open:
All year.

Address:
38500 Voiron.

Reservations:
Made with deposit for min. 1 week for July/Aug.

3803 Camping La Cascade, Bourg d'Oisans, nr Grenoble

Small site amongst the mountains, with heated sanitary facilities.

Although very much among the mountains, with the ski resorts of Alpe d'Huez and Les Deux Alpes close at hand, Bourg d'Oisans, which is in the Romanches valley at 725 metres above sea level, presents no access problems at all for caravanners. You simply drive from Grenoble along the wide N91 Briancon road with no passes or steep gradients. La Cascade is close to, and within sight and sound of, the waterfall from which it takes its name. It has about 130 individual pitches of varying but quite adequate size on mainly flat ground. The two heated sanitary blocks are of top quality with mainly British toilets, washbasins in private cabins with light, mirror, free hot water; good free hot showers, fully controllable. The heated municipal swimming pool is very close but the site now reports the construction of its own pool. Shop. Snack bar. Children's playground. General room with TV. Animation some evenings. Games/TV room. Table tennis. Volleyball. Boules. Washing machine.

Directions: Site is about 400 m. along the road towards Alpe d'Huez which leads off from the N91 just east of Bourg d'Oisans.

Charges 1994:
-- Per unit inc. 2 persons Ffr. 84.00, 3 persons 105.00; extra adult 18.00, or child (under 10) 12.00; camper on foot, bicycle or m/cycle 36.00; local tax (15/6 - 31/8) 1.00; electricity (6A) 15.00 (more in winter - 25.00 - 30.00).

Open:
1 Feb - 30 Sept

Address:
38520 Bourg d'Oisans.

Tel:
76.80.02.42.

Reservations:
Essential for July/Aug; made for any length with deposit and fee.

CAMPING – CARAVANNING

LA CASCADE ★ ★ ★ ★NN
Open from 1 February – 30 September
Caravans and Chalets for Hire
Swimming Pool
CLEAN – CALM – COMFORTABLE
38520 Bourg d'Oisans
Tel 76.80.02.42   Reduced rates outside July/August

3804 Camping La Rencontre du Soleil, Bourg d'Oisans, nr Grenoble

Small, friendly site in mountain area.

Situated almost opposite Camping La Cascade, this site is somewhat smaller with 80 enlarged pitches. There is little to choose between them. Rencontre de Soleil is an informal and friendly site, again with individual, mainly flat pitches of varying size. It has a good heated toilet block with British toilets, basins with free hot water, shelf and mirror, mostly in private cabins, and preset free hot showers; it should be large enough. Torches required at night. Bar with terrace. No shop; supermarket 1½ km. in town. Self-service restaurant, with takeaway. Pizzeria. Tennis. General room for sitting and TV, children's play room adjoining. Drying room. Swimming pool. Bourg d'Oisans is situated at the foot of France's largest National Park - Le Parc des Ecrins. A haven for cycling enthusiasts, it is at the centre of the staging points for the Tour de France.

Directions: Situated almost opposite no. 3803 on the Alpe d'Huez road from the N91, just east of the town.

Charges 1994:
-- Per unit incl. 2 persons Ffr. 87.00 - 106.00; extra person 25.00, or child (under 5) 15.00; electricity 15.00 - 23.00, acc. to amps; local tax 2.00.

Open:
23 March - 9 Sept.

Address:
38520 Bourg d'Oisans.

Tel:
76.80.00.33.

Reservations:
Made with deposit and fee (min. 1 week) and essential in peak season as site has many regular clients.

FRANCHE COMTE
Haute-Sâone - Doubs - Jura - Tre. de Belfort

This beautiful region, tucked up against the Swiss border, is best visited in Autumn when the forests are so colourful. However there is a great deal for the holidaymaker to do in all the seasons - the mountains of the Jura, in the south of the region, cater for winter sports and watersports in summer, with an extensive range of facilities and activities. If you like mountains, the Jura is relatively undiscovered, and the traditional way of life still exists in many areas. Franche-Comté, like Alsace, has seen many invasions in its history, and this is reflected in its differing architectural styles. For lovers of mountains and history this region is well-worth a visit, and it really is an area (as yet) not subjected to 'mass tourism'.

2500 Castel Camping Caravaning Le Val de Bonnal, Rougemont
Well managed, attractive site in large country estate.

This is an impressive site, harmoniously designed in keeping with the surrounding countryside, well away from main roads and other intrusions. Having said that the site itself is very busy, with a wide range of activities and amenities. The pitches, all of a good size and with electricity (5A), are separated by a mixture of trees and bushes, carefully landscaped. Some of the newer pitches are less secluded, but the ambience generally is peaceful despite the size of the site (200 pitches in 37 acres) and its deserved popularity.

The four toilet blocks, very clean when visited, provide free hot showers (some with separators) washbasins in private cabins and British WCs. There are separate washing up blocks, with sinks and free hot water, and coin-operated washing machines, ironing boards and sinks for hand washing clothes. Amenities include La Forge restaurant, situated beyond the river in the adjoining leisure park, on-site snack bar/takeaway, bar, terrace, shop, situated in sympathetically converted former farm buildings, well equipped children's play areas, and a range of sport facilities including table tennis, boules, bicycle hire, etc, but the main attraction is the variety of watersports on the 3 large lakes and nearby river. These include swimming, pedaloes, and fishing as well as water skiing, windsurfing and canoeing. In fact, the range of activities available at this site is almost inexhaustible, not to say exhausting - you can even go hot air ballooning! There are also 150 hectares to walk in and it is ideally placed for day trips to Switzerland.

Directions: From Vesoul take the D9 towards Villersexel. After approx. 20 km. turn right in the village of Esprels at sign for Val de Bonnal. Follow for 3½ km. and site is on the left.

Charges 1993:
-- Per pitch with electricity, incl. 2 persons Ffr. 111.00, without electricity 91.00; extra person 25.00; child (2-7 yrs) 12.00; local tax 1.00 per day.

Open:
15 May - 15 September.

Address:
Bonnal, 25680 Rougemont.

Tel:
81.86.90.87.

Reservations:
Only made for pitches with electricity. Contact site.

All the camp sites featured in this guide are regularly inspected by our team of experienced site assessors.

FRANCHE COMTE - Jura

3900 Camping Les Bords de Loue, Parcey, nr Dole
Satisfactory camp on the banks of the River Loue.

The Jura has many types of landscape, but here the countryside is green and flat, stretching almost as far as the eye can see. The River Loue, by which this camp is situated, meanders across the plain and provides a bathing beach along one side of the site. There is much natural beauty and historical interest in this region and Les Bords de Loue could well provide a base for investigating these. The site is under new management - the third change in as many years - and they are busy updating, improving and adding to the facilities. We can therefore only comment on expectations and not what has actually been achieved.

The 200 pitches on flat grass are being increased to 350 on either side of gravel roads with electricity in all parts. There are trees around the camp but not too much shade. The four sanitary blocks (2 new and 2 old) are being improved and increased with a mix of British seatless and continental toilets. Bar with takeaway service and full restaurant (from 1993). There is swimming in the river and a pool is under construction. Mobile butcher and baker call - small shops in village, larger ones in Dole (8 km.). Tennis. Table tennis. Fishing. Boating. Volleyball. Horse riding near. Minigolf 1 km. Children's play area. Washing machines and dryers. The pleasant owners hope to welcome more British visitors and our readers comments would be welcome.

Directions: Site is 1 km. west of Parcey. Leave autoroute A36 at Dole exit and follow ring road signed Geneva to the N5. Parcey is just after where the N5 joins the D405 from the centre of Dole. Camp is signed in the village.

Charges 1994:
-- Per person Ffr. 19.00 + local tax 1.50; child (under 7 yrs) 13.00; pitch 25.00; electricity (3A) 13.00.

Open:
15 April - 15 Sept.

Address:
39100 Parcey.

Tel:
84.71.03.82.

Reservations:
Write to site.

3903 Le Domaine de Chalain, Doucier, nr Lons-le-Saunier
Large lakeside site with many sports and amenities available.

Doucier lies east of Lons-le-Saunier among the wooded hills of the Jura, and rather away from the main routes. This large, park-like site is situated on the edge of a lake surrounded on three sides by woods and some cliffs. Large areas are left for sports and recreation. The lake shelves gently at the edge but then becomes deep quite suddenly; there is a small shallow pool for non-swimmers. Day visitors can be very numerous on fine weekends.

The site is divided into two parts, one (nearer the lake) with larger pitches (costing rather more). You should find room in the other part, but from 5/7-16/8, it is better to reserve to make sure. Over 200 electrical connections; little shade. There are 8 sanitary blocks which have been improved over the years. Continental and seatless WCs; washbasins with warm water mainly in private cabins; free hot showers in separate blocks. Shops, takeaway (no restaurant) both 31/5-31/8. Bar. Large community room. Tennis courts. Table tennis. Paddling pool. Minigolf. Small electric boats and pedaloes for hire. Animals and birds in enclosures. Organised activities. Cinema. Disco for young. Washing machines. Medical centre with nurse. Used by tour operators.

Directions: The site can only be approached via Doucier: from Switzerland via N5 (from Geneva), then the N78 and D39; from other directions via Lons-le-Saunier or Champagnole.

Charges 1993:
-- Per unit incl. 3 persons: lake pitch Ffr 66.00 - 109.00, central area 102.00, hill area 94.00; electricity 14.00; pitch with 3 services 85.00 - 130.00; extra person 12.00 - 16.00; child (under 10 yrs) 6.00 - 8.00; extra small tent 6.00; local tax 1.00.

Open:
At least 1 May - 15 Oct.

Address:
Doucier, B.P. 96 F. 39003 Lons le Saunier.

Tel:
84.24.29.00.
FAX: 84.24.94.07.

Reservations:
Made with deposit (Ffr 320) and fee (80) for min. 5 days.

3901 La Plage Blanche, Ounans
Attractive riverside site with good amenities.

Situated in open countryside, along the banks of the River Loue with its own small beach, this site has 120 good sized pitches (marked out) on level ground, most with electricity (3A). Trees have been planted, although as yet there is little shade. It is said to be possible to swim in the river and we are told that this is normally safe for children although, when we were there, the river was in flood after heavy rain. New sanitary facilities in two unusual blocks have tiled hot showers, separate washcabins, ample hooks, mirrors etc, and with both seatless and continental WCs. Bar/snack-bar, with terrace. River fishing. Launderette. Table tennis. Riding. Bicycle hire. TV. Children's play area. Caravans for hire.

Directions: Ounans is about 20 km southeast of Dole. The site is best approached from Dole via the D405 to Parcey, thence via the N5 towards Poligny, turning left after 7 km. onto D472 to Ounans from where site is signed.

Charges 1993:
-- Per person Ffr 18.00 plus local tax 1,00; child (under 7 yrs) 10.00 plus 0.50; pitch 22.00; extra car 12.00; dog 4.00; electricity (3A) 14.00.
Open:
1 April - 30 Sept.
Address:
39380 Ounans.
Tel:
84.37.69.63.
Reservations:
Write with Ffr. 200 deposit.

3902 Camping de Surchauffant, La Tour du Meix, nr Orgelet
Comfortable site situated on the shores of Lake Vouglans.

This site is one of a group which includes site no. 3903 but is much smaller, having only 200 pitches. It may appeal to those who prefer a more informal/intimate atmosphere. It is pleasantly situated above the beaches bordering the Lac de Vouglans, which also offers a variety of watersports activities, boat trips etc. and is used for swimming, being guarded in high season as it shelves steeply. The pitches are of reasonable size, informally arranged, and most offer electricity; they are divided by hedges, and there is some shade. The sanitary installations are adequate rather than luxurious, with seatless WCs, hot showers and some washbasins in private cabins. Restaurant/bar. Laundry. Shops nearby. Children's games. Watersports on lake.

Directions: From Lons le Saunier take the D52 to Orgelet. Site is situated adjacent to the D470, at La Tour du Meix, about 4 km. east of Orgelet.

Charges 1993:
-- Per unit incl. 2 persons Ffr 47.00 - 60.00; with electricity 61.00 - 74.00; with 3 services 63.00 - 79.00; extra adult 11.00 - 14.00; child (under 10 yrs) 6.00 - 7.00; local tax 1.00.
Open:
1 May - 30 Sept.
Address:
39270 La Tour du Meix.
Tel:
84.25.41.08.
Reservations:
Write with deposit (Ffr. 620) and fee (80).

3904 Camping La Pergola, Marigny, Lac du Chalain
Hillside, terraced site overlooking lake.

Lac de Chalain sparkles amidst the undulating, cultivated countryside of this part of the Jura. Not on any main route, it is worth a detour if you are seeking the restful peace of the countryside. Having said that, the lake could well be crowded at weekends in summer. The 300 pitches at La Pergola are on numerous, level, stony terraces, with steep steps between, giving an excellent view over the lake from all places. Hedges of small conifers separate the numbered pitches but there is little shade. A tall wire fence protects the site from the public footpath which separates the camp from the lake but there are access points. A large restaurant at the entrance is shared with members of the public who use the lake for watersports. The five new sanitary blocks (mixed British and continental WCs) are distributed about the camp but if you pitch on a terrace without one, there are steep steps to negotiate. Supermarket. Swimming pool. Table tennis. Volleyball. Disco (high season). Washing machines, dryers and irons. Facilities for the disabled but site not really suitable.Used by three British tour operators.

Directions: Site is 2½ km. north of Doucier on Lake Chalain, on road D27.

Charges 1993:
-- Per unit incl. 2 persons, electricity and water: lake pitch Ffr. 70.00 - 140.00, plus supplement 6/6-5/9 30.00; standard pitch 70.00 - 120.00; extra person 25.00; child 10.00; extra car 15.00; local tax 1.00.
Open:
1 May - 30 Sept.
Address:
39130 Marigny.
Tel:
84.25.70.03.
FAX: 84.25.75.96.
Reservations:
Write to site.

> see advertisement in previous colour section

LANGUEDOC-ROUSSILLON
Lozère - Gard - Hérault - Aude - Pyrénées-Orientales

Essentially two regions (Languedoc and Roussillon) somewhat artificially 'cobbled together' some years ago for mainly administrative reasons, Languedoc-Roussillon, with its Mediterranean coastline, stretches from the Spanish border in the west to the Rhône in the east, and from the under-populated Lozère in the north, to its cosmopolitan regional capital, Montpellier in the south. It contains areas of high mountains, the Pyrénées and the Cevennes, and stark and quite arid uplands, and fertile vine-covered coastal plains. Sleepy villages and fascinating towns such as Nîmes, Beziers, Carcassonne and Perpignan, the tranquility of the famous Canal du Midi, the Minerve and the Route of the Cathars, the awe-inspiring Gorges du Tarn, ultra-modern coastal resorts such as La Grande Motte, Cap d'Agde and Canet, somehow combine (and contrast) to give this large region a fascination all of its own.

1101 Camping Eden II, Villefort, nr Chalabre/Ariege
Potentially most attractive site in spectacular scenery, near the Pyrénées.

Set in beautiful surroundings, this well equipped new site is situated in the foothills of the Pyrénées and provides an ideal location to explore this area; there is a ski station 30 km. away. Growing trees planted around the site provide a number of shady pitches. When visited there were 75 marked pitches on mainly level ground, the majority having electricity and drainage of which 8 are 'super-pitches' with their own sanitary facilities, including hot showers. These and the main, large sanitary block have been built to very high standards and are among the best we have seen; the amenities include a small unit for the disabled, laundry and ironing facilities and even hairdryers. There is an attractive, partly shaded, swimming pool and sun bathing terrace adjacent to the small bar/restaurant and takeaway. Mini-shop at present. Refrigerator for ice packs. Archery. Table tennis. Volleyball. Tennis. Golf practise. Children's playground. Bicycle hire. Riding, fishing, watersports near. Comprehensive literature and ideas about activities in the area are provided. Mobile homes and chalets for hire.

Directions: Site is situated between Quillan and Lavelanet, off the D117. Take the D16 north at Puivert; site is on left before village of Villefort.

Charges 1993:
-- Per pitch, incl. 2 adults: basic (tent) Ffr 52.00 - 59.00; pitch + electricity (6-10A) 73.00 - 83.00; with 3 services 94.00 - 107.00; plus sanitary facility 115.00 - 132.00; extra person 13.00; extra small tent (high season) 6.00 - 10.00; local tax 1.00.

Open:
Mid-March - mid-Oct.

Address:
Domaine de Carbonas, Villefort, 11230 Chalabre.

Tel:
68.69.26.33.
FAX: 68.69.29.95.

Reservations:
Made with min. Ffr. 200 deposit, Sat.-Sat.

1102 Camping Le Moulin du Pont d'Alies, Axat, nr Quillan
Site for visiting the Pyrénées or night halt on the way to Spain.

For those travelling from Toulouse to the Spanish frontier at Le Perthus, the route via Limoux and Quillan is more pleasant than the main road, though not so quick. This site is on this route and makes a good night stop, or a base for exploring the Pyrénées. It is on a flat piece of ground between the N117 road and the river Aude, and 1½ km. north of Axat. Shade available and many electrical connections. A small swimming pool was built in 1992. Two sanitary blocks which have been refurbished, part tiled, have vanity style washbasins, some in private cabins, seatless toilets and free hot showers. Cleaning may be variable. Improved washing up and laundry sinks. Facilities for the disabled. Washing machine. Small shop (July/Aug). Large general room with bar. Table tennis. Mountain walks. Trout fishing. Children's playground. Petrol station. Watersports including canoeing, rafting, hydrospeed. Caving and climbing nearby and the site is popular with young people for canoeing. Chalets for hire.

Directions: Site is off the N117, 11 km. east of Quillan, by junction with N118.

Charges 1993:
-- Per unit, incl. 2 persons 58.00 Ffr; tent pitch incl. 1 person on foot or with m/cycle 40.00; extra person 14.00; child (under 6) 7.00; electricity (4A) 13.00; dog 6.00.

Open:
1 June - 10 Sept.

Address:
St Martin Lys, 11140 Axat.

Tel:
68.20.53.27.

Reservations:
Made if some deposit sent.

1103 Camping Municipal La Pinède, Lézignan-Corbières

Satisfactory site by the Narbonne-Carcassonne road next to swimming pool.

A modern little municipal site, within walking distance of the little town and only 35 km. from Narbonne Plage, having transit trade in addition to longer term. La Pinède has been laid out in terraces on a hillside, with good internal access on made-up roads. The 94 individual pitches vary quite a bit in size and are divided up mainly by various shrubs and bushes with electricity available. Outside the gates are a good sized municipal swimming pool, open 1/7-31/8, and tennis courts. The 3 sanitary blocks make up an excellent provision and they are of quite reasonable quality; mostly continental toilets, but free hot water between certain hours morning and evening in the washbasins (in private cabins) and in the numerous hot showers. Many water points. Small shop with bar and hot food (open 1/7-31/8). Washing machine. Mobile homes for rent.

Directions: Access directly off main N113 on west side of Lézignan-Corbières

Charges 1993:
-- Per adult Ffr. 15.50; child 9.50; pitch 15.50; electricity 14.00.
-- Less outside 17/6 - 16/9.

Open:
1 April - 15 Oct.

Address:
11200 Lézignan.

Tel:
68.27.05.08.

Reservations:
Advisable in season.

1104 Camping Le Martinet Rouge, Brousses-et-Villaret, nr Carcassonne

Very pretty, rather quaint retreat in Aude countryside north of Carcassonne.

LE MARTINET
ROUGE ★ ★ ★

BROUSSES-ET-VILLARET, 11390 CUXAC-CABARDÈS, France
Tél: 68/26.51.98. domicile: 26.50.80

35 emplacements sur 2 ha. Propriétaires Mr et Mme MARTY

A shady, quiet, clean site suitable to visit the medieval walled city of Carcassonne or enjoy the surrounding rich countryside with rivers, forests, caves and gorges. An area with many traces of its historic past including the "Cathar Castles" and well worth visiting.

This is a very pretty, little site with a rather old-fashioned feel - this extends to the sanitary blocks which, on first sight, look rather antiquated but on closer inspection were immaculate. They have British WCs, large hot showers, washbasins (hot water) in private cabins, dishwashing and laundry facilities, including a washing machine. The most striking features of the site are the massive granite boulders (outcrops of smooth rock) throughout the area used for sunbathing and by children for playing on - some look potentially dangerous! Fossils have been collected and displayed in the little shop and there is a small shrine, the history of which we did not discover. The site offers only 35 pitches in two contrasting areas - one is well secluded with irregularly shaped, fairly level pitches created amongst a variety of trees and shrubs, while the other is on open meadow more typical of English rather than French sites. There are said to be electrical connections throughout and more have now been added (when we last visited boxes were well spaced out, sometimes requiring a long cable). Small bar/café serving only snacks but a number of restaurants in the surrounding villages. Small, quite well stocked shop. Useful also as a possible overnight stop. Tennis, swimming, riding, fishing quite close. Caravans and bungalows to let. The site reports the addition of a swimming pool.

Directions: Using the N113 going west from Carcassonne, turn right onto the D48 just after the village of Pezens (6 km). Follow D48 for 8 km. (surface not so good) and site is signposted just before the village of Brousses-et-Villaret.

Charges 1994:
-- Per pitch incl. 2 persons and car Ffr. 55.00; person 17.00; extra car 10.00; electricity 16.00.

Open:
1 May - 30 Sept.

Address:
Brousses-et-Villaret
11390 Cuxac-Cabardes.

Tel:
68.26.51.98.

Reservations:
Made with deposit of 20%.

1106 Camping Au Pin d'Arnauteille, Montclar, nr Carcassonne

Peaceful, small, developing site with superb views to the Corbières and beyond.

Enjoying some of the best and most varied views of any site we have visited, this rather unusual site is ideally situated for exploring, by foot or by car, the little known Aude Dèpartement, the area of the Cathars and for visiting the walled city of Carcassonne (a 10 minute drive). However, access could be difficult for large, twin axle vans. The site itself is set in some 115 hectares of farmland and is on hilly ground with the mere 75 large pitches (all with electricity at 3 or 6A) arranged on grassy and gently sloping terraces with some shade. There is a new 25 x 10 m. swimming pool with paved sunbathing area in a hollow basin surrounded by green fields with some newly developed pitches. The sanitary facilities are modern and unisex, the main one part open, part enclosed, another under the pool and one behind reception. They are well located for all areas and provide modern facilities including British WCs, hot showers with dressing areas, washbasins in cabins with hot water, dishwashing under cover (with hot water) and laundry facilities with washing machine. Facilities for the handicapped and a baby bath are other features in what amounts to a good overall provision.

A new restaurant has been constructed in a converted old building (snacks and takeaway also). The reception building is vast; originally a farm building, subsequently a new top floor being added by former owners (to create a nursing home) but later converted to apartments. Although architecturally a disaster, from some angles it is quite attractive - any estate agents among our readers who would like to provide a description for us? Mature trees soften the outlines. Shop. Table tennis. Volleyball. Horse riding. Fishing 2 km. Chalets, mobile homes and bungalow tents to let. This is a developing site with enthusiastic owners who also keep horses for riding.

Directions: Using D118 from Carcassonne, after bypassing the small village of Rouffiac d'Aude, there is a small section of dual carriageway. Before the end of this, turn right to Montclar up a rather narrow road for 3 km. Site is signposted sharp left and up hill before the village.

Charges 1993:
-- Per person Ffr. 17.00;
child (under 7 yrs) 11.00;
pitch 20.00; car 11.00;
electricity 15.00; dog 4.00.
-- Less 10% outside 18/6 -
14/9.

Open:
1 April - 30 Sept.

Address:
11250 Montclar.

Tel:
68.26.84.53.
FAX: 68.26.91.10.

Reservations:
Made with deposit of 35%
of charges.

1105 Camping La Bernede, Rennes-Les-Bains

Pleasantly sheltered municipal site within easy walking distance of small spa town.

Situated in a sheltered position alongside the river, within 10 minutes walking distance (along either river bank) of the town, this is a small site ideal for a visit to this interesting little spa town and little known area steeped in Cathar history. The 50 pitches are of reasonable size, all with electricity (10A) and on fairly level grass with easy access, although access to the site itself is over a rather narrow, unfenced, low bridge/ford. There is a modern sanitary block with British and Turkish style WCs, hot showers, washbasins (3 with hot water) and washing up facilities. Although there is no restaurant or shop on site, bread is delivered daily and the site is within easy reach of the several bars, restaurants and shops in Rennes Les Bains, including the local bar/restaurant in the town square which we found to offer good value. Readers tell us there is a good English owned restaurant further up the valley at Bugarach. It is also possible to use the thermal pool and other facilities (cheaper rates over longer periods).

Directions: Using D118 from Carcassonne, 12 km. before Quillan going south, turn right onto D613 at Couiza. Turn right again after 5½ km. to Rennes-les-Bains (3 km.). Follow through village and site is signposted on left past the houses.

Charges 1993:
-- Per pitch Ffr. 16.00; person 13.00; child (under 12 yrs) 7.00; electricity 9.00; animal 5.00.

Open:
15 April - 31 Oct.

Address:
c/o Les Thermes de la Haute Vallée, Grand rue des Thermes, 11190 Rennes Les Bains.

Tel:
68.69.87.01.
FAX: 68.69.80.38.

Reservations:
Write to site

3005 Camping L'Eden, le Grau-du-Roi, nr Montpellier

Good modern site close to beaches and Camargue, with swimming pool.

The Eden is a good example of a modern, purpose built 4-star camp. It is on flat ground about 500 m. from a sandy beach, with 400 individual pitches in regular boxes surrounded by hedges. Shade is available on many of them and electricity on most. Reservation is advisable for the main season. The five sanitary blocks, a good supply, have free hot water everywhere; toilets as so often in France are much shorter than washbasins, which are in cubicles or private cabins; free preset hot showers with pushbutton which runs on. One block has been rebuilt and enlarged, with baby bath and facilities for the disabled. There is a small swimming pool (18 x 8 m.) with water slide and children's pool. Supermarket, boutique, bar and restaurant with takeway (all open all season). TV room. Half court tennis. Minigolf. Archery. Table tennis. In season organised events, sports, excursions, etc. for children and adults. Marina, with sailing lessons, and riding, tennis near. Bicycle hire. Laundry facilities. Free bus service to beach in main season. Some tour operators.

Directions: There is now a road bypassing Le Grau-du-Roi from the west, as well as the approach from Aigues-Mortes. Turn left at sign to `Port Camargue' and `Campings' just northeast of Grau-du-Roi. At next crossroads go left again towards `Phare de l'Espiguette' and after 200 m. right at second sign for l'Eden. **Note:** It is not the site with entrance where you turn; for l'Eden go hard right onto access road and further 200 m. to site on left.

Charges 1994:
-- Per pitch incl. 2 persons: simple (for small tents) Ffr 110.00, with electricity 108.00 - 167.00, with electricity and water 127.00 - 182.00, all acc. to season; extra person 10.00 - 30.00; extra car, small boat 20.00; extra small tent 15.00; local tax 1.00.

Open:
Easter/1 April - 10 Oct

Address:
Port Camargue, 30240 Le Grau-du-Roi.

Tel:
66.51.49.81.
FAX: 66.53.13.20.

Reservations:
Made from Sat. to Sat. only with deposit and fee. Write between 1/1 and 15/5.

LANGUEDOC-ROUSSILLON - Gard

3001 Camping Domaine de la Bastide, Nîmes
Convenient site for visits to Nîmes and other antiquities.

This municipal site has 230 individual pitches on flat ground, 150 fully marked out for caravans in circular groups with electricity (6 or 16A), water and drainaway, and the others for tents. Like many municipal sites, it has workers as well as holiday-makers among its clients. The copious sanitary installations consist of three blocks, one of which can be heated, with British and continental WCs, washbasins in private cabins with shelf, most but not all with hot water, and free hot showers with single push-button at preset temperature (rather too cool when tested). Facilities are provided for the disabled. Self-service shop. Public restaurant/bar with takeaway, open all year and catering for routiers-type lunches. Children's playground. Washing machines. Studios and caravans for hire.

Directions: Site is 5 km. south of city centre on D13 road towards Générac; well signposted from junctions on ring road.

Charges 1993:
-- Per caravan pitch incl. car, electricity Ffr 47.00 (1 person) - 130.00 (6 persons); tent pitch + car 31.50 (1 person) - 120.00 (6 persons); extra person 20.00; extra car 12.00; extra caravan or tent 16.00.
Open:
All year.
Address:
30900 Nîmes.
Tel:
66.38.09.21.
Reservations:
Any length with deposit and large fee for July/Aug.

3006 Domaine des Fumades, Les Fumades, Allègre, nr Alès
Attractive, medium sized site with many activities and near thermal springs.

This is a very pretty site with large pitches (all with electricity) on flat grass, attractively laid out in bays amongst a wide variety of trees. Located in the Cevennes, it is conveniently situated for excursions into the Ardèche, Provence, and the Camargue and within easy reach of the Mediterranean beaches. It has an extensive and varied activity and entertainment programme. There is a good sized swimming pool, with smaller children's pool, and another pool should now be open. Surrounded by terracing, providing ample sunbathing facilities, the pool is overlooked by the restaurant and terrace, located in the attractive original Provencal style buildings, which also house the bar, takeaway, reception, shop and a small sanitary block serving the pool area. The main sanitary block is centrally situated and provides free hot showers in cubicles with separators, including some with washbasin also, British WCs, washbasins in cabins, baby baths, facilities for the disabled. Washing up and laundry facilities are provided. Minigolf. Volleyball. Petanque. Library. American motorhomes are not accepted. Apartments, chalets and caravans for hire. There is one British and one Dutch tour operator.

Directions: From Alès take the D16 through Salindres, continue towards Allègre until you see signs for Fumades (and the thermal springs) on the right.

Charges 1994:
-- Per pitch Ffr 60.00; person 25.00; child (0-7 yrs) 10.00; local tax 1.00; electricity (2A) 10.00 or (4A) 18.00; animal 8.00.
-- less outside July/Aug.
Open:
1 April - 30 Sept.
Address:
Les Fumades,
30599 Allègre.
Tel:
66.24.80.78.
Reservations:
Made with deposit (Ffr 500) and fee (80).

Please show reception staff this Guide when you arrive at a site
- it helps them, us and eventually you too

THE ALAN ROGERS'
Good camps guide

3003 Camping Abri de Camargue, Le Grau-du-Roi, nr Montpellier

Pleasant site with both indoor and outdoor swimming pools.

This is a well organized and agreeable site, which has two free swimming pools, one 250 sq.m. and a smaller indoor heated one (12 x 6 m.) which is overlooked by the restaurant/bar (with heating and air conditioning) and sheltered terrace. The 300 flat pitches are said to average 100 sq.m., but there is some variation in size, and electricity and water are available on most. The camp is now well shaded, with trees and flowering bushes quite luxuriant in parts. The six toilet blocks are of nice quality and should be a good provision. They have British WCs, washbasins in private cabins, adjustable showers and sinks, all with free hot water. Facilities for dishwashing.

The site is 800 m. from two different beaches, those at Port Camargue and L'Espiguette (in July and Aug. a free bus to L'Espiguette beach stops outside). There is a summer fair within walking distance. Le Grau-du-Roi is 1½ km. and the old town of Aigues-Mortes 9. TV room. Takeaway. Washing machines. Children's playground. Bicycle hire. Security guard. All facilities open or available when site is open. Caravans and mobile homes for hire. Used by tour operators. All languages are said to be spoken at reception, although we did not put it to the test.

Directions: There is now a road bypassing Le Grau-du-Roi from west as well as the approach from Aigues-Mortes. Turn left at sign to `Port Camargue' and `Campings' just northeast of Grau-du-Roi. At next crossroads go left again towards `Phare de l'Espiguette/Rive Gauche' and after 200 m. you come to site on right. If approaching via the D979 from north, turn onto D62 and D62A towards La Grande Motte at junction north of Aigues-Mortes.

Charges guide:
-- Per unit with 1 or 2 persons incl. electricity Ffr 85.00 - 155.00; with 3, 4 or 5 persons 95.00 - 165.00, all acc. to season; extra person 10.00; extra car/trailer 20.00.

Open:
1 April - 31 Oct.

Address:
2 Rte. du Phare de l'Espiguette,
Port Camargue,
30240 Le Grau-du-Roi.

Tel:
66.51.54.83.
FAX: 66.51.76.42.

Reservations:
Made for min. 2 weeks and Sun. - Sun. only during 15/7-19/8, otherwise any period, with deposit and sizeable fee for main season.

N3010 Domaine de la Sablière, Saint-Privat-de-Champclos, nr Barjac

Spectacularly situated naturist site in the Cèze Gorges.

This site, occupying a much larger area than its 300 pitches might suggest, enjoys a spectacular situation and offers a wide variety of facilities, all within a really peaceful, wooded and dramatic setting. The pitches are grouped in three main areas - at the bottom of the gorge (mainly for tents) alongside the fast flowing river (good for swimming and canoeing), at various points close to the main access road, which is well surfaced but steep and winding, and in a newer area near the top of the hill, the whole side of which forms part of the site. The pitches themselves are mainly flat on terracing with many of good size, with 3, 6 or 10A electricity. There is a further group of pitches along the river for caravans. During high season cars are banned in one of the areas by the river (used mainly for tents) but parking is provided some 100 - 200 m. away. All the pitches are attractively situated among a variety of trees and shrubs.

There are six sanitary blocks of good quality with excellent free hot showers arranged in typical open plan, naturist site style and washbasins (cold water). Washing up and laundry sinks are also open plan. Toilets are mainly British seatless type. Laundry with 2 washing machines and a dryer. An open air, covered restaurant (1/5-30/9) provides good value, waiter service meals in an attractive setting and a takeaway service. A supermarket (open 28/3-30/9), charcuterie, bureau de change and swimming pool complex, dynamited out of the hillside and built in local style and materials, complete the facilties. The complex provides two large pools and a children's pool, sunbathing terraces, bar, sauna, TV room and a disco (situated about halfway up the hill).

This is essentially a family run and family orientated site. The owner/manager, Gaby Cespedes, and her team, provide a personal touch that is unusual in a large site and this no doubt contributes to the relaxed and very informal atmosphere. First time naturists would probably find that this site would provide a gentle introduction into naturism without any pressure. The activities available at La Sablière are varied and numerous and include walking, climbing, swimming, canoeing, fitness track, fishing, archery, tennis, minigolf, boules (including special floodlit area), table tennis and pottery lessons. Activity and entertainment programme for adults and children (28/6-31/8). Mobile homes, caravans and tents to hire. You must expect some fairly steep walking between pitches, swimming pool complex, restaurant and supermarket and a torch would also be handy.

Directions: From Barjac take D901 for 3 km. Site is signed just before St. Privat-de-Champclos and is 3 km. on narrow roads following camp signs.

Charges 1993:
-- Per regular pitch incl. 2 persons Ffr. 75.00 - 110.00, acc. to season; extra adult 14.00 - 26.00; child (under 8 yrs) 10.00 - 18.00; pet (not accepted in peak season) 9.00 - 13.00; leisure card (for activities) free - 5.00; electricity 3A 20.00, 6A 27.00; local tax (over 16 yrs) 1.00.

Address:
Saint-Privat-de-Champclos 30430 Barjac.

Tel:
66.24.51.16 or 66.24.55.72. FAX: 66.24.58.69.

Reservations:
Made with deposit (Ffr. 250 per week booked) and fee (110).

LANGUEDOC-ROUSSILLON - Lozère

4801 Camping Couderc, Ste. Enimie

Small, family run site on banks of the River Tarn.

Not so well known to the British as Millau, Ste. Enimie is the place in the Gorges of Tarn for the French. The views from the roads either side of Ste. Enimie are quite spectacular, even if the driving is relatively dramatic! Camping Couderc is about 1½ km. from the town and is situated literally on the banks of the Tarn itself. It has been developed from the Couderc family's former vineyard and the level pitches of reasonable quality are on four long terraces, in fact separated by vines. There is also a number of additional pitches on a gently sloping field which also accommodates the children's play area. They are all of roughly 100 sq.m. and electricity is available on most, albeit in some case requiring a long lead.

There is a swimming pool with paved sunbathing area and swimming is also possible in the river (quite fast flowing). The site has canoes for hire but, for the less active or adventurous, boat trips are available from the town of Malène further down the river. Although there is no restaurant at the site itself (snacks are occasionally available in high season and there is a bar) there are several restaurants in the town including one run by the Couderc family. Sanitary facilities, in two new and one older block, include pre-set, pushbutton hot showers with dressing area, some washbasins in private cabins (H&C), British WCs, facilities for the handicapped, under cover washing up area and a washing machine. Petanque. Mobile homes for hire.

Directions: From Ste. Enimie, take the D907 in the direction of Peyreleau. Site is 1½ km. on the left. When the new, free autoroute is completed (following the route of the N9) exit from La Canourgue and take D998 to Ste. Enimie.

Charges 1994:
-- Per person Ffr. 17.00; child (under 7 yrs) 8.00; caravan or tent 15.00; car 15.00; motorcaravan 25.00; electricity 12.00; local tax 1.00.

Open:
April - mid-Oct.

Address:
Rte de Millau, 48210 Ste. Enimie.

Tel:
66.48.50.53 or 66.48.50.07.

Reservations:
Made with Ffr. 60 fee (July/Aug.).

4802 Camping du Lac, Morangies, Villefort

Unpretentious, small site situated right beside the lake, near Gorges du Chassezac.

Lozère is a relatively little known département so far as British visitors are concerned but the small town of Villefort is popular with the French both for summer holidays and as a winter sports resort. Camping du Lac is situated at what amounts to a tiny port (boats for hire and launching facilities) on the lake, about 2½ km. from the town, close to the medieval village of La Garde Guérin.

This small site of only some 60 pitches in total is officially divided into two either side of a small road, with one part designated as a 2-star campsite, the other as a 3-star caravan site - such are the mysteries of the French classification system! The lower part, bordering the lake, provides some 40 level, terraced pitches, separated by small railings, with electricity and shaded by chestnut trees. Elsewhere there is artificial shade and there are some pitches with hardstanding. It has its own small, modernised sanitary block with pushbutton hot showers, some Britsh type WCs, washbasins with cold water and washing up facilities under cover. The higher part with 20 artificially shaded pitches has its own sanitary block also. Although a railway line runs fairly close and trains can be heard during the day, we heard none during the hours of darkness. No restaurant but some dishes to order in season and many restaurants close by. Bread and milk to order. Small children's playground. Fishing, swimming and watersports in lake. Tennis, archery, bicycle hire 2½ km. Ski-ing. Mobile homes and chalets for hire - also in winter.

Directions: From Villefort, go north avoiding D901 to Mende and following D906 in direction of La Garde-Guérin. Site is signposted beside the lake.

Charges 1994:
-- Per normal pitch incl. 2 persons Ffr. 45.00 - 55.00, with electricity 55.00 - 65.00, with electricity, water and drainage 65.00 - 75.00; tent pitch without car 30.00 - 35.00; extra person 15.00; child (7-12 yrs) 8.00; extra car 10.00; animal 5.00.
-- Less 20% in June and Sept. for stays of over 8 days.

Open:
All year

Address:
Av. des Cévennes, 48800 Villefort.

Tel:
66.46.80.59 or 66.46.81.27.
FAX: 66.46.82.01.

Reservations:
Contact site for details.

LANGUEDOC-ROUSSILLON - Hérault

3401 Camping Lous Pibols, La Grande Motte, nr Montpellier

Site with good installations, close to sea and yachting resort.

La Grande Motte, 7 km. west of Le Grau-du-Roi, has been turned into a very large yachting marina. Camping Lous Pibols, on the edge of the resort, is neatly laid out and has first class sanitary installations with British toilets, individual basins in private cabins with shelf and mirror, free hot water for showers and for washing up and clothes sinks. Except for a small section for short visits, the camp is divided into marked-out and numbered pitches of fair size (100 sq.m.), mostly well shaded and on firm ground with sandy topsoil (there are tarred access roads with flat and easy access). Electricity is available on caravan pitches. From late June to late August early arrival may be needed to find a place. The beach here is 300 m. from the camp (you can also take the car and park alongside). It is a long sandy one, with gentle slope and safe bathing, though the loose sand may blow about at times. Self-service shop, restaurant/bar and takeaway (May - August). TV room. Table tennis. Washing machines. Children's playground. Doctor calls. There is a new swimming pool with paved sunbathing terrace and a snack bar on site. Mobile homes for hire.

Directions: Camp is well signposted at La Grande Motte.

Charges 1993:
-- Per pitch incl. up to 3 persons, with electricity, water and drainaway Ffr. 150.00, extra person 25.00; pitch without services 110.00, extra person 20.00; local tax 1.00.
-- Less 20% outside 1/7-1/9.

Open:
1 April - 30 Sept.

Address:
34280 La Grande Motte.

Tel:
67.56.50.08.

Reservations:
Not made.

3404 Camping Lou Village, Valras-Plage, nr Beziers

Good value site with direct access to beach and bathing lagoon.

Valras itself is a smarter and much larger resort than Vias and also offers a wide choice of camp sites. Our selection of Lou Village has been influenced by several factors - direct access to the beach, a rather unusual lagoon for bathing (with lifeguard) and in another part windsurfing, a new swimming pool with quite elegant terrace bar/restaurant (serving a wide range of meals) and cost. Prices at Lou Village (when we visited at least) are very competitive and seem to provide better value than other nearby sites of comparable quality. Like all the better sites in the area, Lou Village becomes crowded in the high season. The pitches further inland are partly separated by tall trees which provide good shade. Nearer the beach the pitches are smaller, many separated by bushes, bamboo hedges, etc.

The site has many attractive features and a pleasant, relaxed atmosphere. It is let down somewhat by the sanitary blocks. These provide a few British seatless WCs, although mostly continental, free hot showers in cabins without separators. They do have about half the washbasins in private cabins. Bearing in mind that older types of facilities are more difficult to keep clean, maintenance (in July) seemed satisfactory. Takeaway. Shop. Tennis. Volleyball. Boules. Minigolf. Football field. Children's playground. Bathing and windsurfing (with school) lagoons. Entertainment and activities organised.

Directions: Site is south of Beziers. From autoroute, take Beziers-Ouest exit for La Yole and Valras Plage. Continue for 13-14 km. Sign to Lou Village is just past Camping de la Yole before the built up area of Valras Plage.

Charges guide:
-- Per unit incl 2 persons Ffr. 100.00, 3 persons 110.00, 4 persons 125.00; extra person (over 7 yrs) 12.00 (under 7 free); extra car 8.00; electricity 13.00; dog 12.00; local tax 1.10 (over 4 yrs).
-- Less 30% outside July/Aug.

Open:
10 May - 20 Sept.

Address:
B.P. 30, 34350 Valras-Plage.

Tel:
67.37.33.79.
FAX: 67.37.53.56.

Reservations:
Made with deposit (Ffr. 600).

3402 Camping Le Garden, La Grande Motte, nr Montpellier

Site with good installations quite close to sea.

This is a site of equal standing to no. 3401 (see opposite), perhaps less crowded and slightly nearer the sea, and provides a further opportunity to holiday in this unique resort. No reservations are made and it becomes full for most of July/August. Possibly some road noise. There are two new sanitary blocks, a shop and restaurant/bar (open June - mid-Sept). Shopping complex. Laundry facilities.

Directions: Next to no. 3401 (shared entrance area).

Charges 1993:
-- Per unit incl. 1-3 persons Ffr 110.00, with 3 services 142.00; extra person 26.00; extra person 21.00; local tax 1.10.

Open:
1 March - 31 Oct.

Address:
34280 La Grande Motte.

Tel:
67.56.50.09.

Reservations:
Not made.

3403 Camping International Le Napoleon, Vias Plage

Small family site bordering the Mediterranean.

Le Napoleon is a family owned and managed site, 150 m. from a wide sandy beach. It offers a range of facilities including swimming and paddling pools, half tennis courts and volleyball. Vias town is in the wine growing region of the Midi, (close to the famous Canal du Midi), an area which includes the Camargue, Beziers, the medieval town of Carcassonne and the modern resort of Cap d'Agde. The 200 pitches here are level and grassy, with shade and are 80 - 100 sq.m. in size. Electricity is available on most pitches. Three toilet blocks provide British toilets, hot showers, with shelves and hooks, and washbasins in cabins. There is a well maintained toilet for the handicapped with ramps, and a baby bath. Supermarket and other shops outside camp entrance, including a British pub, bazaar, pizzeria and fish restaurant. On site is a bar/restaurant next to the small swimming pool mainly for children (with attendant in high season - pool games are organised). Minigolf. Volleyball. Bicycle hire. Boules. TV room (satellite). Organised entertainment. Disco nearby. Three washing machines (ironing boards also). Chalets, bungalow, mobile homes and caravan to hire. English, German and Dutch spoken.

Directions: From Vias town, take the D137 towards Farinette beach. Site is on the right near the beach.

Charges 1994:
-- (Probable) Per pitch incl. 2 persons and electricity Ffr. 120.00; tent pitch incl. 2 persons 105.00; extra person 25.00; electricity 6A 17.00, 10A 20.00; extra tent, extra car, boat or pet 17.00; local tax 1.65 per person (child 0.85).
-- Less 30% outside 25/6-31/8.

Open:
Easter - 30 Sept.

Address:
Farinette Plage, 34450 Vias sur Mer.

Tel:
67.21.64.37.
FAX: 67.21.75.30.

Reservations:
Taken from 1 Jan. with deposit (Ffr. 400) and fee (100).

N3405 Camping Naturiste Le Mas de Lignieres, Cesseras, nr Olonzac

Small, rural naturist site with pool and very large pitches, in the hills of the Minervois.

Enjoying some marvellous views to the Pyrénées, the Corbières and the coast at Narbonne, this site provides some 40 large (c. 200 sq.m.) pitches with electricity (6A), water and drainage, on mainly level grass, separated by small hedges. There are also some smaller pitches (100 sq.m.) for tents, with cars parked elsewhere. There is some shade, although as the site is fairly new, the many trees are mainly young. There is a variety of flora, including four types of orchid. Within the confines of the site there are some good walks with superb views and, although the camping area is actually quite small, the very large pitches and young trees and hedges give an impression of spaciousness and freedom, creating a very relaxing ambience.

There is a swimming pool with sunbathing area, tennis, volleyball and boules courts (all free) and a small shop selling the usual range of essentials (including fresh bread and croissants to order). Although at present there is only a bar/snackbar, a restaurant and also a sauna are planned for future years. The sanitary installations include hot showers in cabins, British WCs, washbasins with H&C, washing up and laundry facilities in 2 blocks. Tennis. Volleyball. Boules. Table tennis. Children's playground. Sailing, riding, canoeing, bicycle hire near. Mobile homes and caravans for hire. No dogs allowed.

Directions: From the A61 autoroute take the Lezignan-Corbières exit, through the town via the D611 to Homps, then via the D190 to Olonzac. Go through the village following the signs to Cesseras, from where the site is signposted.

Charges 1993:
-- Per large pitch, incl. 2 persons and electricity, water and drainage Ffr 87.00; tent pitch 66.00 (electricity 17.00); extra person 17.00; child (2-7 yrs) 9.00; extra car or tent 10.00.
-- Reductions of 15% before 14/6 and after 31/8 or 20% from 1/10 - 14/5.

Open:
All year.

Address:
Cesseras-en-Minervois, 34210 Olonzac.

Tel:
68.91.24.86.

Reservations:
Made until 25/6 with deposit (Ffr 300) and fee (70).

6602 Camping Caravaning Ma Prairie, Canet, nr Perpignan

Site 3 km. back from sea among the vineyards, with various amenities.

The Gil family provide a warm welcome and pleasant atmosphere at Ma Prairie. It lies some 3 km. back from the sandy Canet beaches, with two swimming pools - a small children's one (120 sq.m.) and a large one for adults (10 x 22 m.), across a small road from the camping area. There are 260 pitches of nearly 100 sq.m. average, on flat grassy ground with separations. The 180 in the older part have good shade, the rest is more open. Most have electricity and water and drainage are available on 35. The three sanitary blocks have mixed British and continental WCs, washbasins in private cabins with shelf and mirror and hot showers (with pushbutton). Baby bath. Ample free hot and cold water in basins, showers, washing-up sinks and clothes sinks. There may possibly be some noise on pitches adjacent to road. Quite a few pitches are taken by tour operators and there is a busy atmosphere. A large, newly built bar/restaurant overlooks the terraced pool area and satellite TV has been installed on the site. Shop. Takeaway food service. Tennis. Table tennis, billiards and amusement machines; disco, dancing etc. about 3 times weekly in season. Washing machines. Children's play area. Mobile homes and equipped tents for hire. Bus service to Canet, where there are first class restaurants, etc. including one owned and run by the same family.

Directions: Site access is from the D11 Perpignan road close to the junction with D617 in Canet-Village.

Charges 1993:
-- Per unit with 2 persons 110.00 Ffr; extra person 29.50; child (under 7) 16.50; local tax 1.00; electricity (6A) 24.00 or (3A) 18.00; dog 15.00; extra car 14.00.
-- Less 30% in May, June and Sept.

Open:
1 May - end-Sept.

Address:
66140 Canet en Roussillon

Tel:
68.73.26.17.
FAX: 68.73.28.82.

Reservations:
Made from Sat-Sat with 30% deposit and Ffr. 80 fee.

LANGUEDOC-ROUSSILLON - Pyrénées Orientales

6601 Camping-Caravaning California, Le Barcarés, Perpignan
Family owned site with swimming pool, not far from beach.

This small site is attractively laid out with much green foliage (like an orchard) and has some 200 hedged pitches on flat ground. The site is acquiring a mature look with an attractive terraced pool bar area. The pitches vary a little in size and shape but average about 100 sq.m. with shade and electricity on all pitches. The two toilet blocks are of standard modern construction with seatless WCs, free pre-mixed hot water in the washbasins with shelf and mirror, in the showers with pushbutton which runs on a bit, and in the sinks. Baby bath and small toilets. The camp is about 800 m. from a sandy beach and has a swimming pool of 200 sq.m. and children's pool (open from 1 June), with free water slide in a small separate pool. There are barbecue areas on site, but own barbecues are also allowed. Restaurant/bar with takeaway. Shop, wine store and pizzeria at entrance to site. Tennis. TV room. Sailboards and mountain bikes for hire; BMX cycle track on site. Archery. Washing machine. Car wash. Exchange facility. Children's animation in season and some evening entertainment. Some services in main season only. Bungalows and mobile homes to let.

Directions: Site is on D90 coast road 2 km. southwest of Le Barcarés centre.

Charges 1994:
-- Per unit incl. 2 persons Ffr 92.00; extra person 26.00; child (under 7) 16.00; extra vehicle 16.00; electricity (10A) 15.00; local tax (over 4) in Jul/Aug 1.00.
-- Less 20-50% outside July/Aug.

Open:
17 April - 25 Sept

Address:
Route de St. Laurent, 66420 Le Barcarés.

Tel:
68.86.16.08.
FAX: 68.86.18.20.

Reservations:
Any period with deposit (Ffr. 400) and fee (60).

66420 LE BARCARES
Tel. (68) 86.16.08
★★★ NN

Open: Easter till 30th September
(reservations possible)

*SWIMMING POOL FREE OF CHARGE
SMALL POOL & WATER SLIDE*

800 metres from the beach
quiet relaxing – all the comfort of its category

BAR – SNACK BAR – MEALS TO TAKE AWAY
PLAYGROUND – TV – TENNIS – GROCER'S

Bungalows, caravans and mobile homes for hire

PORT-BARCARES – 68.86.16.08

6603 Camping Cala Gogo, St. Cyprien-Plage, nr Perpignan
Site by beach, with own swimming pool and varied amenities.

This site has an agreeable situation by a sandy beach where bathing is supervised and boats can be put on the beach. Also on site is a good-size free swimming pool with children's pool and a pleasant terrace bar area adjoining. The 700 pitches, on flat ground, are individual ones of around 100 sq.m. They are now more fully marked out with easier access and electrical connections everywhere and shade is developing. The five toilet blocks are basically good and provision now includes a large new block with more British toilets, washbasins in private cabins with shelf and mirror and free hot showers, no dividers or hooks but fully controllable. Maintenance may vary in high season. A large bar complex with disco and TV, becomes very busy in season (could be noisy), and an attractive small shopping mall and supermarket. Full restaurant plus self-service restaurant with simple menu and hot takeaway food. Small bar by beach. Organised programme of events in season: sports, etc. during day, dancing or entertainment in bar some evenings. Wine boutique. Courses in skin-diving, windsurfing, sailing. Tennis. Table tennis. Children's playground. Cycle hire. Boat excursions. Treatment room; doctor calls daily in July/Aug.

Directions: Site is to south of St. Cyprien, well signed from roads around.

Charges guide:
-- Per person (any age) 30.00 Ffr, plus local tax; pitch (any unit) 45.00; electricity 13.00.
-- 20% less in June and Sept.

Open:
1 June - 30 Sept, with all services.

Address:
66750 St. Cyprien-Plage.

Tel:
68.21.07.12.
FAX: 68.21.02.90.

Reservations:
Made for Sat. to Sat. and necessary for Jul/Aug, with deposit and fee.

6605 Camping Le Haras, Palau-del-Vidre, nr Argelès

Pretty site on edge of village in Roussillon countryside.

A very 'French' site, Le Haras is situated midway between the coast (about 8 km.) and the Pyrénées on the edge of a village, in quiet countryside removed from the bustle of the coastal resorts. It has some 90 individual pitches, most with electricity and drainage, arranged informally in the grounds of an old manor house with a mixture of trees, shrubs and flowers providing colour and shade. It is within earshot of a railway line which has trains on it at intevals during the day. The two adjoining modern, rather unusual sanitary blocks provide a mixture of British and continental WCs, hot showers and washbasins with hot water in cabins (cold water in open basins beside the toilets), clothes and dishwashing sinks (cold water) plus facilities for the disabled. This provision is now supplemented by a new small block near the pool area. An open air, covered bar/restaurant provides a range of home cooked meals including local specialties, which is situated adjacent to the swimming pool (20 x 10 m.). There is also a good restaurant, L'Ancienne Ecole, in the village centre run by an English couple for more formal occasions. Small shop (open main season only - village shops near). TV. Table tennis. Entertainments in season. 2 washing machines.

Directions: Approaching from the north on the N114, turn right onto the D11 just south of Elne, immediately after crossing the River Tech. The site is adjacent to the D11, just east of Palau del Vidre.

Charges guide:
-- Per pitch Ffr. 35.00; person 18.00; child (under 7 yrs) 12.00; electricity 3A 13.50, 6A 17.50, 10A 21.50; water connection 6.00; extra car 10.00.
-- Less 20% for May, June and Sept, 30% in low season.

Open:
All year.

Address:
Domaine St. Galdric, 66690 Paulo del Vidre.

Tel:
68.22.14.50 or 68.22.29.13.

Reservations:
Recommended for July/ Aug and made with deposit (Ffr. 300) and fee (50).

6606 Camping Les Dunes de Torreilles-Plage, Torreilles, nr Perpignan

Seaside site near Perpignan with swimming pool and pitches with own sanitation.

This is an unusual site in several respects. It is quite large, with some 600 pitches, all of 100 sq.m. minimum but of varying size and shape, all having electricity and drainage. The pitches are all marked and most are separated by foliage except near the beach and dunes where vegetation is sparse. The site has the advantage of direct access to sandy beaches with good bathing and boating, including a naturist beach. The facilities on site are numerous including a swimming pool (20 x 10 m. 15/5-30/9), with children's pool, a restaurant, bar, pizzeria and several takeaways. A 'Centre Commercial' with supermarket, shops and small restaurant is adjacent. Tennis courts. Windsurfing lessons; boards for hire, also pedaloes. Kiosk/bar by beach. Disco. Launderette. Treatment room; doctor calls June to Sept. Entertainment programme and organised excursions. Another unusual feature of the site is that each pitch has its own sanitary unit with shower (heated and adjustable), washbasin, British WC, mirror and hooks. Clients keep these units clean during their stay but the site takes a deposit to ensure that they are left clean, however they are cleaned for incoming clients. There are a number of static units on the site devoted to tour operators, some leased on a semi-permanent basis and others for hire. However, there are over 300 pitches for tourists and, apart from the mid-July to mid-August peak season, there is usually ample space and the opportunity to choose your own pitch. In many respects this is an ideal site for families, in a developing tourist area, with plenty of activities on the site and nearby but without being too intrusive for those who prefer just to relax. There may be some evening noise on pitches at one side from an adjoining campsite which operates a disco. This is not a site you are likely to forget - we like it, but it may not be to everyone's taste - it can be windy and dry.

Directions: From autoroute A9 take exit for Perpignan-Nord, then D83 towards Le Barcares for 9 km. then south on D81 towards Canet for 3 km. before turning left to site.

Charges 1993:
-- Per unit all-inclusive with electricity Ffr. 68.00 - 179.00, acc. to season; deposit refunded on departure 300.00; local tax 1.00.

Open:
15 March - 15 October

Address:
66440 Torreilles-Plage.

Tel:
68.28.30.32 or 68.28.38.29.

Reservations:
Made from Sun. to Sun. with deposit and Ffr. 85 fee.

6610 Camping Les Galets, Argelès-sur-Mer

Smaller, distinctively French site with views of the Pyrénées.

This site, unlike its large `international' neighbours, is distinctively French in character and will appeal to readers seeking a more tranquil situation, yet within easy reach (1½ km. by road or `train') of this very busy resort. Although to some extent dominated by mobile homes, these are mostly well established and rather informally situated with well developed foliage, gardens and trees providing a surprisingly pretty environment. There are large, level touring pitches mainly with ample shade, the reception being in the newer part of the site where shade is undeveloped, although trees have been planted. In season there is an attractive, mainly open air restaurant/bar, Les Capucines, providing a good selection at good value with both waitress service and takeaway. There is a rectangular swimming pool (15 x 7 m. and open June - Sept) with adjacent, covered leisure area for evening entertainment programmes, table tennis, a larger than average children's play area, volleyball court and boules pitch.

Sanitary facilities are in two blocks - one in the newer part with modern fittings including pushbutton hot showers with dressing area, washbasins in private cabins (hot water) and British WCs. The other block is older with more old fashioned fittings including some continental WCs, showers without separated dressing areas and only cold water to washbasins. Facilities for the handicapped. Shop (1/6-30/9). Riding, minigolf, archery near. Laundry facilities. Mobile homes and chalets for hire. `Train' service to Argelès.

Directions: Site is in Taxo area, set back from Argelès. Approaching from St. Cyprien on D81 after crossing River Tech, watch for new roundabout and take right fork to Taxo (d'Avall minor road) then first right. Continue past Camping La Sirène and turn right to site opposite minigolf.

Charges 1994:
-- Per pitch incl. 2 persons Ffr. 99.00; extra person 25.00; child (under 3 yrs) 15.00; extra car 5.00; electricity (3A) 20.00; dog 9.00; local tax 1.50.
-- Less 40% outside 4/7-5/9.

Open:
All year.

Address:
Rte. Taxo - d'Avall, 66700 Argelès-sur-Mer.

Tel:
68.81.08.12.
FAX: 68.81.68.76.

Reservations:
Write to site.

6611 Camping Le Dauphin, Argelès-sur-Mer

Quieter site with views of the Pyrénées and good swimming pools.

Situated near Taxo in the quieter, northern part of Argelès (a somewhat frenzied resort in season), this site enjoys good views of the Pyrénées, particularly from the terrace area surrounding its excellent complex of swimming pools. About a third of the 300 level, grassy and well shaded pitches (all with 3A electricity) have the benefit of what amounts to their own individual sanitary block with hot shower, washbasin and WC and with an adjacent washing up sink. The other pitches are served by a central sanitary block which, although quite old, has been refurbished to provide excellent, modern facilities including a number of showers and washbasins en-suite, British WCs, etc.

The site has a good range of facilities in addition to the swimming pools, including a bar/restaurant with takeaway, tennis courts, half courts, shops, a large children's play area and from 1994, minigolf. Table tennis. Entertainment twice weekly in Jul/Aug. Although located some 1½ km. from the town and beach, there is a regular connecting `train' service to and fro throughout the day and evening up to midnight. Used by tour operators.

Directions: Follow directions for Les Galets but continue past minigolf and site is on right.

Charges 1994:
-- Per pitch incl. 2 persons Ffr. 125.00; extra person 27.00; child (under 5 yrs) 15.00; electricity 22.00; water and drainage 20.00; individual sanitation 50.00; extra car 10.00; animal 10.00; local tax (over 10 yrs) 2.00.

Open:
22 May - 30 Sept

Address:
Rte. Taxo d'Avall, 66701 Argelès-sur-Mer.

Tel:
68.81.17.54.

Reservations:
Write to site.

N6612 Camping Naturiste La Clapère, Maureillas

Very attractive naturist site in the lower ranges of the Pyrénées.

Situated in a valley in the Albères, this site occupies a large area (50 hectares), includes a fast flowing small river and offers a choice of good sized pitches on no less than eight separate terraces. They are all slightly different in character; two for example are alongside the river, one is among greengage trees, another amongst vines. Electricity is available on five of the terraces, the others being more suitable for tents.

There is a large swimming pool with smaller children's pool, and ample paved sunbathing areas, alongside which is the attractive bar and restaurant (with simple, basic `plat du jour' menu and takeaway) and the shop which, although small, is very well stocked. Table tennis. Boules. Volleyball. Organised rambles. Children's playground. Fishing. Caravans for hire. There are three modern sanitary blocks of unusual design providing first class facilities including some of the best (open plan) hot showers we have come across. Washbasins have hot and cold water as do the washing up and laundry sinks - there is also a washing machine. This is one of a small number of very attractive, unspoiled naturist sites located in beautiful, wild countryside and it is little wonder that more and more campers and caravanners are turning to naturist sites for their holidays in these more environmentally conscious times.

Directions: Take the last autoroute (A9) exit before Spain (Boulou exit). Leave Boulou on N9 in the direction of Le Perthus for 3 km. Turn right onto the N618 to Maureillas, then the D13 in the direction of Las Illas. Site is 2 km.

Charges 1993:
-- Per pitch Ffr. 21.00 -
30.00; adult 21.00 - 30.00;
child (0-14 yrs) 12.00 -
18.00; animal 5.00 - 8.00;
electricity 15.00; local tax
1.00, child (4-10) 0.50.

Open:
1 April - 31 Oct.

Address:
Route de Las Illas,
66400 Maureillas.

Tel:
68.83.36.04

Reservations;
Made with deposit (30% of
charges).

6613 Hotel de Plein Air L'Eau Vive, Vernet-les-Bains

Well kept small site at the spa town of Vernet in the Pyrénées.

Enjoying dramatic views of the towering Pic du Canigou (3,000 m.), this site is situated 1½ km. from the centre of Vernet-les-Bains. It is approached via a rather uninspiring and not too well made up lane through a residential area, which should not be allowed to put you off. The site is well kept with first class sanitary facilities in two modern blocks with British WCs, hot showers with dressing area, washbasins (hot water) in private cabins, dishwashing (hot water) under cover, facilities for the handicapped and laundry with washing machine.

The 58 tourist pitches, all with electricity (4 - 10A) and water, are on level grass, hedged but without a lot of shade. Although there is no swimming pool as such, the site has a more or less natural pool (created by pumping and circulating running water from the nearby stream - very attractive) and even providing a tiny beach with water slide, cordoned off for children. There is an attractive open air (but under cover) bar/restaurant with waiter service and takeaway and although there is no shop as such, fresh bread can be ordered. Well situated for touring this area of the Pyrénées and with very comfortable amenities, this small site quickly becomes fully booked in season and advance reservation is essential. Chalets to let.

Directions: Following the N116 to Andorra, 6 km. after Prades, take the turning at Ville Franche de Confleut (old walled town) for Vernet-les-Bains. Continue up hill for 5 km. to one way system. Follow this round and turn right over bridge in direction of Sahorre. Immediately, at one end of the small block of shops, turn right into the Avenue de Saturnin and follow for about 1 km. past houses to more open area and site is signposted.

Charges 1994:
-- Per pitch incl. 3 persons
and electricity (4A)
Ffr.105.00 for 10/7-22/8,
otherwise incl. 2 persons
79.00 - 89.00; extra adult
15.00; child (4-16 yrs)
10.00; animal 5.00;
electricity (10A) 9.00.
-- Discounts for weekly
stays.

Open:
1 Feb - 30 Nov.

Address:
Chemin de Saturnin,
66820 Vernet Les Bains.

Tel:
68.05.54.14.

Reservations:
Made with deposit (20% of
charges) and Ffr. 70 fee
(high season only).

6614 Hollywood Camping International, Amélie-Les-Bains

Pretty, small site with pool on outskirts of famous spa town.

Do not be misled by the name - this is an unpretentious little site in a rural setting. It enjoys good views of the nearby mountains (Mont Albères), yet is within 2 km. of the rather elegant spa town of Amélie-les-Bains. There are some 100, mainly level pitches, all with electricity, water and drainage, arranged on small, grassy terraces with a variety of trees and shrubs providing variable amounts of shade. The site has the benefit of a recently built pool (14 x 8 m.) with paved sunbathing area and a modern sanitary block. This has free hot showers, with dressing area, washbasins in cabins with hot and cold water, washing up sinks (H&C) and a laundry with washing machine and ironing board. WCs are mainly continental (Turkish) with some British seatless. Although the site does not claim to have its own restaurant, it is adjacent to an auberge run by the same family providing a range of meals and takeaways. Children's playground. Caravans, tents and bungalows to let.

Directions: Site is between Amélie les Bains and Pont Céret on the D115. Turn left up partly made-up road immediately after the small village of La Forge de Reynés approaching from the direction of Le Boulou.

Charges 1993:
-- Per unit inc. car and 2 persons Ffr. 60.00; extra person 20.00; child (under 7 yrs) 10.00; extra tent 6.00; extra car 8.50; animal 5.50; electricity (4A) 15.00 (6A) 18.00; drainage 4.00.
-- Less 10% outside 1/5-15/9.

Open:
All year.

Address:
B.P. 3,
La Forge de Reynès,
66110 Amélie-Les-Bains.

Tel:
68.39.08.61.

Reservations:
Made with deposit (Ffr. 370) and fee (40).

LIMOUSIN
Creuse - Corrèze - Haute-Vienne

This region, traversed by several major roadways, is best explored by taking the quieter back roads. There are few large towns, Limoges and Brive (both worth a visit) being exceptions, but many delightful smaller settlements on the banks of the numerous rivers in the region. The area is steeped in history, much of it violent, from the harsh life of the prehistoric cave-dwellers to civilian massacres during the second World War, but the overwhelming impression today is of peace and tranquility - far removed from the frenetic activity which characterizes so much of twentieth century life (and even some holidays). This is a land of lakes, forests and farmland between the mountains and the sea.

8702 Castel Camping du Château de Leychoisier, Bonnac la Côte
Elevated site in the grounds of a château, 10 km north of Limoges.

Just 2 km. from the A20/N20, yet very quiet and secluded, the Château de Leychoisier makes an ideal staging point or a good base for a longer stay in the region. Pitches are very large, individual ones on grassy ground, marked out by trees. Of the 80 pitches, some 55 have electrical connections and some with water and drainaway too. The sanitary facilities are not all modern, but all the toilets are of British type and washbasins are in private cabins with mirrors and free hot water. The showers are good, also with free hot water. There are baby bath and nappy changing facilities and provision for the disabled. There is a restaurant and a pleasant bar with terrace in an old open-ended barn. Small shop selling basic foodstuffs and fresh bread every morning. Mini-market at 2 km, supermarket at 5 km. Swimming pool (unsupervised) and a 4 ha. lake with free fishing and a marked off area for swimming. Tennis, table tennis, TV room, babyfoot and bar billiards. The large estate is available for walks and there is good terrain in the area for mountain bikes, but none for hire. It is a friendly, quiet site where you have plenty of space and where there are no letting units and many people like it for these reasons.

Directions: Take the exit (west) signed Bonnac-La-Côte from the A20/N20. The site is well signed from the village.

Charges 1994:
-- Per pitch Ffr. 38.00; person 25.00; child (under 7) 17.00; extra car 13.00; dog 6.00; electricity (4A) 19.00.
-- Less 15% April, May, 1-15 June and Sept.

Open:
1 April - 30 Sept.

Address:
87270 Bonnac-La-Côte.

Tel:
55.39.93.43.

Reservations:
Made with deposit (Ffr. 100) and fee (80), although short reservations accepted without charge in low season.

Improved cover less cost than AA or RAC

for all Continental Motoring Holidays

"THE BEST ALL-IN-ONE POLICY YOU CAN BUY"

If you're taking your car on holiday you need this insurance

* Holiday Insurance

* Personal emergency assistance

* Optional motoring breakdown and accident service by EUROP ASSISTANCE
Europe's leading assistance service.

* Cancellation
  - Unlimited

* Medical Expenses
  - £2,000,000

* Personal Accident
  - £20,000

* Baggage & Money
  - £1,200

* Legal Liability
  - £2,000,000

* Legal Expenses
  - £25,000

* Full Emergency Assistance
  -Unlimited

* Optional Motoring Breakdown & Accident Service
  (For vehicles not more than 15 years 11 months old up to GVW 3.5 tons, length 7m, height 3m and width 2.2m). A 24 hour on-the-spot service. Includes roadside help, hire car, accommodation, repatriation, bail bond etc. - there's no better.

* Supplement
  - for a small sum this doubles the Hire Car limit from £750 to £1,500 and increases Alternative Accommodation allowance from £100 to £200 per person.

10% OFF your GOLD COVER PREMIUM *THROUGH* **GOOD CAMPS** *See over.*

for all Continental Motoring Holidays

Use the application form below to claim 10% discount on your Gold Cover Insurance protection for any continental motoring holiday you take in 1994.

Easy Cost Calculator

HOLIDAY INSURANCE		Period up to 3 days £	Period up to 6 days £	Period up to 9 days £	Period up to 17 days £	Period up to 24 days £	Period up to 31 days £	Each Extra Week or Part £
ADULTS	CHILDREN							
1	Nil	6.60	9.80	12.50	19.60	22.90	26.20	4.50
	1	11.60	17.20	21.90	34.30	40.10	45.80	7.90
	2	16.60	24.60	31.30	49.00	57.30	65.40	11.30
	3	21.60	32.00	40.70	63.70	74.50	85.00	14.70
	4	26.60	39.40	50.10	78.40	91.70	104.60	18.10
2	Nil	13.20	19.60	25.00	39.20	45.80	52.40	9.00
	1	18.20	27.00	34.40	53.90	63.00	72.00	12.40
	2	23.20	34.40	43.80	68.60	80.20	91.60	15.80
	3	28.20	41.80	53.20	83.30	97.40	111.20	19.20
	4	33.20	49.20	62.60	98.00	114.60	130.80	22.60
3	Nil	19.80	29.40	37.50	58.80	68.70	78.60	13.50
	1	24.80	36.80	46.90	73.50	85.90	98.20	16.90
	2	29.80	44.20	56.30	88.20	103.10	117.80	20.30
	3	34.80	51.60	65.70	102.90	120.30	137.40	23.70
	4	39.80	59.00	75.10	117.60	137.50	157.00	27.10
4	Nil	26.40	39.20	50.00	78.40	91.60	104.80	18.00
	1	31.40	46.60	59.40	93.10	108.80	124.40	21.40
	2	36.40	54.00	68.80	107.80	126.00	144.00	24.80
	3	41.40	61.40	78.20	122.50	143.20	163.60	28.20
	4	46.40	68.80	87.60	137.20	160.40	183.20	31.60

Double these rates if Winter Sports cover is required

MOTORING SERVICE	Vehicles up to 15 years 11 months (back to 'S' registration)						
	20.00	25.00	32.00	40.00	44.00	48.00	8.00
SUPPLEMENT	8.00	9.50	10.50	14.00	16.00	18.00	4.00
CARAVANS/TRAILERS	12.00	12.00	12.00	12.00	12.00	12.00	No charge

Instructions

1. Work out the period of insurance you will need - be careful, departure sailing on the 2nd June, with return sailing on the 11th June is 10 days NOT 9 days.

2. Using the line which corresponds with the number in your party, will tell you the cost of the Holiday Insurance for the 'Period' you will need. Don't include children under 4 - they go free!

3. Add the Motoring Breakdown Service cost (if needed) and, if you wish to take the Supplement or include your caravan or trailer, add the cost for these.

Going on more than one holiday? Ask for another form.

APPLICATION FORM
BLOCK CAPITALS PLEASE

If you would like the protection Gold Cover Insurance can offer please complete the application below and return it to Deneway Guides & Travel, Chesil Lodge, West Bexington, Dorchester DT2 9DG.
For immediate cover phone 0308 897809.

Details of Holiday

Outward Voyage	Day	Month	Year		Inward Voyage	Day	Month	Year

| No. of Adults in party | | No. of Children in party (4 & under 14) | | Tick if cover required for Winter Sports Activities | |

Cover Required
Please insert premium in box(s) for cover required.

PREMIUM

Holiday Insurance	£	
Motoring Service (Only available as an extension to Holiday Insurance)	£	
Motoring Supplement (Only available in conjunction with Motoring Service)	£	
Caravan/Trailer (Only available in conjunction with Motoring Service)	£	
TOTAL PREMIUM	£	
LESS 10% SPECIAL DISCOUNT DUE	£	
NET DUE	£	

Name

Address

Postcode   Daytime Tel. No.

Payment

Choose your method of payment and tick box:

I enclose cheque for £

Cheques payable to Deneway Ltd.

Access/Visa Credit Card   Expiry Date

No.

Name of Cardholder:

Signed

Date

THREE
of the
BEST

ON SALE
EVERY MONTH
at your local newsagent

8701 Camping de Montréal, Saint Germain-les-Belles
Pleasant lakeside site between Limoges and Brive.

Situated on the edge of the town with good views across the small lake, this pleasant municipal site is ideal for an overnight stop or a for a longer stay in the beautiful Limousin countryside. There are 60 tourist pitches, all over 100 sq.m. and separated by well kept hedges, which afford good privacy and views of the lake. They are arranged on two grassy terraces but have little shade. Some 15 pitches have electrical connections. The modern toilet block is well designed to be quiet and draught free and is well appointed. The toilets are British and the washbasins, some communal, some in private cabins, have razor points, mirrors and hot water. The showers are controllable and there is space for dressing, but it is not partitioned. Good facilities for the disabled. There are undercover washing up and laundry basins but no washing machine or dryer. A restaurant with terrace and bar overlooks the lake (open to the public) and there is a takeaway service. The site has no shop but the baker calls mornings in July/August and there are a supermarket, restaurants and a good range of shops in the town 10 minutes walk away.

Leisure facilities on the site are centred on the 5 hectare lake with its 150 m. long sandy beach. A bathing area is marked out by two diving boards, there are pedaloes for hire, a large children's play area and two tennis courts. The tourist office on site gives updated information to local events.

Directions: From Limoges take the N20 south and shortly after Magnac-Bourg turn left at the crossroads onto the D7. Continue about 6 km. to St Germain-les-Belles from where site is well signposted on a side road to La Porcherie.

Charges 1993:
-- Per person Ffr. 10.00; child (under 7 yrs) 5.00; vehicle 5.00; pitch 5.00; electricity 9.00.
Open:
1 April - 30 Sept.
Address:
87380 St Germain-les-Belles.
Tel:
55.71.86.20.
Reservations:
Made by phone or letter (letter preferred) to the Tourist Office (address as site); no booking fee.

1901 Camping Intercommunal de l'Abeille, Merlines, nr Ussel
Pleasant site for a short halt between Clermont-Ferrand and Brive.

This camp is part of a `village de vacances' complex which has many solidly built bungalows. The site itself is fairly small, having around 75 individual pitches, all with hardstandings (a little weedy) and a grassy area for tents, with about 34 electrical connections in one section. There was some space in early August. The two modern small toilet blocks have continental toilets for men, British for women, washbasins with shelf, mirror and cold water, some in private cabins, and pre-mixed free hot showers. To use the facilities of the village de vacances, which include restaurant, bar and organised activities for both the young and adults, you have to join the Association that runs it, at a fee which would probably only be justified for stay of a few days or more. It is possible that the small swimming pool in the village section may be free to campers. Laundry room with dryer. Canoes for hire on nearby lake. Mountain bike hire. Tennis. Riding nearby. 10 chalets for hire.

Directions: Site is signposted on the eastern edge of the village of Merlines which lies 20 km. northeast of Ussel on the N89 road.

Charges 1993:
-- Per pitch incl. 4 persons Ffr. 45.00 - 58.00; extra adult 12.00; child 6.00; electricity 12.00; pet 10.00.
Open:
mid-June - mid-Sept.
Tel:
55.94.31.39.
Reservations:
Situation uncertain; write to Village VAL 'L'Abeille', 19340 Eygurande or try phoning 73.43.00.43 (head office, Clermont-Ferrand) or site in season. Probably easiest just to turn up.

LOIRE VALLEY - Eure et Loir

VAL DE LOIRE
Eure-et-Loire - Loiret - Cher - Indre - Indre-et-Loire
Loir-et-Cher

This beautiful region, with its mild climate, is at the very heart of France, yet still within an easy day's drive from the Channel ports. It is no wonder that so many châteaux, using the attractive local stone, were built here; many, like Chinon and Clemonceaux are well known, but there are more than one hundred others, so the choice of which to visit is very wide. A good way to make the most of a visit to this region is to use the 'routes touristiques', which not only lead you to beautiful churches and châteaux, but also take you through an ever-changing landscape of picturesque villages, with many spectacular views of the River Loire itself. Visits to places such as Amboise, Blois, Chartres, Orleans, Tours and many other attractive and historic towns could be a holiday in itself.

2801 Camping du Parc de Loisirs, Cloyes-sur-le-Loir, Châteaudun
Pleasant staging post on the N10 south of Châteaudun

This site, conveniently but quietly situated near to the old N10, has been improved and makes a good stop-over for a night or maybe a bit longer - some of the Loire châteaux are not all that far. The site is now in three parts: a permanent section (about 50%), a longer-stay tourist section consisting entirely of individual 'special' pitches with electricity, water and drainaway, and an overnight area, with electricity, but where pitches are not marked and units can be packed rather close. Two sanitary blocks serve the site well; one is new and modern and well-appointed, with private cabins and pushbutton showers; the second, by the reception, is older, but still in good condition but has few toilets. The 'Parc de Loisirs' itself, also open to the general public on payment, but free of charge to campers, consists of a large children's playground, with inflatable castle, a swimming pool, water chute and splash pool, minigolf, tennis, pedaloes, canoes and boats and pony rides. Small shop. Spacious restaurant and bar, with upper dining and disco rooms, and terrace, open all summer and some winter weekends. Discos some evenings in high season. Washing machine.

Directions: Site is well signed in Cloyes, 12 km. south of Châteaudun, on N10.

Charges 1994:
-- Per person 25.00 Ffr; child (under 7) 15.00; pitch 35.00; electricity (5A) 15.00.
-- Individual pitches cost more.

Open: All year.

Address: 28220 Cloyes.

Tel: 37.98.50.53. FAX: 37.98.33.84.

Reservations: Made for min. 1 week for individual pitches with substantial deposit and fee.

Camping Parc de Loisirs

CLOYES-SUR-LOIRE

FREE Attractions:
Pedalos – Minigolf
Ponies – Swimming Pool
Waterslide
Canoes – Games
Ping-pong...

98

3701 Camping de la Mignardière, Ballan-Miré, nr Tours

Pleasant little site quietly situated just southwest of Tours.

The situation of this little site may appeal to many - only 8 km. from the centre of the city of Tours yet in a peaceful spot, within easy reach of several of the Loire châteaux notably Azay-le-Rideau, and with various sports amenities on or very close to the site. There are now 150 numbered pitches (30 in a new area) all with electricity and 100 with drainage and water also. They are on flat grass and are of good size. Four modern sanitary blocks have British WCs, free hot water in the washbasins (in private cabins) and the sinks, and premixed hot water in the showers. There are also two portable units with 2 showers, 1 toilet, 1 washbasin and 2 dishwashing sinks crammed into each. Unit for the disabled and a baby bath in the heated block near to reception. Laundry facilities.

Amenities on the site include a shop, two new swimming pools with sunbathing terrace, a good tennis court and table tennis. There is a bar and restaurant/crêperie with takeaway. Just outside the site is a small 'parc de loisirs' with pony rides, minigolf, small cars, playground and some other amusements. An attractive lake catering particularly for windsurfing is 300 m. away (boards can be hired, or your own put on, but not other boats) with restaurants also, and there is a family fitness run. Barrier gates with card (100 Ffr. deposit), closed 2230 - 0730 hrs. Reservation is essential for most of July/Aug. Virtually half the pitches are taken by tour operators. Mobile homes and chalets for hire.

Directions: Site is difficult to find due to new roads and general housing and industrial developments. It lies between, not in, Ballan-Miré and Joué-les-Tours and is signposted north off the D751, though the sign is hard to spot. Better to follow the D751 Joué-les-Tours road and signs to 'Lac' or Campanile Hotel and pick up camp signs (300 m. northwest of lake) from there.

Charges 1994:
-- Per unit Ffr. 36.00;
person 28.00; child (under 7) 18.00; fully serviced pitch incl. 4 persons 175.00; electricity 18.00.
-- Less outside July/Aug.

Open:
1 May - 30 Sept.

Address:
37510 Ballan-Miré.

Tel:
47:53.26.49.
FAX: 47.53.94.89.

Reservations:
Made for any length with deposit (Ffr. 220) and fee (80).

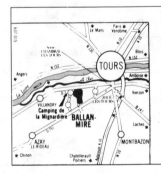

CAMPING ★ ★ ★ ★
DE LA MIGNARDIERE

37510 Ballan-Miré. Tel: 47 53.26.49

' All the comforts of a 4-star camp with a wide range of activities for enjoyment and relaxation of adults and children: swimpool and tennis on site, water sports lake, ponies and minigolf very close, the Loire châteaux and all the attractions of Tours. From autoroute take exit for Chambray-les-Tours. 2 Mobile Homes and 8 Chalets for hire.

3703 Camping Le Moulin Fort, Chenonceaux

Tidy riverside site with pool close to Château.

Le Moulin Fort is situated on the banks of the river Cher, on flat grass with some 100 pitches marked out by shrubs and trees. The two toilet blocks are well appointed and clean when seen. There is a small swimming pool (with paddling pool) and canoes can be hired from a small river beach, from which fishing is also possible. The reception also houses a small terrace bar, also providing takeaway meals, open lunchtime but shut after 8.00 in the evening. A few provisions, including bread, can be purchased at reception, but there is a supermarket across the bridge in Chisseaux. The site is less than 2 km. from one of the most beautiful châteaux, and in season there is a `son et lumiere' spectacle every evening. It is a good touring base for this and other sights, as well as an ideal location for a short stay en-route to the Auvergne or points further south.

Directions: Take the D40 Tours - Chenonceaux road, go through the village and after 2 km. turn right onto the D80 to cross the river at Chisseaux. Site is on the left just after the bridge.

Charges 1993:
-- Per pitch Ffr 24.00; adult 24.00; child 6.00; electricity 19.00.

Open:
Easter - 15 Sept.

Address:
37150 Chenonceaux

Tel:
47.23.86.22.
FAX: 47.23.80.93.

Reservations:
Write to site.

4102 Castel Camping Château de la Grenouillère, Suevres

Comfortable site with good amenities on the N152 midway between Orléans and Tours.

This site is well situated for visiting many of the Loire châteaux and makes a good stopover, but there are also enough attractions on site and locally to make it suitable for a longer stay. It is set in a 28 acre park and the 250 pitches are in three distinct areas. The majority are in a well wooded area, with about 60 in the old orchard and the remainder in open meadow, although all pitches are separated by hedges; 200 of the pitches have electricity (5A) and there is one water point for every 4 pitches. Additionally, there are 15 'grand comfort' pitches with a separate luxury sanitary block in the outbuildings of the château itself. The three other sanitary blocks, one for each area, are modern and well appointed. All the toilets are British with handwashing facilities nearby. Other washbasins are in private cabins with hot water, mirror and shelf. Some showers are pre-set, some controllable and all have dressing area, hooks and shelf. Razor points in the men's and hair dryers are provided. Site facilities include a shop, a well appointed bar, 2 supervised outdoor swimming pools, tennis, squash, minigolf, table tennis, pool, baby foot and video games. Bikes and canoes may be hired in July/August and guided tours are organised once a week. There are washing machines and dryers. The site is popular with tour operators.

Directions: From the A10 coming west from Paris, take Meung exit and N152 in the direction of Blois. Coming east from Tours, take Blois exit and N152 in direction of Orléans. Site is on the north side of the road.

Charges 1993:
-- Per unit incl. 2 persons, standard pitch Ffr. 100.00; extra person 30.00; child (under 5 yrs) 20.00; electricity (5A) 20.00.
-- Per unit incl. 2 persons, 'grand comfort' pitch 150.00; extra person 30.00; child 25.00.

Open:
15 May - 15 Sept.

Address:
41500 Suevres.

Tel:
54.87.80.37.

Reservations:
Made for min. 5 days with Ffr. 500 deposit of which Ffr. 100 is booking fee.

Sites marked with a small Alan Rogers' logo

make various special offers or discounts to members of the

ALAN ROGERS' TRAVEL CLUB

4101 Le Parc du Val de Loire, Mesland, nr Blois

Family owned site with swimming pools, situated between Blois and Tours.

This site is quietly situated away from the main roads and towns, but is nevertheless centrally placed for visits to the châteaux; Chaumont, Amboise and Blois (21 km.) are the nearest in that order. It has some 250 pitches of reasonable size, either in light woodland marked out by trees, (30 occupied by British hire tents) or on open meadow with separators. Some 50 pitches have electricity, water and drainaway. The two original toilet blocks are of very fair quality and have British WCs (with external entry), washbasins all in private cabins with free hot water, shelf and mirror, free hot showers at preset temperature, and hot water also in sinks. A third toilet block has been built with modern facilities. Units for the handicapped and new baby bath facilities. Water points around. On site there are 3 swimming pools, the newest (200 sq.m.) with sunbathing area, and heated all season; also a smaller pool, open mid-May to mid-Sept. and a small children's pool. Tennis court with floodlighting, and the good children's playground enlarged with skate board facilities. Barbecue area - some organised or DIY (free wood). Large shop. Limited hot takeaway food all season. Bar adjacent to pools, with snack service and TV room. Pizzeria with takeaway. Laundry facilities. Bicycle hire. Pony rides. Table tennis. Minigolf. BMX track. Tennis training wall. Football practice pitch. Basketball. Some organised sports and competitions in July/August. Wine tasting opportunities twice a week. Local walks on marked footpaths (maps Ffr.2). Mobile homes for hire and some tour operators. Watch for the Rabbit family!

Directions: The little village of Mesland lies 5 km. northwest of Onzain and is accessible from the Château-Renault/Amboise exit of the A10 autoroute via D31 to Autrèche, continue 5 km. then left at La Hargardière at camp sign and 8 km. to site.

Charges 1993:
-- Per unit incl. 2 persons: standard pitch (100 sq.m.) Ffr. 110.00, large pitch (150 sq.m.) with water and drainage 140.00; extra person 30.00; child (2-7 yrs) 20.00; electricity (6A) 20.00; extra car 10.00.
-- Reductions in low season.

Open:
1 May - 15 Sept.

Address:
41150 Mesland.

Tel:
54.70.27.18.
FAX: 54.70.21.71.

Reservations:
Made for min. 4 days with deposit and fee (Ffr. 100).

4103 Sologne Parc des Alicourts, Pierrefitte sur Sauldre

Secluded 21 hectare site in the heart of the forest with many sporting facilities.

This site is situated in a very secluded, forested area midway between Orleans and Bourges, about 20 km. to the east of the A10. There are 250 pitches of which 200 have electricity (2-6A) and provisions for water are good. Most pitches are 120 sq.m. (min. 100) and vary from wooded to more open areas, thus giving a choice of amount of shade. There are 3 sanitary blocks, the oldest of which has British and 'Turkish' type toilets, whilst the two newer ones have all British. The washbasins (open and in private cabins) have razor points, hair dryers and hot water. The showers in the old block are pre-set, those in the new blocks are controllable. In addition, there are three baby/toddler bath rooms plus washing machines and drying facilities. There is a restaurant using fresh produce and traditional cuisine (July/Aug) plus a takeaway service in a pleasant bar with terrace. The shop has a good range of produce in addition to the basics (essential as the nearest good sized town is some distance).

Leisure facilities are exceptional: two swimming pools (one for adults, one for children) with 25 m. shute, plus a paddling pool, a 7 hectare lake with fishing, bathing, canoes, pedaloes and children's play area, a 5 hole golf course (a very popular feature), football pitch, volleyball court, tennis, minigolf, table tennis, boules, cyclo-cross and mountain bikes and a way marked path for walking and cycling. In addition, there are lots of organised competitions for adults as well as children. In high season there is a club for children with an animateur twice a day, a disco once a week and a dance for adults. Some 26 pitches are taken by tour operators.

Directions: Site is on a back road, 5 km. from Pierrefitte sur Sauldre and is well signed from this village. From the A71 take the Lamotte-Beuvron exit.

Charges 1993:
-- Charges outside July/Aug. in brackets.
-- Per unit (incl. 2 persons) Ffr. 98.00 (74.00); extra person over 18 yrs 35.00 (29.00), 7-18 yrs 22.00 (17.00), (under 7 free); electricity 15 (2A), 19 (4A) or 24 (6A).

Open:
1 May - 20 Sept.

Address:
Domaine des Alicourts, 41300 Pierrefitte sur Sauldre.

Tel:
54.88.63.34.

Reservations:
Made for min. 7 days for July/Aug. only.

LORRAINE-VOSGES
Moselle - Meurthe-et-Moselle - Vosges - Meuse

This is a region of great contrasts with hills, valleys, plateaux and mountains stretching into the distance. It has not always been so, but now it has a peaceful feeling - the beautiful valley of the Moselle, with its vineyards, fascinating towns and large cities like Metz and Nancy, the lakes and waterfalls of the Vosges and the numerous castles, evidence of the regions history. Easily reached from the Channel ports by using the Autoroutes, it is well situated for excursions into both Luxembourg and Germany

8801 Camping Les Deux Ballons, St. Maurice-sur-Moselle
Good mountain site for summer and winter activities.

St. Maurice-sur-Moselle is in a narrow valley 7 km. from the source of the River Moselle in the massif of Hautes Vosges on the main N66 which leads to the Col de le Bussang. This is a pleasant leafy area for winter ski-ing and summer outdoor activities. Les Deux Ballons lies in a small valley surrounded by mountains and under a cover of trees which give shade in most parts. The 180 pitches are on stony ground under the firs or on two terraces, and all have electrical connections. Motorcaravan service area available.

Three sanitary blocks of average quality (British seatless WCs) are spread around the site; a further block is planned. There is a bar/restaurant with terrace and with waiter service in July and August, and a takeaway. The large swimming pool measures 30 x 20 m. and there is a smaller one for children. In July and August there are games competitions, organised walks, fishing, bowls, cycles for hire, horse riding, summer sledging and grass ski-ing. Ski hire in winter. TV rest room. Tennis. Table tennis. Volleyball. Bowls. Washing machines and dryers. Chalets and caravans for hire.

Directions: Site is on the main N66 Le Thillot - Bussang road on the northern edge of St. Maurice near Avia filling station.

Charges 1994:
-- Per person Ffr. 18.00; child (under 7 yrs) 11.00; pitch 21.00; electricity 4A 19.00, 15A 26.00; water connection 15.00; dog 6.00; local tax 1.50.

Open:
1 March - 31 Oct and Xmas.

Address:
17 Rue du Stade, 88560 St. Maurice-sur-Moselle.

Tel:
29.25.17.14.

Reservations:
Necessary for winter and July/Aug. Write with deposit (Ffr. 100) and booking fee (50).

8802 Camping de Belle Hutte, La Bresse, nr Gerardmer
Pleasant mountain site for summer and winter sports.

La Bresse, in the heart of the Vosges mountains, makes a good base for winter ski-ing and summer walking and although a little off the beaten track, is on one of the southern routes to the Col de la Schlucht. Camping de Belle Hutte, although surrounded by mountains and trees, occupies an open hill slope (900 m. above sea level) with grass pitches on six terraces. Places of about 90 sq.m. are divided by hedges, but not numbered, and all have electrical connections. The reception office at the entrance carries basic food supplies with larger shops and restaurants in the village about 400 m. away.

The well built, brick sanitary block is centrally placed, of excellent quality and heated in cool weather. Here is also found a laundry room with washing machines and dryers, a drying room, a play room with table tennis, rest room with open fire and TV and a ski storage room. Children's plaground. To reach the camp you would have to depart from the usual main through routes but it is a good site in pleasant surroundings.

Directions: Site is about 9 km. from La Bresse on the D34 road towards the Col de la Schlucht.

Charges 1994:
-- Per person Ffr. 13.50; child 10.00; car 7.50; caravan 9.50; tent 8.00; motorcaravan 19.00; dog 8.00; extra small tent 6.50; electricity 2-10A 7.50 - 31.00; local tax 1.10.
-- Prices higher in winter.

Open:
All year.

Address:
88250 La Bresse.

Tel:
29.25.49.75.

Reservations:
Necessary in winter. Write for booking form and return with Ffr. 150 deposit.

MIDI-PYRÉNÉES - Ariège

MIDI-PYRÉNÉES
Lot - Aveyron - Tarn - Haute-Garonne - Ariège - Haute-Pyrénées - Gers - Tarn-et-Garonne

This is France's largest administrative region and it encompasses many different, often contrasting, areas, from the majestic peaks of the Pyrénées, to the sunny farmlands of the Midi, to the breathtakingly beautiful river valleys and gorges in the Dèpartements of Lot and Aveyron. The region caters for many tastes and types of holiday - the nature lover, the explorer, the historian, the sportsperson, the food-lover, the wine-lover, or anyone who likes to sit and watch the world go by. A region to return to time and again.

N0901 Domaine Naturiste de Pauliac, Saverdun

Superbly situated, Dutch owned naturist site with glorious views.

Situated in attractive countryside, the views from the terrace and swimming pools at this site are exceptional including the distant Pyrénées across the Ariège landscape. The 286 pitches (many of which have electricity) are informally arranged on small terraces throughout the large and varied grounds which include semi-wooded and more open areas giving a choice of amount of shade. The site and swimming pools have been attractively landscaped around the old manor house (Domaine) and outbuildings which now form the reception, bar, restaurant and the oldest of the several sanitary blocks. The conversions have been sympathetically carried out with the result that the appearance of the old and attractive buildings is largely unimpaired.

The bar provides quite a focal point for informal gatherings and is pleasantly cool, while the smart French restaurant specialises in a number of well prepared dishes at reasonable prices. There is a well stocked shop including fresh bread, essential because the nearest village is some kilometres away. Sanitary facilities, particularly in the new, nicely tiled blocks are good with the usual naturist site style open-plan hot showers, British WCs, washbasins (open and in private cabins), dishwashing and laundry facilities (including washing machine) under cover and facilities for the handicapped. Facilities in the older block are similar but betraying their age. Both have winterised sections. In the height of the season there is an extra mobile block in the wooded area.

At most naturist sites, particularly the larger ones, the range of leisure activities (sporting and cultural) on offer is extensive and Domaine de Pauliac is no exception. Apart from two large swimming pools, plus a child's pool and sauna, there are facilities for boules, table tennis, volleyball, archery and a sauna. Drawing, painting, pottery and massage classes in the main season. Further afield, the site owners organise mountain walking, climbing, caving and cycling. The site is also quite conveniently situated for day excursions to places such as Carcassonne, the Route of the Cathars, the Pyrénées or even Andorra. Bungalows, cabins, mobile homes and tents to let.

Directions: Site is signposted in village of Saverdun which is bypassed by the N20 between Auterive and Pamiers. It lies on a small un-numbered road branching off the D14 WSW of the village.

Charges 1993:
-- Per pitch Ffr. 33.00; person 25.00; child (under 7 yrs) 12.00; animal 10.00; electricity 15.00.
-- Discounts (except electricity) 20% before 15/6 or after 15/9 or 10% before 30/6 or after 1/9.

Open:
All year.

Address:
09700 Saverdun.

Tel:
61.60.43.95.

Reservations:
Made with deposit (50% of charges) plus Ffr. 85 fee.

1200 Camping Peyrelade, Rivière sur Tarn, nr Millau

Situated by a pebble beach in the Gorges du Tarn.

Peyrelade is at the foot of the Gorges proper, and the campsite is situated on a bend in the river which has thrown up a natural pebble beach. Bathing is safe and the water is clean. Canoes can be hired and the site can arrange for rafting trips and 'canyonning' excursions. There are some 180 level, grassy tourist pitches, all with electric connections, marked out by trees and shrubs. Shade is very good in most parts. There is a small pool, and childrens' play area, and the site abuts a leisure centre with minigolf and tennis courts, which can be booked at the camp reception. A friendly bar and restaurant/pizzeria provides sustenance, including a full takeaway service. The site is ideal for visiting the Tarn Gorges and other attractions in the area include Roquefort of cheese fame, La Couvertriade (a Knights Templar village) and the eastern Cevennes. The Mediterranean coast is just within range for a day trip.

Directions: From the N9 Sevérac - Millau road, turn east from Aguessac (follow Gorges du Tarn signs). The site is 2 km. past Rivière sur Tarn, on the right. The access road is quite steep.

Charges 1993:
-- Per unit incl. 2 persons Ffr 90.00; extra adult 17.00; child (under 5) 13.00; electricity 16.00.

Open:
1 June - 15 September.

Address:
12640 Rivière-sur-Tarn.

Tel:
65.62.62.54 or 65.60.08.48 (low season).

Reservations:
Write to site.

1201 Castel Camping Val de Cantobre, Nant d'Aveyron, nr Millau

Attractive, terraced site in the valley of the Dourbie.

This site, set in the lovely high Causse and Gorge country, offers many excursion possibilities to places like the Gorges du Tarn. It is not as remote as it might at first seem, since the N9 Clermont-Ferrand to Mediterranean road has been much improved. The 170 individual pitches, some a little threadbare, are on flat terraces set on a steep hillside, so up-and-down walking to various facilities is needed; all have electricity and water. The 3 toilet blocks are of mixed type. The new modern one at mid-levels has 24 (12M and 12F) cabins housing both a washbasin and a shower, plus 6 or so WCs and a fully appointed room for the disabled, a ladies make up room and baby bath. The oldest block, by reception will have more toilets, thereby evening out some imbalance in the provision. The uppermost block has only minimal washing facilities but is due to be renovated for 1994.

The restaurant, bar, small shop and reception are all housed in beautiful, old regional buildings. There is a small swimming pool (19 x 7 m. unheated) and paddling pool which are very popular. The site is building up its activities with enthusiasm, offering an impressive list of outdoor pursuits (mostly off-site), including rafting and river trekking. Organised events in season: guided walks, sports competitions, some dances, etc. Takeaway and pizzeria. Laundry room. Caravans for hire. Tour operators take 15-20% of pitches. The administration copes well with the pressure of popularity in high season and good English is spoken throughout the site.

Directions: Site is 4 km. north of Nant, on D991 road to Millau.

Charges 1993:
-- Per unit incl. 2 persons and electricity 125.00; extra person (over 4 yrs) 20.00.

Open:
1 May - 21 Sept.

Address:
12230 Nant d'Aveyron.

Tel:
65.62.25.48.
FAX: 65.62.10.36.

Reservations:
Made for any length with deposit (Ffr. 82) and fee (18).

1202 Les Rivages, Millau

Large site on town outskirts close to Tarn Gorges with good range of sporting facilities.

This site is a very popular and well organised, being close to the high limestone `Causses' and the various river Gorges - particularly the Tarn - and their associated attractions, such as caves, remote villages, wildlife refuges, etc. Some 314 pitches occupy flat ground adjacent to the Dourbie river, close to its confluence with the Tarn. There is safe river bathing from the river beach. Pitches in the older part of the site are arranged in fours and tend to be a little crowded, with a bare 100 sq.m. space. In a newer, though less shaded part of the site (Camp 2), campers have more room. All pitches have electricity (6A) whilst 98 also include water and drainaway points. Pitch quality varies and shade is available according to taste. Sanitary facilities are good, the 4 modern blocks providing washbasins in private cabins, showers and toilets (British and continental), dishwashing and laundry sinks, rooms for the handicapped, baby bath, children's toilets and a laundry.

The current management is committed to providing a wide range of sporting and cultural options (said to be 26 different activities). On site there are indoor and outdoor tennis courts, 2 badminton courts, 2 squash courts, volleyball and two swimming pools. Table tennis. Football. Petanque. Activities on the river, mountain biking, walking, fishing and many more. Cyclo-cross track. All are exclusively for campers in high season. Children's play area and entertainments - child minding (3-6yrs) is available. Off-site organised activities are extremely varied and efficiently publicised through an excellent Information Bureau. Shop. Snack bar. Restaurant. Gates shut 10 pm. - 8 am, with nightwatchman. A few pitches (8%) are occupied by tour operators.

Directions: Site is on the Nant (D991) road out of Millau.

Charges 1993:
-- Per pitch incl. 2 persons: normal Ffr 90.00, with electricity 105.00, with all services 115.00; extra person (over 3 yrs) 18.00; pet 12.00; local tax (15/6-15/9) 1.00.
-- Less 25% in low season, 15% in mid season.

Open:
1 May - 30 Sept.

Address:
Avenue de l'Aigoual, 12100 Millau.

Tel:
65.61.01.07.

Reservations:
Advisable for Jul/Aug. with deposit (Ffr. 400) and fee (100).

1203 Camping Val Fleuri, Belmont-sur-Rance

Satisfactory small, grassy site close to town centre.

Belmont is somewhat remote, either from through routes or the well known tourist attractions, yet it is nonetheless a pretty little town and this part of Avreyon is well worth a short stay. The site is on the banks of the river (though bathing at this point is not recommended) and is well grassed with small hedges between the 69 flat, fairly standard sized pitches, mostly arranged in pairs. 44 pitches have electricity (2, 4 or 6A) and shade is minimal. With the town so close there are few on-site amenities, but the restaurant/bar (Relais Routiers) opens at lunch times and evenings all the year. There are organised activities 2 or 3 times a week in season.

The single sanitary block in two parts is not luxurious but is well cleaned and just about adequate for the numbers on site. Toilets are the seatless type, washbasins are in private cabins and there are dishwashing and laundry sinks (with H&C). Ironing room. Facilities for the handicapped. Fishing from site. Good large grassy play area. Children's pool. Swimming pool, tennis, canoe school, karting, riding and the facilities of the town are close. Boules. Table tennis. Bungalows (3) and tents (3) for hire.

Directions: Site is on the south bank of the Rance on the road to Lacaune.

Charges 1993:
-- Per pitch incl. 1 or 2 persons Ffr. 52.00; extra person 20.00; electricity 2A 8.00, 4A 10.00, 6A 12.00; pet 7.00.

Open:
15 March - 31 Oct.

Address:
12370 Belmont-sur-Rance.

Tel:
65.99.95.13.

Reservations:
Made for min. week with 20% deposit.

1204 Castel Camping Les Tours, St Amans des Cots
Attractive, friendly and efficiently run site on shores of Lac de la Selves.

This is an impressive campsite, set in beautiful countryside very close to the Truyère Gorges, Upper Lot valley and the Aubrac Plateau. There are 250 pitches, all of approx. 100 sq.m. and with 5A electrical connections. Some 100 pitches also have individual water points. About 20% of the pitches are for static caravans - reserved for tour operators or owned by the site, but these are well spaced. The site has a spacious feel about it, enhanced by the thoughtful terraced layout. The sanitary facilities are good, with four blocks, all with free hot showers, individual washing cubicles, British and continental toilets, and seem more than adequate for the number of campers. They were spotlessly clean when seen in main season.

The central complex, including office, restaurant, bar, swimming pools (650 and 40 sq.m.), shop and modern children's play area is most attractive. There are volleyball and tennis courts, a putting green and table tennis. The site arranges a varied programme of daytime and evening activities. Lake activities available include canoeing, pedaloes, windsurfing, water ski-ing and there is provision for launching small boats. Riding and golf near. Takeaway. Room for films and videos. Shop and greengrocer. Exchange facilities. The owner and his staff are helpful. Used by tour operators.

Directions: Take D34 road from Entraygues-sur-Truyere to St. Amans-des-Cots (14 kms.). In St. Amans turn right onto D599 (site is signposted), then left on to a long, twisting descent to the lake and site.

Charges 1994:
-- Per unit, incl. 2 persons Ffr 108.00, 3 persons 132.00; extra person 23.00; child 16.00; electricity 15.00; services 8.00.
-- Less 20% outside July/Aug.
Open:
15 May - 30 Sept.
Address:
12460 St. Amans-des-Cots.
Tel:
65.44.88.10.
FAX: 65.44.83.07.
Reservations:
Made and are advisable for July/Aug. - write for details.

1205 Camping Les Terraces du Lac, Pont de Salars, nr Rodez
Family run site overlooking lake between Millau and Rodez.

Situated at an altitude of some 2,000 ft. on the plateau of Le Lévézou, this site enjoys attractive views over Lac de Pont de Salars and also has the benefit of a swimming pool. The site is terraced, providing 180 good sized, level pitches with or without shade, all with electricity. There are presently no tour operators and the site seems largely undiscovered by the British.

There is an attractive, quite large (200 sq.m.) pool and children's pool, with paved and grass sunbathing terraces and good views over the lake which has direct access from the site at two places - one for pedestrians and swimmers, the other for cars and trailers for launching small boats. There is a large bar/restaurant serving full meals during the high season and snacks at other times. There are four sanitary blocks, all quite modern including a new 'state of the art' one. All have free hot showers, seatless WCs and some washbasins (H&C) in private cabins, plus washing up areas under cover and laundry facilities including a washing machine. Takeaway. Solarium. Children's playground. Volleyball. Pétanque. Table tennis. Billiards. Games and TV rooms. Tennis 3 km. Entertainment and activities in high season. This site is well situated for excursions into the Gorges du Tarn, Caves du Roquefort and nearby historic towns and villages.

Directions: Using D911 Millau - Rodez road, turn north at Pont de Salars in the direction of the lake on the D523. Follow camp signs. Ignore first site and continue following lake until Les Terraces (approx. 5/6 km).

Charges 1994:
-- Per pitch incl. 2 persons Ffr. 65.00 - 95.00; extra person 16.00 - 21.50; child (under 7 yrs) 11.00 - 14.50; electricity (5A) 16.00 - 19.00; water, drainage and electricity 22.00 - 26.50; local tax 1.00.
Open:
1 June - 30 Sept.
Address:
Rte. du Vibal, 12290 Pont de Salars.
Tel:
65.46.88.18.
FAX: 65.46.85.38.
Reservations:
Made with deposit (Ffr. 400) and fee (70).

N6501 Domaine Naturiste L'Eglantiere, Aries-Espénan, nr Castelnau-Magnoac

Pretty riverside site in the Vallée du Gers.

This site is situated in the valley between the Pyrénées and the plain, within easy reach of Lourdes and the mountains. The site itself is in a hollow alongside a small, fast flowing river, surrounded by oak trees. It comprises 12 ha. for camping and caravanning, with a further 28 for walking and relaxing in woods and fields. The river is said to be suitable for swimming and fishing. The 100 or so pitches, all of a good size, are on fairly level grass and are very secluded, being separated by a variety of tall trees and bushes. About 40 have 12A electrical connections. There is a medium sized swimming pool, with sunbathing areas both on paving and grass, and a children's pool. A clubhouse is attractively designed and built by traditional methods, in traditional materials, including locally grown oak. beams. It provides a bar and crêperie with terrace, an indoor activities area, further sanitary facilities and eventually perhaps also an indoor pool. There is a range of restaurants in the nearby village. The existing sanitary facilities are in typically naturist style, providing under cover, open plan hot showers, washbasins (H&C) in vanity units, seatless WCs and sinks for washing up (cold water). Shop. Children's play area and a rather elderly Shetland pony. Volleyball. Badminton. Table tennis. Pétanque. Archery. Boating on river. Trekking and cross-country cycling. Studios, mobile homes and tents to rent.

Charges 1993:
-- Per pitch incl. 2 persons
- 'traditional' Ffr. 69.30 - 99.00, acc. to season, 'wild' 63.20 - 89.00; extra person 17.50 - 25.00; child (3-8 yrs) 9.80 - 14.00, under 3 yrs free; electricity 18.00.

Open:
1 April - 15 Oct.

Address:
65230 Aries-Espénan.

Tel:
62.99.83.64 or 62.39.88.00.
FAX: 62.39.81.44.

Reservations:
Made with Ffr. 600 deposit.

Directions: From Auch take the D929 southward to Castelnau-Magnoac and then follow signs to the hamlet of Aries-Espénan from where site is signposted.

3203 Camping Château Le Haget, Montesquiou

Mature site in parkland setting on Pilgrims Route to Santiago.

Charm and a certain, if slightly faded, elegance seem to characterize this site which is situated in the grounds of a romantic-looking, restored château. The grounds contain a wide variety of mature trees, some of them immensely tall and impressive, as well as many of the more old fashioned and fragrant rose bushes. There are some 100 pitches of good size on fairly level grass of which about half have electricity. Although there are many big trees and shrubs, the site is not oppressive and shade varies.

A secluded, hedged swimming pool with sunbathing area and a separate, quite large children's pool, children's play area, table tennis, bicycle hire, occasional discos in the former stables and an 'animation' programme provide entertainment for youngsters. The owners (who are Dutch although the site has a distinctly French atmosphere) arrange excursions to destinations such as the Pyrénées, Armagnac châteaux (including tastings!), etc. The sanitary facilities are perhaps unique in having the showers upstairs - the actual facilities including hot showers, washbasins, some British seatless WCs, washing up sinks and washing machine are mainly housed in wooden cabins within the large, old buildings, one of which was the original Orangerie. They are certainly not of the latest design but seem to operate satisfactorily and were very clean when seen on our visit in July. There is a small bar/restaurant serving a 'menu of the day' situated in another of the original outbuildings. Tennis 2 km. Rooms, caravans, tents and chalets to hire.

Charges 1994:
-- Per person Ffr. 25.00; child (under 7 yrs) 15.00; pitch 35.00; car by unit 10.00; car in parking place 6.00; electricity (6A) 12.50; drainage 10.00; dog 6.00.
-- Less 25% outside 15/6-31/8.

Open:
15 May - 15 Sept.

Address:
32320 Montesquiou.

Tel:
62.70.95.80.
FAX: 62.70.94.83.

Reservations:
Write to site for details.

Directions: From Auch take the road to Bayonne (124). After about 3 km. turn left on the D943 - Route des Bastides et Castelnaux. At Montesquoiu pass the village and turn left at camp site sign.

3201 Castel Camping Le Camp de Florence, La Romieu
Small site in undulating countryside of woods and fields of wheat and sunflowers.

A warm welcome awaits visitors to the Camp de Florence, now part of the Castels chain, from its Dutch owners who have sympathetically converted the old farmhouse buildings to provide facilities for the site. There are 120 pitches of 100 sq.m, most with electricity and terraced where necessary, some with shade. There are two toilet blocks, one heated for winter use. They have British toilets, free hot water, showers with hooks, stools, and washbasins, some in cabins; they should suffice. Washing machine. A restaurant, for visitors as well as campers, provides a range of food plus a good value à la carte menu. It is only open at midday in winter. The site also provides a swimming pool (built with a beach effect so one can walk in on 3 sides), a paddling pool, children's play area, games area and pets area typical of Dutch owned sites. Barbecues are permitted. Takeaway. Games room. Tennis. Table tennis. Petanque. Volleyball. Clay shooting. Video shows. Discos. Picnics. Musical evenings. Excursions. Exchange facility. Supermarket in nearby village. On Sunday mornings in the summer there is a small market of regional products on the terrace. The historic village of La Romieu is less than 300 m. away, the Pyrénées are 2 hrs. drive, and the Atlantic coast a similar distance. Fishing, riding, tennis, bicycle hire nearby for those seeking a quiet holiday. Mobile homes and chalets for hire.

Directions: Site is signed on the D931 Agen - Condom road 3 km. before Condom in the direction of La Romieu (D41).

Charges 1994:
-- Per unit Ffr. 35.00, with water and drainage 45.00; person 28.00 Ffr; child (0-3 yrs) 10.00, (4-7 yrs) 20.00; electricity 15.00; dog 6.00.
-- Less 30% on person charges outside high season.

Open:
All year.

Address:
32480 La Romieu.

Tel:
62.28.15.58.
FAX: 62.28.20.04.

Reservations:
Write or phone for information (English spoken).

LE CAMP DE FLORENCE 32480, LA ROMIEU, GERS
SUN ★ COMFORT ★ NATURE ★ WATER

The Gers – A county waiting to be discovered, an unspoilt landscape of rolling hills, sunflowers and historic fortified villages and castles.
Peace, tranquility, the home of Armagnac, Fois Gras and Magret Duck.
A four star campsite with bungalows, mobile homes and trigano tents for hire.

Tel 62 28 15 58   Fax 62 28 20 04

4603 Camping Les Pins, Payrac-en-Quercy
Site in wooded parkland, suitable for a Dordogne holiday or overnight stop on way south.

Camping Les Pins named after its pine trees, has impressive views. The level pitches (100 sq.m) are clearly marked, all have electricity and 34 water and drainage connections also. Most are shady but there is a fair number of sunny places. A heated pool (15 x 17 m.), with sunbathing area and a smaller children's paddling pool are on site and a separate, small leisure park (Aqua Follies) adjoins the site with water chute, jacuzzi pool, contra-current pool and trampoline which is free for campers. Tennis court (charged).

An attractive bar/restaurant with views over surrounding area also provides takeaway meals. The three toilet blocks are very well maintained providing British WCs, showers, complete with stools, washbasins in cabins, hooks, shelves and full length mirror. Hot water for dishwashing sinks and laundry. Washing machines and dryers. Shop. TV. Library. Table tennis. Pétanque. Boules. Volleyball. Some entertainment in season. Nearby fishing, horse riding and canoeing on the Dordogne. Discos. Mobile homes to let.

Directions: Site is by N20 south of Payrac-en-Quercy, 16 km. from Souillac.

Charges 1993:
-- Per person Ffr. 29.00; child (under 7) 16.00; local tax 1.00; pitch 43.00; electricity 16.00.
-- Less 30% outside 15/6 - 31/8 (not for electricity).

Open:
1 April - 30 Sept.

Address:
46350 Payrac.

Tel:
65.37.96.32.
FAX: 65.37.91.08.
UK: (0722) 322583.

Reservations:
Made for min. 1 week with deposit (25%) plus fee (Ffr. 90).

MIDI-PYRÉNÉES - Lot

4602 Les Reflets du Quercy, Crayssac
Family run site with Tahitian flavour 16 km. from Cahors.

Les Reflets is a purpose built site, attractively laid out on a hillside with 95 terraced pitches. All have electricity, water and drainaway and are on levelled hardstanding. This can cause some problems with pegs for tents and awnings but drills are supplied on arrival. Three modern toilet blocks give an ample service and have mostly British WCs, washbasins in cabins with free hot water, shelf and light and well equipped hot showers. Hot water in sinks also, washing machine in each block. There is an excellent swimming pool with diving board, small shop and an imaginative restaurant with takeaway service. Two tennis courts, table tennis and volleyball number among many leisure facilities. The site now has a high proportion of mobile homes and tour operator pitches (mostly French) and has only a small number of touring pitches. However a Tahitian flavour gives a special ambience.

Directions: Site is signposted from the main D911 about 16 km. west of Cahors. Turn south opposite D23 to Catus, then 2 km. to site following signs.

Charges guide:
-- Per pitch Ffr 40.00 - 70.00; adult 15.00 - 18.00; child (3-12) 10.00 - 14.00.
-- Special weekly rates.
Open:
Easter - 12 Nov.
Address:
Crayssac, 46150 Catus.
Tel:
65.30.91.48.
FAX: 65.30.97.87.
Reservations:
Write with deposit (20-30%).

4604 Moulin de Laborde, Montcabrier
Small site developed round an old watermill, with swimming pool.

The watermill and its outbuildings at Moulin de Laborde have been sympathetically developed to provide a courtyard and terrace with a small bar, restaurant (with takeaway) and a shop. There are 60 pitches of 100 sq.m on level grass all with electricity and bordered by woods, hills and a small river. Trees and shrubs have been planted so shade is developing. Swimming pool with sunbathing area and paddling pool. The good sanitary block has well designed showers, British WCs and washbasins in cabins. Free hot water for dish and clothes washing also. Washing machine and dryer. Unit for disabled. Mountain bike hire and mountaineering lessons available. Rustic children's play area on grass. Volleyball. Badminton. Boules. Petanque. Recreation room. Table tennis. Barbecue facilities. Riding, tennis and canoeing on the Lot near.

Directions: Site is near Montcabrier, just south of the D673, 12 km. from Fumel. Follow the D673 north for 2-3 km. towards Cazals; site is on the right.

Charges 1993:
-- Per person 24.00 Ffr; child (under 7) 12.00; pitch 30.00; electricity 12.00.
-- Less outside 15/6 - 31/8.
Open:
15 May - 30 Sept.
Address:
46700 Montcabrier.
Tel:
65.24.62.06.
Reservations:
Made with deposit (Ffr. 30 per night, min. 300) by Eurocheque or postal draft.

4605 Camping La Rêve, Le Vigan
Very peaceful, clean site with pool far from the madding crowd.

La Rêve is situated in the heart of rolling countryside where the Perigord runs into Quercy. Pitches are divided by low shrubs which, like most of the trees on the main camping field, have been planted fairly recently. The use of acacias means the shade level will improve in future years. There is plenty of space for all units and some pitches are very large. Most have access to electricity and there are now 8 new pitches in the woods. The modern toilet block is kept very clean, with free hot showers, washbasins in private cabins, special cubicles for the disabled and a baby room. The small swimming pool was also very clean, about 1½ m. depth throughout, with a separate children's paddling pool. The reception area houses a small shop, a pleasant open-air, but covered, bar and terrace takeaway/restaurant, serving snacks and more substantial dishes. A small children's playground, boules area, table tennis and volleyball facilities complete the amenities. La Rêve impressed us with its tranquillity and the young Dutch owners are keen to develop the site in such a way that this would not be lost. A site particularly suitable for families with very young children.

Directions: Follow N20 from Souillac towards Cahors About 3 km. south of Payrac, turn right onto D673 (signposted Le Vigan, Gourdon). After 2 km, La Rêve is signed on the right down a small lane and site is some 3 km. further on.

Charges 1994:
-- Per adult Ffr. 18.00; child 9.00; pitch 22.00; electricity 3A 8.00, 6A 12.00.
-- Less 10-25% outside July/Aug.
Open:
May - Sept.
Address:
46300 Le Vigan.
Tel:
65.41.25.20.
Reservations:
Made for any length with deposit (Ffr. 250) and fee (20).

4601 Castels Camping de la Paille Basse, Souillac, nr Sarlat

Site in high situation with panoramic views and good swimming pools.

Lying some 8 km from Souillac, this family owned and managed site is easily accessible from the N20 and well placed to take advantage of excursions into the Dordogne. It is part of a large Domaine of 80 hectares, which is available to campers for walks and recreation. The site itself has a high location and there are excellent wide views over the surrounding countryside. The 250 pitches are in two main areas - one is level in cleared woodland with good shade, and the other on grass in open ground without shade. They are all a minimum 100 sq.m., numbered and marked, with about 80 having electricity, water and drainaway; electricity is available near all the others. The site has a good swimming pool complex, with a main pool (25 x 10 m.), a second one (10 x 6) and also a paddling pool; they are not heated. Solarium and a crêperie adjacent to the pools. Shop. Restaurant, bar with terrace and takeaway food. Disco room (twice weekly in season). TV rooms (with satellite) and cinema room. Archery and tennis (charged). Children's playground. Laundry facilities. Doctor calls.

The main sanitary installations (there is also a small night unit at one end of site) are in 3 different sections, all centrally located close to reception and kept very clean. They have British WCs, washbasins in private cabins with shelf, mirror and light and pre-set hot water, and a good supply of free hot showers (in one block) with pre-set hot water. The latest block is of an excellent standard. Activities and entertainment organised in season. The site can get very busy in main season and is popular with tour operators.

Directions: From Souillac take D15 road leading northwest towards Salignac-Eyvignes and after 6 km. turn right at camp sign on 2 km. approach road.

Charges 1994:
-- Per person Ffr. 30.00; child (under 7) 18.00; pitch 48.00 or with 3 services 60.00; electricity 17.00 - 30.00.
-- Less 20% outside 15/6-5/9.

Open:
15 May - 15 Sept.

Address:
46200 Souillac-sur-Dordogne.

Tel:
65.37.85.48 or 65.32.73.51.

Reservations:
Made for min. 2 weeks with deposit and Ffr. 90 booking fee.

8101 Camping Relais de l'Entre Deux Lacs, Teillet, nr Albi

Small, quiet family run site between the Lakes of Rassisse and Bancalié.

The Belgian family of Lily and Dion Heijde-Wouters have developed this small, pretty site, situated in part meadow, part semi cleared woodland, over a period of 11 years. The site now offers a range of modern amenities including a good sized swimming pool and an excellent bar/restaurant specialising in Belgian cuisine. It also serves a range of no less than 30 different Belgian beers as well as French wine. Special family orientated attractions include a weekly barbeque evening, children's activity programme and 'Its a Knockout' contests.

The 54 pitches, all with electrical connections, are on level terraces with the possibility of ample shade. They are of varying size, up to 100 sq.m. The site and activities are very well managed and the owners are at pains to ensure that the generally tranquil atmosphere is not disrupted by noise late at night. Late arrivals or those wishing to leave before 8.00 am. are therefore sited in an adjacent small meadow. There are two sanitary blocks, the main one being of new construction with the latest fittings including free, pre-set hot showers, washbasins in private cabins, British WCs and dishwashing sinks under cover (H&C). The older, smaller block, in the converted pigeon house, has similar, though older style fittings and is heated in winter when the new block is closed. Volleyball. Table tennis. Boules. Children's farm and playground. Shop. Bicycle hire. Canoes and kayaks for hire on Rassisse lake. Caravans and small chalets to let. This site is well situated for a variety of interesting excursions in an area not that well known to British visitors.

Directions: From Albi ringroad, take the D81 going southwest to Teillet (approx. 20 km). Continue through village on D81 and site is on right.

Charges 1994:
-- Per person Ffr. 20.00; child (under 7 yrs) 9.50; tent or caravan 11.50; car or m/cycle 10.50; motorcaravan 25.00; extra tent 8.50; electricity (3A) 9.50, (6A) 18.00.
-- Less 20% outside 15/6 - 31/8 for stays of min. 5 days.

Open:
All year.

Address:
81120 Teillet.

Tel:
63.55.74.45.
FAX: 63.55.75.65.

Reservations:
Made with deposit (Ffr. 100 per week booked) and fee (70).

NORD / PAS DE CALAIS - Nord

NORD/PAS DE CALAIS
Pas-de-Calais - Nord

There is a temptation to drive quickly through this region en-route to destinations further south, or at best, to make a night-stop close to the Channel ports. To do so is rather a pity, as there is much to see and do, and it is an ideal area for a short break or for an extended stay at the start or end of a long holiday. The region is an intriguing combination of busy market towns, ferry and fishing ports, seaside resorts, sleepy villages and pretty countryside, all within easy reach of the Channel Tunnel.

5901 Camping Perroquet Plage, Bray Dunes, nr Dunkerque

Very large, seaside site with many activities, on the Belgian border.

This 30 ha. sized camp has something of a novelty value in its association with the frontier which runs down one side of the camp and even through the entrance - the shop is in Belgium but the office is in France. Split very much into two, a wooded inland section with shade but rather tight access roads is very different from the dunes camping some 1 km. distant, by the sea where tractors place your caravan for you in the sand. There are about 800 pitches altogether, although only 120 for tourers, and pitch is a somewhat arbitrary term in the dune areas where the majority of touring units are placed, although there is always electricity nearby.

Six toilet blocks serve the site. Two are inland, where one is of good quality and size, but the one furthest from the entrance is best avoided. The four in the dunes are of surprisingly fair quality considering the potential usage. Hot water is free to showers (preset, pushbutton type with seat and hook). Washbasins are all in private cabins, with similar preset supply of hot water. Toilets are all of the seatless type. Many dishwashing sinks in outdoor covered locations but with cold water only. The total provision appears adequate and the blocks are said to be cleaned regularly during the day. The site has many activities although surprisingly the nearest swimming pool is 1½ km. distant in Bray Dunes. Animation is almost continuous every day in July and August. Café, bar, restaurant and takeaway in Dunes complex - plus basic food store, newsagent and souvenirs. Also small shop by entrance. 3 tennis courts. Boules. Volleyball. Golf practice nets. Putting surface. Mountain bike hire. Archery and shooting areas. Table tennis. Riding from site. Surfing, sailing and shore fishing catered for.

Directions: Follow signs to Bray Dunes from the N39/N1/E40 coast road. From Bray Dunes centre, follow camp signs or road to De Panne (in Belgium) and camp is seawards of the Customs Post at the frontier.

Charges 1994:
-- Per person Ffr 20.60 + local tax 2.40; child (under 7 yrs) 10.30; car 9.00; caravan 12.00; tent 9.00; electricity 12.50.

Open:
1 April - 30 Sept.

Address:
59123 Bray Dunes.

Tel:
28.58.37.37.

Reservations:
Recommended for July/Aug.

Please show reception staff this Guide when you arrive at a site

- it helps them, us and eventually you too

6201 Castels Camping Caravaning de la Bien-Assise, Guînes, nr Calais

Site with pool and excellent amenities close to cross channel links, worth a longer stay

This site is probably a good choice for those looking for a camp close to Calais (15 mins) and the Channel Tunnel exit (less than 8 km.). Boulogne is also only 20 mins away. It provides 150 pitches, all numbered but not fully marked out, on flat grass and of a good size with many electrical connections. The three sanitary blocks are of excellent quality - the newest with facilities for small children. There is also provision (new) for disabled visitors. The facilities provide amply for the size of the site and are of a standard one would expect from a site of this quality. They provide British toilets, washbasins all in private cabins with free hot water in these and also in good, fully controllable showers, a small bath, and sinks for clothes and washing up. There is a launderette.

The site is run personally by the proprietors who are constantly striving to improve it. There is a heated swimming pool (16 x 6 m.) in an enclosed position and a small pond which may be developed for fishing. The sporting facilities include tennis, minigolf, table tennis, a children's playground and mountain bikes for hire. There is a crêperie/snack bar on site as well as an excellent restaurant, `La Ferme Gourmande' which provides quality service and food at reasonable prices (open all year, closed Mondays). Hotel rooms are available also (all year). TV room and library. Shop. Some entertainment in July/Aug. This is a popular site making a real effort to further upgrade its already very good facilities so reservations at peak times may be advisable. Reception is open long hours to meet the requirements of those crossing the Channel. Limited use by one UK tour operator.

Directions: Site is situated on the D231 southwest of Guînes and is signposted in the town.

Charges 1994:
-- Per pitch Ffr 44.00; adult 20.00; child (under 8) 15.00; electricity 15.00.
-- Less 7% in low season.

Open:
1 May - 25 Sept.

Address:
62340 Guînes:

Tel:
21.35.20.77.
FAX 21.36.79.20.

Reservations:
May be advisable for July/Aug: deposit required for stays of about a week or more.

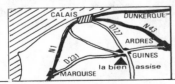

6202 Camping Le Canchy, Licques, nr Calais

Small, unpretentious, rural site in peaceful chalk downland.

Ideally situated for the tunnel, this small, recently developed site (1988) provides a reasonably priced stopover en-route south, but anyone looking for rural tranquillity may be tempted to a longer stay. The 72 grassy pitches of fair but variable size, are set on a flat meadow, mostly around a gravelled circular perimeter track. All areas have electricity (3 or 4A) and water and waste disposal points are plentiful and decorative. The trees and shrubs are beginning to mature and provide some shade and the site has a pleasing ambience with a warm welcome. This is only marred by one thing - the small children's play area has an unfortunate view of the men's urinals section of the toilet block. This centrally located block is very clean and has free hot water to the basic pre-set pushbutton showers, but not to the washbasins to which it has to be ferried by bucket or container from a single tap within the block. Toilets are British and continental type and there are good facilities for the handicapped. The block is not heated in winter. There are few on site amenities and most requirements have to be served by shops in the village some 1 km. distant, though the office does stock some drinks and ice creams, and bread, milk and basics can be ordered. Freezer for ice. Washing machine. Boules. Telephone. Fridge for ice.

Directions: Site is about 1 km. south east of Licques from where it is signposted. Licques is on the D224, some 24 km. SSE of Calais and is a village on the Route de Drap d'Or - a tourist route. Calais, 25 km. Boulogne 26 km.

Charges 1994:
-- Per person Ffr 14.00; child (under 7) 7.00; pitch 14.00; electricity 8.50.
-- Less outside July/Aug.

Open:
15 March - 31 Oct.

Address:
Rue de Canchy, 62850 Licques.

Tel:
21 82.63.41.

Reservations:
Usually space available.

6203 Camping Château de Gandspette, Eperleques, nr St Omer

Family run site in grounds of château with swimming pools.

Conveniently situated for the Channel Ports and the Tunnel, this family run site provides useful overnight accommodation as well as offering a range of facilities for a longer stay. It has the benefit of a large new (1993) heated swimming pool - an addition to a smaller older one with paved sunbathing area. There is also an attractive bar and grill restaurant and takeaway situated in a 17th century building adjacent to the château.

There are 120 pitches in all (100 sq.m.), half of which are semi-permanent French holiday caravans which intermix with the touring pitches giving a real French ambience. All have electricity (3 or 4A) and are delineated by trees in the corners and some hedging with circular gravelled access road. There is a central open space and the pitches are surrounded by woodland so that it is possible to have shade or sun. The sanitary block is somewhat utilitarian looking but appears quite satisfactory providing seatless WCs, some wash-basins in cabins with H&C, others with cold only and free push-button operated hot showers in good sized tiled cubicles with separators. Covered dishwashing sinks with hot water point. Washing machine. Other facilities include a children's play area, with a play field; riding nearby - in the campsite at weekends if reserved, walks in the site's own woods. Petanque, tennis, children's room with electronic games and darts! Entertainment in season.

Directions: From N43 St Omer - Calais road (southeast of Nordausques) take D221 (east) and follow camp signs for 5-6 km.

Charges 1994:
-- Per unit incl. 2 persons Ffr. 90.00; extra person (over 4 yrs) 25.00, under 4 free; extra car 10.00; electricity (3A) 12.00.

Open:
1 April - 30 September.

Address:
62910 Eperlecques.

Tel:
21.93.43.93.
FAX: 21.95.74.98.

Reservations:
Necessary for July/Aug - write to site.

NORMANDY
Seine-Maritime - Eure - Orne - Calvados - Manche

As the history of Normandy is so closely linked with our own, it is not altogether surprising that so many British visitors feel comfortable in this fascinating and diverse region. Apart perhaps from the weather, which can often be rather too like our own, Normandy has everything for a first rate holiday; a superb coastline, stretching from near Dieppe in the east, round the Cotentin penninsular, almost to Mont St. Michel in the west, with towering cliffs, vast sandy beaches and a variety of resorts. Normandy is famous for its rich cuisine, lush countryside, interesting historic towns and cities, and the famous 'landing beaches' of 1944, but it also has a few 'secrets', such as the Suisse Normandie, the Pays d'Auge, and the forested Orne Valley, all of which amply reward a visit; and of course there are the 'three C's' - Creme, Camembert and Calvados!

1401 Camping de la Côte de Nacre, St. Aubin sur Mer, nr Caen
Large new site just back from the sea, with swimming pool.

This stretch of the Normandy coast comprises a long series of towns which tend to run together. Nonetheless, the beaches and bathing are good, and are within walking distance of the site. There are some 350 standard sized, disc marked pitches here, laid out adjacent to semi-circular gravelled access roads; 250 of them have electricity (4, 6 or 10A). There are 52 super pitches with water, drainage, electricity, telephone and TV connections. Because the site is fairly new, the trees and shrubs planted have not yet had much time to grow, so there is not much to separate pitches or to give shade and there is a somewhat bare appearance at present. The two sanitary blocks are of modern construction and style. Washbasins are in cabins and all hot water is free. The provision should be good and the blocks are well cleaned. In winter a small block is opened in the reception complex. Given its situation, on site activities are not extensive although there is a small pool with child's pool and some animation and excursions are organised in season. The reception complex houses a bar, restaurant (open all year), TV and games room and a small shop (basics only in winter). Scattered children's play equipment. Boules. Table tennis. Bicycle hire.

Directions: Camp is on the southern side of the town centre relief road and well signposted from the approach roads to St Aubin, but make sure you leave the adjacent towns first.

Charges 1994:
-- Per pitch Ffr 25.00 - 28.00, acc. to season; adult 23.00 - 25.00; child (under 7) 12.00 - 13.00; electricity 17.00 - 30.00, acc. to amps (4, 6 or 10); extra car or tent 12.00 - 13.00.

Open:
All year.

Address:
Rue du Camping, BP 18, 14750 St. Aubin sur Mer.

Tel:
31.97.14.45.
FAX: 31.97.22.11.

Reservations:
Advisable for July/Aug. and made with deposit (Ffr. 500) of which 100 is non-returnable.

1402 Camping Municipal, Bayeux
Well kept municipal site making a good night halt.

Whether or not you want to see the tapestry, this site makes a very useful night stop on the way to or from Cherbourg, and in addition it is only a few kilometres from the coast. It is a good site, pleasantly laid out with grassy lawns and bushes, and its neat, cared for appearance makes a good impression. The 225 pitches are a mixture of shade and open, well marked and generally of good size, 170 with electricity. The three toilet blocks have British and continental WCs, troughs for washing, free hot showers, units for disabled, and are of fair quality (one newish good one), but some washing facilities are not fully enclosed. Large public swimming pool close to the site. Mobile shop with takeaway food July/Aug. Large supermarket opposite (closes 8 pm). Children's playground. Reading room with TV. Games room. Laundry room. The site is busy over a long season - reservation, particularly for electricity, is advised.

Directions: Site is on the south side of northern ring road to town.

Charges guide:
-- Per person 11.50 Ffr; child (under 7) 6.20; pitch and car 14.10; extra vehicle or pitch 6.20; electricity 11.70.
-- Less 10% over 5 days.

Open:
15 March - 15 Nov: warden full-time 15/6-15/9.

Address:
14400 Bayeux.

Tel:
31.92.08.43.

Reservations:
Min. 3 nights without deposit. (See editorial).

1403 Castel Camping de Martragny, Martragny, nr Bayeux

Site adjoining château in parkland setting, close to Bayeux and D-Day landing beaches.

Martragny is particularly convenient for those using the port of Cherbourg and has facilities to encourage longer stays as well as stopovers. Taking 140 units on the pleasant lawns surrounding the château, it does not have marked out pitches but, with numbers strictly limited, overcrowding is unlikely. There are 120 electrical connections. The sanitary installations are constructed to top standards and a further block is provided in the extension. Facilities include British toilets, individual basins mainly in private cabins with mirror and light and free hot water in basins, showers and sinks. Provision is made for the handicapped. There is a small (12 x 6½ m.) free swimming pool which is well heated (open from about mid-May) with children's paddling pool. Shop and hot takeaway food and delivery service all season. Crêperie near the pool (July and Aug). Play areas. Minigolf. General rooms, one with TV. Breakfast served, rooms (en-suite) to let and bar, with billiards room adjacent, in château (all year). Table tennis. Laundry facilities. Quietly situated, the site is 12 km. from the sea, and one can visit the Bayeux tapestry, Caen, and the wartime landing beaches and Arromanches museum. The site is popular with tour operators. As 1994 is the 50th anniversary of the D-Day landings, reservations will be essential for at least June, July and August.

Directions: Site is off N13, 8 km. southeast of Bayeux. Take Martragny exit from dual carriageway.

Charges 1994:
-- Per person Ffr. 25.00; child (under 7) 16.00; pitch 45.00, plus 5.00 for caravan or motorcaravan; extra car 10.00; electricity (6A) 18.00.

Open:
1 May - 15 Sept

Address:
14740 Martragny.

Tel:
31.80.21.40.
FAX: 31.08.14.91.

Reservations:
See text - made for min. 3 nights; deposit and small booking fee required.

1407 Camping de la Vallée, Houlgate

Fresh, well kept site, close to lively little resort of Houlgate.

Camping de la Vallée's owners provide a warm welcome to all visitors and the site has good, well-maintained facilities. The 150 pitches are large, open and grassy, with hedging planted and all have electricity. Part of the site is sloping, the rest level, with some tarmac roads, the rest gravel. An old farmhouse has been converted to house a rustic bar and comfortable TV lounge and billiards room. A heated swimming pool and new tennis court have been added to the facilities. Shop. Small snackbar/takeaway in season. Children's playground on grass. Volleyball. Football field. Tennis. Bicycle hire. Petanque. Organised entertainment in Jul/Aug. There are 3 toilet blocks, one of which is large, new and excellent, but all provision is good. Free hot water in the controllable, well fitted showers; wash basins in cabins; mainly British toilets. Facilities for the handicapped are provided. Washing up and laundry provision with machines, dryers and ironing boards. Washing lines are not allowed. The beach is 1 km. and town 900 m. and a championship golf course is nearby. English spoken in season. Popular with tour operators.

Directions: Site is 1 km. from Houlgate, along D24A (route de Lisieux). Turn right onto D24, rue de la Vallée and look for site sign.

Charges 1994:
-- Per person 25.00 Ffr; child (under 7) 15.00; pitch 35.00, with services 40.00; dog on lead 15.00; extra car 10.00.
-- Less 10% outside main season.

Open:
1 April - 30 Sept.

Address:
88 rue de la Vallée, 14519 Houlgate.

Tel:
31.24.40.69.
FAX: 31.28.08.29.

Reservations:
Write to site.

see advertisement opposite

1405 Castel Camping-Caravaning Le Colombier, Moyaux, nr Lisieux

Normandy site with swimming pool and other installations of high quality.

Le Colombier is a site of quality with the aspect of a spacious country estate. Pitches are large, and it has a free heated swimming pool (25 x 12m.) in a very attractive landscaped setting between the manor house and the `colombier' - a circular building which houses the bar, library and TV room. The 170 pitches, all with electricity and some with water connections also, are marked out by trees at the corners but otherwise have nothing between them.

The central toilet block is of the very best quality, with everything in private cabins and free hot water for all services. A new smaller block of similar quality has now been opened on the opposite side of the camp, mainly for the benefit of the new extension, with British toilets and an unit for disabled. Shop. Crêperie. Takeaway in main season. Special dinners (limited numbers) served some days in château. Bar open latter part of evening. TV room. Large general room for reading, cards, etc, with TV. Tennis court. Minigolf. Volleyball. Free fishing on nearby lake. Washing machine and dryer. Baby sitting available. You do pay for the quality, and there are no off-peak reductions, but all the site's main amenities (pool, crêperie, bar, etc.) are open for the whole season and the château and its surroundings do have a certain elegance. Reservation is advisable for main season. Used by a tour operator. American motorhomes not accepted. Lisieux is 16 km., and places on the coast such as Deauville and Honfleur 30 to 40. Excursions to Paris also available.

Directions: Site is 3 km. northeast of Moyaux on D143, well signposted from the Cormeilles-Lisieux road.

Charges 1994:
-- Per person Ffr 30.00; child (under 7) 15.00; pitch 60.00; electricity 15.00.

Open:
1 May-15 Sept with all services.

Address:
Le Val Séry.
14590 Moyaux.

Tel:
31.63.63.08.
FAX: 31.63.15.97.

Reservations:
Made for min. 5 days with Ffr. 100 fee.

5000 Camping L'Etang des Haizes, St. Symphorien-le-Valois, La Hayes-du-Puits

Small, attractive, informal site with heated pool.

L'Etang des Haizes offers 150 good size pitches on level ground with 100 electrical connections (3 or 6A). They are set in a mixture of conifers, orchard and shrubbery, with some very attractive slightly smaller pitches near a private lake. There are 45 mobile homes inconspicuously sited, 25 of which are for hire. Sanitary blocks are of modern construction, open plan and mixed, with British WCs, one with free controllable showers and washbasins in private cabins. There are plans to install showers in the smaller block for 1994. Unit for the disabled, washing up under cover and small laundry with 2 washing machines. The lake offers good coarse fishing for huge carp (we are told!), swimming (with a long shute) and pedaloes. Other facilities include a heated swimming pool, an attractive bar with terrace overlooking the lake and pool, 2 children's play areas, table tennis, TV lounge, pool table, boules, volleyball and minigolf. Only milk and bread available on site, but supermarket in La Haye-du-Puits (1 km). Gate locked 22.00-06.00 hrs. Site is just 8 km. from a sandy beach and a 25 km. drive will take you to the Normandy landing beaches.

Directions: Site is signed off the D900 from St. Sauveur le Vicomte, 1 km. before La Haye-du-Puits.

Charges 1994:
-- Per adult Ffr 27.50; child (under 9 yrs) 14.00; pitch plus car 38.00; electricity 3A 18.00, 6A 25.00; dog 12.00.
-- Less 20% outisde July/Aug.
-- Special offers for D-Day commemorations.

Open:
15 March - 15 October.

Address:
50250 St. Symphorien-le-Valois.

Tel:
33.46.01.16.
FAX: 33.47.23.80.

Reservations:
Made with 25% deposit.

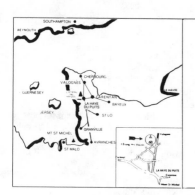

L'ETANG des HAIZES
★ ★ ★ ★
50250 LA HAYE DU PUITS
★ Special D-Day Tariff
★ Mobile Homes to Hire

For your first night in France, test the comfort, rest and atmosphere. During your stay visit Bayeux, Mont St Michel and enjoy our typical Normandy meals with a bottle of real Calvados. *Don't miss the opportunity of visiting this very beautiful campsite.*

5001 Camping-Caravaning L'Ermitage, Barneville-Carteret

Family oriented site close to beach.

This corner of Normandy is short of good sites either for overnight stops before or after the ferry or for longer stays. Most of the 150 pitches here have electricity (3 or 6A) and 80 also have water and drainaway. The oldest part of the site has been supplemented by three additional fields nearer the beach where shade and hedges are not as developed. The one central toilet block is well maintained and provides free hot water, showers with dividers, washbasins (some in cabins), British toilets (fewer in number), baby bath and laundry facilities. Washing-up and clothes sinks have hot water. Near the entrance and reception is a bar with takeaway service in season and the owner's family run a good restaurant nearby (Le Clos Rubier). There is a children's play area on sand and a tennis court. Table tennis. Pin-table. Pool. Horse riding, golf, fishing and sailing nearby. A hydrofoil service to the Channel Islands runs from either Carteret or Portbail and there is an attractive beach at Carteret.

Directions: Site is signposted from the D903 after Barneville-Carteret and before Portbail.

Charges guide:
-- Per person 17.50 Ffr; child (under 7) 11.50; pitch including vehicle 20.00; electricity 13.00 (3A) - 22.00 (6A).

Open:
1 May - 15 Sept.

Address:
St. Jean de la Riviére, 50270 Barneville Carteret.

Tel:
33.04.78.90.

Reservations:
Made for a min. of 1 week, with Ffr. 200 deposit. (Please do not ask for reservations for less than a week).

5002 Camping Pré de la Rose, Villedieu-les-Poëles

Good, reasonably priced municipal site a short walk from town centre.

Villedieu, 28 km. inland, lies on a route followed by many of those who use the port of Cherbourg, and to a lesser extent Le Havre. The Pré de la Rose is a small site taking some 100 units on individual pitches; these are of good size, marked out and separated by low hedges. Electrical connections available in all parts. One good-sized toilet block with continental WCs for men and British for women, and a smaller one with British WCs for all, make up a good provision. A few washbasins are in private cabins with free hot water, the others are not enclosed and with cold. Free hot showers preset and chain-operated (water does not run on). Like the site itself, the blocks have a cared-for look. Tennis adjacent. TV room. Children's playground on sand. Shops are 400 m. in town centre. This is one of those good, well kept municipal sites with very moderate prices that one sometimes comes across in France. It becomes full in main season but there are departures each day and places for early arrivals.

Directions: The site is an easy walk from the town centre; entrance past market place car park.

Charges 1993:
-- Per adult Ffr 12.00; child (under 7) 5.00; pitch 12.00; car 4.00; electricity 10.00.

Open:
Easter - 15 Sept.

Address:
50800 Villedieu.

Reservations:
Made for about a week or more without deposit.

5004 Camping Municipal Ste. Mère Eglise

Useful municipal site for overnight stay or to visit Second World War area.

A typically unpretentious municipal site, providing 70 pitches on level grass, all with electricity (8A) this site is adjacent to tennis courts and the gymnasium. The sanitary facilities are adequate rather than luxurious, providing hot showers, some basins in cabins (cold water only) and seatless flushing toilets. This site is ideally situated within about 5 minutes level walking distance of the centre of this historic little town, (the first town in France to be liberated by the Allies), with its war museum and strategic position near to the Normandy landing beaches. Look for the parachutist hanging from the 13th century church! (He was taken down in summer 92 - but a reader tells that he is back!)

Directions: Site is signposted from town centre.

Charges guide:
-- Per person Ffr 9.00; child 4.50; tent/caravan + car 13.50; motorcaravan 15.00; electricity 10.00.
-- Less approx 10% out of high season.

Open:
All year.

Address:
50480 Ste. Mère Église.

Tel:
33.41.35.22.

Reservations:
Not normally necessary.

5005 Camping Municipal Le Haut Dick, Carentan

Small site near main N13 road 50 km. from Cherbourg for convenient night stop.

Out by the marina part of Carentan and well away from main roads, this very satisfactory municipal site should provide a quiet overnight stop at reasonable prices for those crossing via Cherbourg. There is usually space; 115 individual, numbered pitches on flat grass which vary in size, 40 with electrical points. There is also unmarked space for a further 20 or so units. The one sanitary block is large, airy and spacious, with British WCs, free hot water to basins with shelf and mirror (some in private cabins) and to the showers. No shop (town close). Small children's playground. Barbeque. Minigolf. Canoes and bicycles for hire. No other on-site amenities. Much is being done to improve the site by way of tree and shrub planting and one receives a friendly welcome at reception. Gates closed 10 pm.- 8 am.

Directions: Site is northeast of the town centre, by the racecourse and a canal marina. It is signposted from main junctions in town (`Camping' or `Port de Plaisance').

Charges 1993:
-- Per person Ffr 9.50; child (under 7) 5.50; car 6.50; pitch 11.00; electricity 11.00.

Open:
All year

Address:
50500 Carentan.

Tel:
33.42.16.89.

Reservations:
For a few days min. could be made with deposit through La Mairie.

5003 Castel Camping Lez Eaux, Granville

Family site with swimming pools just back from sea on Cotentin coast.

This site, in the spacious grounds of a château, lies in a country situation 3 km. from the nearest beach, 4 from St. Pair, 7 from Granville and under 2 hours from Cherbourg. With pleasant rural views, it has 160 pitches, mostly of good size, not separated but marked by trees, etc. on grassy ground either flat or very slightly sloping. All pitches have electrical connections and some drainage also. Some 45% of are taken by British tour operators and a number of special pitches are provided for late arrivals/departures by tour operator clients. Two modern toilet blocks have washbasins in private cabins (set in flat surfaces and with free hot water and mirror) and hot showers. This should be an adequate provision but it is a busy site and the blocks may receive heavy use. Full provision for the handicapped. There is a small heated swimming pool (12 x 6 m.) and a new, attractive fun pool with slide and water shute. Shop. A small bar, cleverly designed, is in part of the old buildings (with tower). Takeaway with set meal each night (order in advance). Adventure play area. Good tennis. Games room with table tennis. Jacuzzi. Fishing in lake. TV room. Washing machine and dryer. Torches required at night. Note: facilities not fully open until 15/5.

Directions: Site access is signposted west about 7 km. southeast of Granville on main D973 road to Avranches.

Charges 1994:
-- Per pitch incl. 2 persons Ffr. 95.00, pitch with all services 130.00; extra person 30.00; child (under 7yrs) 15.00; electricity 21.00 (5A) - 28.00 (10A).

Open:
1 April - 15 Sept.

Address:
50380 St. Pair-sur-Mer.

Tel:
33.57.66.09.
FAX: 33.51.42.02.

Reservations:
Advisable for high season and made for min. 5 days with deposit (Ffr. 200) and fee (100).

CASTEL CAMPING
Lez Eaux

A family site not far from the ports of St. Malo, Caen, Cherbourg and only 3 kilometres from the beach. Set in the grounds of a Chateau with heated swimming Pool, Tennis Court, Bar and small Restaurant. You are ensured of a warm welcome by the owners Monsieur and Madame de la varde.

MOBILE HOMES FOR HIRE

Reservation direct to the site/or through the guide/Eurocamp Independent/Select Sites.

6101 Camping La Campiére, Vimoutiers

Small, well kept municipal site, close to town.

This site is situated in a valley to the north of the town, which is on both the Normandy Cheese and Cider routes. Indeed the town is famous for its cheese and has a Camembert Museum, 5 minutes walk away in the town centre. The 40 pitches here are flat, grassy and mostly openly laid out amongst attractive and well maintained flower and shrub beds. There is some shade around the perimeter and all pitches have electricity. The one central, clean sanitary block provides British WCs, free hot water to showers and open washbasins. There is a separate bathroom for the disabled. Good children's playground complete with thematic sculptures of the region. No shop but large supermarket 300 m. Tennis courts and park opposite. Extensive water sports facilities 2 km., also riding and ski slope.

Directions: Site is on northern edge of town, signposted from main Lisieux/ Argentan road next to large sports complex.

Charges 1993:
-- Per person Ffr 12.60; child (under 10) 6.30; pitch 8.90; car 7.00; electricity 9.20 (14.65 in winter).
-- Reductions for 7th and subsequent days and from 1/10 - 30/4.
Open:
All year.
Address:
Bvd. du Docteur Dentu, 61120 Vimoutiers.
Tel:
33.39.18.86.
FAX: 33.36.51.43 (Mairie)
Reservations:
Not normally necessary.

6102 Camping Municipal, Le Clos Normand, Sées

Well kept, reasonably priced municipal site which makes a good overnight stop.

This small municipal site provides 50 pitches, 35 of which have electricity. Sizes vary up to 100 sq.m. plus and they are all level, grassy and separated by hedges. The two toilet blocks are situated at either end of the site and are attractive modern buildings but in the typical Normandy colombage style. Toilets are continental seatless for both men and women and washbasins, some in private cabins, some communal, have hot water, razor points, mirrors and hooks. Showers are pre-set, pushbutton type and each has a dressing area with hooks. There is no shop but a supermarket is 300 m. away. The site is well situated, a few minutes walk from the centre of this attractive town which has several good restaurants and bars. There is a boules pitch and a large central grass area for children to play, but no other amenities. In the town are tennis, horse riding and golf (8 km.). There are 120 km. of way-marked walks from Sées (pronounced SAY) - details available from the tourist office. The town has a superb cathedral and an interesting museum.

Directions: Site is well marked from all main approach roads to Sées and is the only camp site in the town.

Charges 1993:
-- Per adult Ffr. 13.00; child (over 8 yrs) 8.00, under 8 free; car 10.00; pitch 10.00; motorcaravan 15.00; m/cycle 8.00; electricity 12.00.
Open:
1 May - 30 Sept.
Address:
Rte. d'Alencon, 61500 Sées.
Reservations:
Made by letter to the Syndicat d'Initiative, Place du Général de Gaulle. (No min. length, no deposit or fee).

2701 Camping-Caravaning Le Vert Bocage, Verneuil-sur-Avre

Pleasant site for night stop en-route south, or for visiting Paris.

Situated in attractive countryside, this site is conveniently beside the N26, about 700 m. from the town of Verneuil, some 50 km. northwest of Chartres. There is a nearby railway station with fast trains to Paris (1 hour). The site is small but provides first class facilities in terms of 65 large, level pitches on grass, many separated by hedges and all with electricity (amps as required). The single, tiled sanitary block provides free hot showers, washbasins with hot and cold water, British WCs and dishwashing facilities (H&C) under cover. It is clean and well maintained. Children's playground. Good restaurant in town. Fishing, swimming pool, tennis near. Apartments to let.

Directions: Site is beside the N26 road at Verneuil-sur-Avre, about 50 km. northwest of Chartres.

Charges 1993:
-- Per adult 23.00; child (under 8 yrs) 12.00; pitch 17.00; caravan or tent 12.00; motorcaravan 16.00; electricity 24.00.
-- Reduction for long stays.
Open:
All year.
Address:
Ave. Edmond-Demolins, 27130 Verneuil-sur-Avre.
Tel:
32.32.26.79
Reservations:
Write to site.

7603 Camping International du Golf, Le Tréport, nr Dieppe
Attractive, wooded site on edge of resort near Dieppe.

PARC INTERNATIONAL DU GOLF

★ ★ ★ ★

Private Campsite – Peaceful – Comfortable

Near the Sea on the TREPORT Cliffs

✳ *In a beautiful wooded park with many flowers* ✳

10% reduction on presentation of 1994 Guide

This site is about 1 km. from the centre of the resort of Le Tréport and is well worth considering for a holiday in this area. It has some 250 pitches, all about 100 sq.m., some on flat grass, separated by fencing markers and many in wooded areas giving more privacy and good shade. There are about 70 pitches with electrical connections, ranging from 2-8A. There are two principal sanitary blocks providing British seatless WCs, free hot water to washbasins (many in private cabins with shelf, mirror and light) and to the showers. These facilities are supplemented by three small toilet blocks of rather basic quality; water points around. Shop. Large bar with an hotel opening in 1994. Sports/play field. Bureau de change.

Directions: Site is situated on the southwest edge of Le Tréport, by the D940 road to Dieppe.

Charges 1994:
--Per pitch + 2 adults Ffr 56.00 - 80.00; extra person 20.00 - 24.00; child (1-7) 8.00 - 14.00; electricity 19.00 - 34.00, acc. to amps.

Less 10% on showing this 1994 guide

Open:
Easter/1 April - 30 Sept.
Address:
76470 Le Tréport.
Tel:
35.86.33.80.
FAX: 35.50.33.54.*t*
Reservations:
Made with Ffr 100 deposit.

7601 Camp Municipal Forêt de Montgeon, Le Havre
Satisfactory, well maintained site, very handy for the port.

This is a good spot to spend the first or last night of your holiday or perhaps a bit longer. In a pleasant quiet setting within a wooded park in the upper part of the town, the site is well laid out with tarred access roads. There are 40 caravan pitches on hardstandings with electricity, water and drainaway plus some 35 on grass, and five tent lawns taking well over 220 units. It can become full with much transit trade but you should find space if you arrive early. The 5 identical sanitary blocks provide plentiful facilities which include some washbasins in private cabins and 8 free hot showers. Small shop (open nearly all season) with takeaway snacks. Tennis. Table tennis. Games room. TV room. Good children's play area. Bicycle hire. Animation. Gates closed 11 pm. - 6.30 am. A sandy beach is 7 km.

Directions: The site and the Forêt de Montgeon are not too easy to find as approaches from most directions are circuitous and signposts easy to miss. Approaching from Tancarville Bridge, follow ferry signs and bear left at rotating advert sign along Quai Colbert. Turn right into Cours de la République, following signs to Montvilliers and Fecamp (N115), past Gare Central. From the ferry turn right and then, shortly after, left into Cours de la République. Pass through Tunnel Jenner (taller vehicles keep in right hand lane). Turn right shortly after the tunnel following signs to the Forêt and camp.

Charges 1993:
-- Per caravan and car incl. 2 persons Ffr. 66.00; tent and car 47.00; extra adult 18.00; child 9.00; electricity (5A) 12.00 - (10A) 24.00.
-- Discounts for 2-6 nights, more for over a week.

Open:
Easter/1 April - 30 Sept.
Address:
76620 Le Havre.
Tel:
35.46.52.39.
Reservations:
Only made for the special caravan pitches for 2 or more nights.

7604 Camping La Source, Petit Appeville, Hautot sur Mer, nr Dieppe

Flat shady site, convenient for Newhaven ferries.

This site is situated just 4 km. from Dieppe and is useful for those using the revitalised Newhaven - Dieppe ferry crossing. It is flat, shady and quiet, in a valley with the only disturbance the occasional passing train. A shallow stream flows along one border (not protected for young children). There are hardstandings for motorcaravans and electricity (3, 6 or 10A). The one toilet block (males to the left, females to the right) is good and kept clean, providing washbasins in cubicles (H&C), pre-set showers with dividers and mixed British and continental WCs (less in number). Dishwashing under cover (H&C). Washing machine. Toilet, shower and basin for the disabled but unmade gravel roads may cause problems. Site has an arrangement with Stena Line and stays open for late ferries - there could be some noise late at night. An attractive small bar, recently attractively renovated, also provides snack meals (open for late ferries). Small play field for children. TV room (French programmes only) and room for young people with table tennis and amusement machines.

Charges 1994:
-- Per caravan or motorcaravan Ffr. 22.00; tent 17.00; person 17.00; child 11.00; car 6.00; electricity 10.00.

Open:
15 March - 15 Oct.

Address:
Petit Appeville,
76550 Hautot sur Mer.

Tel:
35.84.27.04.

Reservations:
Write to site.

Directions: On leaving docks, follow one way system bearing left at Canadian War memorial, below the castle. Follow signs to Paris and Rouen and, after long hill, at large roundabout, take first exit on D925, Av. St. Jaures. After 2 km. turn left at traffic lights on D153 (Pourville sur Mer to right). Just past railway station, left under bridge (signed) into narrow road with stream on right. Site short distance on left.

PARIS / ILE DE FRANCE
Paris - Yvelines - Seine-et-Marne - Val d'Oise - Essonne

How many millions of words have been written about Paris? Quite simply, it is a marvelous place of infinite variety - the list of things to do is virtually endless and could easily fill many holidays - window shopping, the Eiffel Tower, Montmartre, the Louvre, trips on the Seine, pavement cafés, the Moulin Rouge, etc, etc! Both the bus and Metro systems are excellent, efficient and reasonably priced, so there is no need to take your car into the centre. The outskirts of Paris sprawl like most big cities but it is not too difficult to get into some attractive countryside like the beautiful forests at Fontaineblleu or to new tourist attractions such as EuroDisney or the Asterix Parc.

7502 Parc de Camping Paris-Ouest, Bois de Boulogne, Paris

Attractively situated site beside the Seine and close to the city limits.

This site is the nearest site to the city, lying in a wooded area between the Seine and the Bois de Boulogne. One can reach the Champs Elysees in 10-15 minutes by car or there is usually a shuttle bus running from the site to the Metro station. The site is quite extensive but nevertheless becomes very full with many international visitors of all ages. There are about 500 pitches of which 280 are marked, with electricity (10A), water, drainage and TV aerial connections. 60 mobile homes (to rent). No reservations are made for the pitches so arrival early (a.m.) in season is necessary. The four toilet blocks are of necessity rather utilitarian and are of mixed type, with various types of WCs, washbasins, some in cabins and free pre-set hot showers. These facilities suffer from heavy use in season and require continuous renovation. Small supermarket and snack bar available April - Oct. Washing machines and dryers. Bureau de change. Children's playground. Organised excursions. No dogs.

Charges guide:
-- Per unit incl. 2 persons Ffr 65.00; special pitch incl. 4 persons and all services 140.00; extra person 15.00.

Open:
All year.

Address:
Allée du bord de l'eau,
75016 Paris.

Tel:
(1) 45.24.30.00.
FAX: (1) 42.24.42.95.

Reservations:
Not made.

Directions: Site is on east side of Seine between the river and the Bois de Boulogne, just north of Pont de Suresnes. Watch signs closely, use a good map.

PARIS / ILE DE FRANCE - Yvelines

7801 Camping Caravaning Int. de Maisons-Laffitte, Maisons-Laffitte, Paris

Busy site on the banks of the Seine with good train service to central Paris; open all year.

Maisons-Laffitte has a good and frequent train service, including an express service, to the Gare St. Lazare (station is 1 km. from the camp). Normally taking about 18 minutes on the journey, it returns until 12.30 am. The camp occupies a grassy, tree covered area bordering the river. Maisons-Laffitte is a pleasant suburb which has a château, a park, a racecourse and some large training stables. Improvements have been made to the site in recent years. Most of the pitches in the tourist parts (there is also a permanent section) are marked out with separators and of good size. Only the meadows at the end of the site, intended mainly for tents, are not marked and could become more crowded. There are three sanitary blocks, all with free hot water in all services. Two are well insulated and heated for winter use, the third is a more open block better suited for the summer months. Self-service shop. Restaurant/bar with takeaway food also; some live entertainment. Launderette. Table tennis. Billiards. Used by all main tour operators. A busy site, facilities could be overstretched at times. Some railway noise.

Directions: From autoroute de l'ouest take exit to Poissy, then follow signs to Maisons-Laffitte. From N14 from Rouen take St. Germain exit from the Pontoise by-pass motorway and turn left at big roundabout in Forêt de St. Germain. From north or east, take boulevard périphérique to Porte Maillot exit then via Pont de Neuilly and Pont de Bezons which is more complicated and map really needed.

Charges guide:
-- Per person Ffr. 26.00 - 30.00, acc. to season; child under 8 free; pitch: motorcaravan 32.00 - 38.00, caravan 22.00 - 30.00, tent 20.00 - 26.00; car 10.00 - 12.00; electricity (4A) 18.00 - 20.00, (10A) 28.00 - 30.00; local tax 1.00.

Open:
All year.

Address:
1, Rue Johnson, 78600 Maisons-Laffitte.

Tel:
(1) 39.12.21.91.
FAX: (1)34.93.02.60.

Reservations:
Advisable for July/August (deposit required).

7803 Domaine d'Inchelin, St. Illiers la Ville, nr Bréval

Quiet, family run site in the Seine valley within 60 km. of Paris.

This area, within easy reach of Paris and Versailles, is one of rolling countryside and small villages. On the outskirts of one of these is Domaine d'Inchelin where an attractive camp site has been developed around charming old farm buildings. The 135 pitches, almost all with electricity and water connections, are large (250 sq.m.) and are arranged amongst ornamental trees and shrubs with well kept hedges providing privacy and shelter. Peacocks (rather noisy in spring!) and other tame birds parade the site and roost in the trees. A wooded area provides play equipment and space for children to play. Tennis and riding are available nearby.

Neatly arranged in the timbered buildings which surround three sides of the old farmyard are a small shop, bar, takeaway (all in season only), an under cover play area and the sanitary facilities. An attractive, new swimming pool lies sheltered in the centre. The sanitary facilities are split into two areas - one room with toilets (mixed), the other with showers, washbasins in cabins, a dishwashing area and a laundry room (lots of sinks and 1 machine). Hot water is free throughout and whilst the high ceilings and old beams remain, the facilities are well kept and clean. The Daniel family provide a friendly welcome and will advise on what to see in the area and how to reach the attractions of Paris and Versailles. Some seasonal caravans and a small number of pitches are reserved by two British tour operators.

Directions: From the A13 autoroute take the Chaufour exit (no. 15) onto the N13. Turn off within 1 km. into the centre of Chaufour and take the D25 to Lommoye, then the D89 to St. Illiers. Take the Bréval road and the road to the site is almost immediately on the left.

Charges 1993:
-- Prices for July/Aug. (otherwise in brackets). Including car, unit and pitch: per adult Ffr. 65.00 (50.00); child under 14 yrs 25.00 (20.00), under 5 yrs free; dog 10.00; electricity (4A) 25.00, (6A) 40.00.

Open:
1 April - 30 Nov.

Address:
St. Illiers la Ville, 78980 Bréval.

Tel:
34.76.10.11.

Reservations:
Write to site for details.

7701 The Davy Crockett Campground, EuroDisney, Marne-la-Vallée

Disney quality site, with excellent indoor pool and free bus service to Disneyland.

EuroDisney's campsite is situated on the south side of the A4 autoroute, but far enough from it to be untroubled by traffic noise. It contains 97 numbered tourist pitches, each with a hardstanding for vehicles and motorcaravans, and a roughly 25 sq.m. sand-topped tent area. Each pitch is separated from the next by an area of small trees and shrubs and the whole site is well endowed with tall trees for shade. Pitches have their own individual electric point, water supply and drain, a large picnic table and an equally robust iron barbecue. The pitches are placed around a wooded oval (the `Moccasin Trail'), at the centre of which is a modern, high quality toilet block of ample proportions and containing every facility, including washing machines (free) and drinks machines.

Other sectors of the site contain log cabins which are very well equipped and quite attractively priced. The touring sector is furthest away from the main services complex, but a 400 m. walk is well rewarded. The shop provides a rather wider choice of Disney souvenirs than foodstuffs, but all the basic requirements can be obtained, and there are a number of supermarkets and hypermarkets within a short drive. However, most campers will be tempted into using the self-service restaurant, which offers both American and some French style food made from top quality ingredients.

A major attraction is the large leisure pool, with flume and jacuzzis, built inside a huge log cabin, which opens out onto a terrace with chairs and sunbeds. The terrace overlooks `Indian Meadows', a large field, with adventure play equipment, basketball and football goals. Organised campfire sessions sound like fun! Bicycles and golf carts can be hired on a daily basis. There are two good tennis courts. On entry, you will be offered a set of payment cards which can be used to pay for anything on the site or at Disneyland, the total being billed to your card account - very convenient, but even though prices were reasonable, the bill can mount up.

The connection with the main EuroDisney complex is by a free bus service which stops at all sections of the campsite, and takes 15 minutes to get to the Magic Kingdom. We avoided queuing to get in by buying entry tickets from the cycle hire shop on the campsite the night before. It is for other publications to review its attractions, but we had a marvellous time. Nowhere else does Coca-Cola taste quite the same, or are staff quite so polite. This politeness and attention to cleanliness, comfort and visitors' needs were equally in evidence throughout the operation of the campground. There may be somewhat cheaper sites within range of EuroDisney, but this one makes you feel the Disney magic throughout your stay. We highly recommend it as a fine site in its own right, and eminently suitable for visits to that other magic city called Paris, only 35 km. away by autoroute or train. In high season you must reserve, and very early.

Directions: From Paris take the A4 eastwards, following signs for Nancy. For EuroDisney itself take exit 14, but for the Davy Crockett Campground, turn right at exit 13. From Calais, follow Paris signs until just before Charles de Gaulle airport, then follow signs to Marne la Vallée - eventually you should join the A4.

Charges 1994:
-- Per pitch, all incl. Ffr. 375.00; 6-berth cabin from 575.00 per night.

Open:
All year.

Address:
B.P. 117, 77777 Marne-la-Vallée, Cedex 4.

Tel:
60 45 69 33.
FAX: 60 45 69 33.

Reservation:
Essential: write to site.

9500 Parc de Sejour de l'Etang, Nesles-la-Vallée, nr L' Isle Adam

Small, informal site in pretty valley 33 km. northwest of Paris.

This family run site is on the southern outskirts of the village of Nesles-la-Vallée in a pretty, tree lined river valley not far from L'Isle-Adam, a popular destination for Parisiens at weekends. In fact, most of the 150 pitches are occupied by seasonal caravans (plus a few British tour operator tents) and there are only 20 pitches available for touring units. However, with its pretty rural location and close proximity to Paris it is a comfortable and peaceful place to stay for a few days. The site is informally arranged around a duck pond with many trees to provide shelter and shade and semi-tame rabbits competing with the ducks for food and attention. Pitches are large and flat and electricity is available. The single, central sanitary block, which is well heated in the cooler months, is a substantial building and although rather dated in style, the facilities are well maintained and kept clean. Hot water to all facilities is free. Plenty of play activities for children are provided including a good playground, volleyball and basketball areas and a good under cover play barn with table tennis tables. There are no other on-site facilities but the village and a restaurant are within walking distance. Fishing permits for the river are available in the village and riding stables are close by. Chantilly, Parc Asterix and Eurodisney are easily reached by car. The nearest station for access to Paris (and EuroDisney) is 15 minutes away.

Directions: From the A15 take exit 10, then the D927 and D79 to Nesles-la-Vallée. From the N1 take the L'Isle Adam exit. The site is situated on the southern outskirts of the village.

Charges 1993:
-- Per pitch Ffr. 20.30; person 20.30; child (under 7 yrs) 10.15; electricity 20.00 - 25.00 acc. to season.
-- Special family price for 5 days 81.20 per day.

Open:
1 March - 31 Oct.

Address:
10 Chemin des bellevues, 95690 Nesles-la-Vallée.

Tel:
34.70.62.89.

Reservations:
Write to site for details.

9100 La Bois du Justice, Monnerville, Etampes

Clean site close to Paris and Versailles.

The site is situated in a wood in the middle of farmland and the 50 tourist pitches are laid out among the trees, well shaded and flat. Electricity is available throughout. The one large toilet block is very well appointed, and spotlessly clean, although it is some way from the furthest pitches. A medium sized pool, children's playground, open air table tennis and volleyball court provide sporting diversions and a bar is open during the day and early evening. There is no shop, but a bread and provisions van calls morning and evening. Shops and restaurants are to be found in the village 3 km. away, or a lttle further in Etampes. The site is ideal as overnight stop, or for touring the area southwest of Paris - Chartres, Fontainbleau and Versailles are in easy range. Paris itself is only an hours drive, EuroDisney not much more.

Directions: From the N20 (Paris-Orleans), turn left going south at Monnerville, then right as you come into the village. Site is signposted, but the access road is very bumpy for 2/3 km.

Charges 1994:
-- Per pitch 30.00; adult 30.00; child (under 7 yrs) 15.00; electricity 15.00.

Open:
1 March - 30 November.

Address:
91930 Monnerville.

Tel:
(1) 64.95.05.34.
FAX: (1) 64.95.17.31.

Reservations:
Contact site.

PICARDY
Somme - Aisne - Oise

Picardy is not simply a region of ruler-straight roads, shaded by the ubiquitous poplars, across rolling plains, it is a great deal more besides. Deep river valleys, numerous forests of mature beech and oak, peaceful lakes and sandy beaches provide plenty of contrast. It is a region steeped in history, recently much of which is tragic, and the acres and acres of immaculately tended war graves are a sobering reminder. The region is dotted with interesting towns characterized by their fine Gothic architecture. At Marquenterre, near the mouth of the River Somme, is France's largest bird sanctuary outside the Camargue, with over 300 species. There is more to Picardy than roses!

8001 Castel Camping Domaine de Drancourt, St. Valéry-sur-Somme, Abbéville

Popular site between Boulogne and Dieppe with swimming pools and other amenities.

This site will be at a convenient distance for many people from one of the Channel ports, but with all the amenities on the site, plenty stay for much longer periods. On fairly flat meadow with some large apple trees at intervals, the original section is marked out in 100 numbered individual pitches of good size. An extension of that area, with some seasonal caravans and taking 50 units, is in light woodland. Two newer sections are on flat or gently sloping grass, with little shade as yet. The total is now some 200 pitches and electricity is available in most parts. Sanitary installations consist of 3 blocks - the original enlarged block, a modern one of quite good quality, and a third in the newest sections. All have British WCs, free hot water (pre-set temperature in the newer blocks) to washbasins (in cabins or cubicles), showers and sinks. Water points on site. Amenities include two free heated swimming pools, (both 17 x 6 m. but of different depths), open 15/5-15/9 plus some weekends when weather is good. Shop. Takeaway all season. Restaurant (late June-end Aug). Bar in château, small bar with longer hours adjoining general room with TV and new bar by the pools. Separate disco for the young with free entry. Games room with table tennis. Tennis court. Golf practice range. Bicycle hire. Washing machines and dryers. Riding in season. Fishing on payment. Organised activities and weekly excursions to Paris in June-Aug. Bureau de change. Well known and deservedly popular, reservation is advisable for main season. Most tour operators present. Sandy beach at Cayeux 8 km. Run very personally by the energetic proprietor, English is spoken. Tents and bungalows for hire.

Directions: Site lies 2½ km. south of St. Valéry, near Estreboeuf, and is signposted from the St. Valéry road N40.

Charges 1994:
-- Per person Ffr. 25.00 + local tax (over 10 yrs) 1.00; child (under 7) 20.00; pitch 38.00; car 10.00; electricity (6A) 13.00.

Open:
Easter - Oct.

Address:
80230 St. Valéry-sur-Somme.

Tel:
22.26.93.45.
FAX: 22.26.85.87.

Reservations:
Made for any length, with deposit for longer stays.

A quiet country touring site within easy reach of the Channel ports.
2 Swimming pools, Golf Driving range and animations, restaurant etc.

Camping du
Domaine de Drancourt
ST. VALERY-SUR-SOMME
*   *   *   *
Member of Chaine Castels et Camping

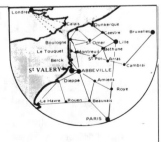

Excursions to Paris every week from June to August

8002 Camping La Croix l'Abbé, St. Valéry-sur-Somme, nr Abbéville
Very French site close to town, with swimming pool.

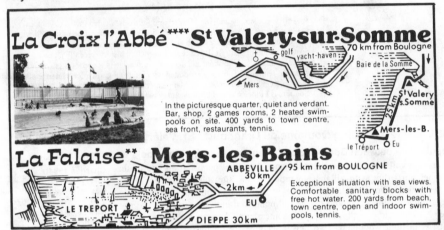

La Croix l'Abbé**** **St Valery-sur-Somme**
70 km from Boulogne
golf — yacht-haven
Baie de la Somme
Mers
St Valery s.Somme

In the picturesque quarter, quiet and verdant. Bar, shop, 2 games rooms, 2 heated swimpools on site. 400 yards to town centre, sea front, restaurants, tennis.

Mers-les-B.
le Tréport   Eu

La Falaise** **Mers-les-Bains**
ABBEVILLE 30 km / 95 km from BOULOGNE
2 km
LE TREPORT
EU
DIEPPE 30 km

Exceptional situation with sea views. Comfortable sanitary blocks with free hot water. 200 yards from beach, town centre, open and indoor swimpools, tennis.

Boulogne and Calais are two of the most used Channel ports, and sites within easy reach on the roads towards Paris and the south are not numerous, so we have included a second site at St. Valéry. The terrain is perhaps less attractive than at nearby Domaine de Drancourt, but it does have the feature liked by many of being only a short walk from town centre. About half the 230 pitches are occupied by permanent caravans, although some are vacated in July/Aug. Tourist pitches are spread around in irregular small groups on flat ground with reasonable privacy but little shade. Two sanitary blocks, one with facilities in a number of separate parts off a central area, the second with segregated facilities, are of fair quality with mainly British, some continental WCs, individual washbasins (partly in cubicles) with free hot water, and free preset hot showers operated by pushbutton or chain. On site is a small heated swimming pool (11½ x 6m.), plus paddling pool, but for those wishing to swim from a beach, the nearest safe one is about 4 km. Shop in July/Aug. with takeaway. Bar. Small children's playground. Games room with table tennis, TV etc. Local radio run from site. Disco. Brasserie and crêperie. Some 'animation' in high season: (sports events, special evenings, etc). The great majority of clients are French.

Directions: Site is within St. Valéry limits on west side close to main road through town; entrance next to Croix l'Abbé bar.

Charges 1993:
-- Per person Ffr 17.00 - 21.50; child (under 10 yrs) 12.00 - 16.00; pitch 16.00 - 26.00; electricity 2A 15.00, 4A 21.00.

Open:
15 March - 15 Oct.

Address:
80230 St. Valéry.

Tel:
22.60.81.46.

Reservations:
Made for min. 1 week with deposit.

8003 Camping-Caravaning Municipal Port de Plaisance, Péronne

Conveniently situated, attractive municipal site.

Even in France some municipal sites have a somewhat 'institutional' feel about them - not so this one which is informally laid out beside the Canal du Nord on the outskirts of the small town of Peronne, on the river Somme. The associations with the Great War (including a museum) are strong and the First World War battlefields and cemeteries are numerous in this area, a vivid reminder of the folly of war. Only some 2-3 hours drive from the Channel ports and Tunnel, this site is conveniently situated for overnight stops en route to or from destinations further south or east. The site itself is surprisingly pretty, being surrounded by trees, with 94 marked pitches of varying shapes and sizes on mainly level grass, some being seasonal. There are 32 electrical connections (5A) so longish cables may be necessary. The sanitary facilities, although in a somewhat antiquated block, are quite adequate, with free hot showers including a divider (but somewhat cramped, some washbasins in private cabins (hot water) and British WCs. There are covered dishwashing sinks with both hot and cold water and a washing machine and dryer. Generally it is a quite adequate provision. Small well equipped children's play area on grass. Though reception is said to be open from 15.00 - 22.00, it is best to arrive before 20.00 hrs. A van with bread and a mobile shop/charcuterie call.

Charges 1993:
-- Per pitch Ffr. 9.75; adult 10.70; vehicle 4.25; electricity 14.25.

Open:
All year
(but check with tourist office).

Address:
Route de Paris, 80200 Peronne.

Tel:
22.84.19.31.
FAX: 22.83.14.58.

Reservations:
Possibly necessary in main season.

Directions: From the north and the ferries, on Autoroute A1, take exit 14 and follow N17 (south) to Peronne. Take signs for town centre and continue through (watching for 3* camp signs). Pass over river Somme and Canal du Nord and site is on right, just past garage at Porte du Plaisance, (2 km. from town centre). From south use exit 13 and follow D79 to Barleux, the D370 to pick up the N17 going north. Watch for site signs on left before crossing Canal du Nord.

0200 Camping Caravaning Vivier aux Carpes, Seraucourt-le-Grand, St Quentin

Small, quiet site, close to A26, 2 hours from Calais, ideal for overnight stop or longer stay.

This new site is imaginatively set out taking full benefit of large ponds which are well stocked for fishing. There is also abundant wild life. The 60 pitches, all at least 100 sq.m. are on flat grass and dividing hedges are being planted. All have electricity (5A), some also with water points and there are special pitches for motorcaravans. The site has a spacious feel although it is close to the village centre (with post office, doctor, chemist and small supermarket). The sanitary block is spacious and spotlessly clean, with separate, heated facilities for handicapped visitors, also available to other campers in the winter months. Laundry facilities. Upstairs there is a large TV/games room which is being further developed and should be ready for 1993. Small children's play area and a petanque court. There is, however, plenty to see in the area - the cathedral cities of St. Quentin, Reims, Amiens and Laon are close, EuroDisney is just over an hour away, Compiegne and the World War 1 battlefields are near and Paris easily reachable by train (1 hr 15 mins from St. Quentin). Day trips arranged for 10 - 18 people to Paris (Ffr 160 p.p) or to EuroDisney with an English speaking guide. The enthusiastic owners speak excellent English and are keen to welcome British visitors. Although there is no restaurant on site, good and reasonable hotels are close. We were impressed by the ambience created and would recommend this site to those seeking tranquillity in an attractive setting. Gates close 10.30 pm.

Charges 1994:
-- Per unit incl. 2 persons and electricity Ffr 70.00; extra person 15.00; child (under 10 yrs) 10.00.
-- Discounts for students with tents.

Open:
All year.

Address:
10 Rue Charles Voyeux, 02790 Seraucourt-le-Grand.

Tel:
23.60.50.10 (French) or 23.60.51.02 (English). FAX: 23.60.51.69.

Reservations:
Write to site for details.

Directions: Leave the A26 (Calais - Reims) road at exit 11 and take D1 to Essigny-la-Grand (4 km.) and then the D72 to Serancourt-le-Grand (5 km.). Site is clearly signposted - it is in the centre of the village.

PICARDY - Aisne / Oise

0201 Camping de Parc de l'Ailette, Chamouille, nr Laon

Modern, lakeside camp site forming part of new outdoor leisure park.

The Parc de l'Ailette has been developed with state, regional and departmental funds as a tourist attraction in an area of open countryside and lakes. Approached through an area of France which has many war grave cemeteries, the Parc is within the triangle formed by the towns of Laon, Soissons and Reims. The development offers many leisure activities but also forms a most attractive nature reserve with abundant wildlife. The 500 acre lake forms the centre for many of the activities including watersports (over some of its area only) and swimming from a sandy beach. Here also are minigolf, tennis and a playground. Elsewhere within the Parc are facilities for boat hire, horse riding, a jogging track, an 18 hole golf course, fishing and miles of signed walks.

Adjacent to the beach is a new, well designed campsite offering 196 large, numbered pitches, all with electricity and marked out by growing hedges of ornamental shrubs. They are arranged in groups with excellent access roads and well kept grass, most with lovely views over the lake. Site buildings are modern and include three sanitary blocks, each divided into small rooms containing either toilets or showers and washbasins (some in cabins). All hot water is free and the blocks are well cleaned. Dishwashing facilities with free warm water are provided outside each block and there is a laundry in the reception block. A snack bar and shop are open in season. There are restaurants at the nearby new hotel and in the local villages. There are a few seasonal units. The Parc and site are said to be crowded in high season when reservation is essential.

Directions: Follow signs to Parc Nautique des Vallées l'Ailette from the N2, N44 and N31 roads which connect Soissons, Laon and Reims. Chamouille is on the D967.

Charges 1993:
-- Per pitch Ffr. 20.00; extra tent 10.00; car 16.00; m/cycle 10.00; adult 15.00; child (4 - 7 yrs) 8.00; electricity 16.00; local tax 1.00.

Open:
1 April - 30 Sept.

Address:
Camping de l'Ailette, 02860 Chamouille.

Tel:
23.24.83.06.

Reservations:
Made with Ffr. 20 fee - details from site.

6001 Camping Campix, St. Leu-d'Esserent, nr Chantilly

Unusual, new site developed in old sandstone quarry, with good access to Paris.

Only opened in 1991 this attractive, informal site is still being developed within the striking confines of an old sandstone quarry on the outskirts of the small town. The quarry provides a very sheltered, peaceful environment and trees have grown to soften the slopes. The 170 pitches are arranged in small groups on the different levels with gravel access roads (fairly steep in places). Electricity is provided on 150 pitches. There are many secluded corners for additional smaller units and plenty of space for children to run around, although parents should supervise as some of the slopes could be dangerous if climbed. A footpath leads from the site to the town where there are shops and restaurants and an outdoor pool (in season). At the entrance to the site a modern building houses the reception, a large social room with open fire and two sanitary units (just one open in low season). These units have free, premixed hot showers and washbasins in rows with hooks and mirrors. Laundry facilities are provided and bread and milk are delivered to the site each day except Wednesdays. Motorcaravan service area. Bungalow tents are available to rent. The friendly, English speaking owner will advise on places of interest to visit which include Chantilly (5 km.) and the nearby Asterix Park. EuroDisney is 70 km. It is possible to visit Paris by train (max. 50 mins) from the station in St. Leu - ask the site for detailed instructions.

Directions: St. Leu d'Esserent is 11 km. east of Senlis, 5 km. northeast of Chantilly. From the north on the A1 autoroute take the Senlis exit, from Paris the Chantilly exit. Site is well signposted in the town.

Charges 1993:
-- Per unit Ffr. 20.00 - 30.00, acc. to season; small tent 5.00 - 25.00, acc. to season and location; person 15.00 - 25.00; child (under 12 yrs) 10.00 - 15.00; electricity 15.00.

Open:
15 March - 30 Nov.

Address:
B.P. 37, 60340 St. Leu-d'Esserent.

Tel:
44.56.08.48.

Reservations:
Advisable for July/Aug. Write for details.

POITOU-CHARENTES
Deux Sèvres - Vienne - Charente - Charente-Maritime

This region is the sunniest in Western France, and is ideal for beach holidays with lively resorts and quiet villages along its extensive Atlantic coastline. The islands off the coast of Charente-Maritime (Ile de Ré and Ile d'Oléron) are popular holiday destinations, particularly with the French themselves. The scenery inland is in marked contrast to the busy resorts and ports of the coast - wooded valleys, the vineyards of Cognac, the Vienne, the agricultural landscape and the heat in summer all seem to make a visit inland an essentially French experience. The towns and cities of the region are also fascinating - La Rochelle (in particular), Poitiers, Angoulême, Saintes, Niort and Cognac are all worth visiting.

1602 Castel Camping Gorges du Chambon, Eymouthiers, nr Montbron
Attractive family site in Charente countryside.

The British owners have further developed this site around a restored Charente farmhouse and outbuildings and it provides high quality facilities in an attractive setting. There are some 120 large marked pitches with electrical connections, on gently sloping grass (shade in parts) and enjoying extensive views over the countryside. The two sanitary blocks are of a good standard with British style WCs, hot showers and washbasins in private cabins. It is a good provision for the number of pitches. There are facilities for the disabled, a baby bath and laundry facilities, including a tumble dryer. The swimming pool (18 x 7 m.) has an adjacent bar selling drinks, snacks and ices. There is a bar and restaurant (in main season only) converted from the barn with an interesting gallery arrangement. Games room with soft drinks, ice creams, TV and table tennis, etc. Games for children are organised daily. Takeaway including pizzas. Small shop for basics in reception. Tennis. Minigolf. Children's play area. Caravans and gite to let. No animals accepted.

Directions: From Montbron village, follow D6 in direction of Piegut-Pluviers. Site is signposted.

Charges 1994:
-- Per pitch Ffr 36.00; person 28.00; child (under 7 yrs) 14.00; car 12.00; electricity (6A) 18.00.
-- Less 15% (not electricity) outside July/Aug.

Open:
15 May - 30 Sept.

Address:
Eymouthiers, 16220 Montbron.

Tel:
45.70.71.70.
FAX: 45.70.80.02.

Reservations:
Necessary for July/Aug. Write to site with min. Ffr. 200 deposit.

1603 Camping Municipal Le Champion, Mansle

Excellent municipal site enthusiastically managed as an integral part of town's activities.

Le Champion is a convenient stop-over on the N10 or a good base to explore the northern Charente area. Situated on a large flat meadow alongside the Charente river with a series of small islands suitable for swimming or fishing (Les Iles) there is provision for 130 good sized pitches marked by young shrubs and numbered boards, with 100 electrical connections (10A). Two sanitary blocks, one older serving the far end of the site and a larger, central, tiled block, have free hot water, some washbasins in cubicles, baby changing facilities and a unit for the disabled. On the whole it is an excellent provision and is very well maintained. Bar/restaurant with outdoor terrace on site (disco at weekends) and an English speaking restaurant at the site entrance - `Le Marmite'. The town with shops is 200 m. over the bridge (but bread van calls in mornings) with a market on Tuesday and Friday mornings and farm produce on Saturday mornings. Swimming pool in town and recreational area and sports ground next to the site with plenty of space for children (where most of the town's social activities are held). The local Syndicate d'Initiative calls at the site to advise on trips and activities, eg. cycle tracking (one or two days), coach trips, open air cinema, climbing tuition, canoeing courses, etc. Trout fishing in nearby lake and river fishing (permits necessary). Canoe and bicycle hire. The site has a busy atmosphere and is well supervised with friendly, helpful staff.

Directions: Site is well signed off the N10 (in town of Mansle), 30 km. north of Angoulême.

Charges 1994:
-- Per pitch Ffr. 15.00; adult 10.00; child 7.00; motorhome, caravan or tent 10.00; vehicle 10.00; electricity 10.00.

Open:
1 June - 1 September.

Address:
16230 Mansle.

Tel:
45.20.31.41.
FAX: 45.20.30.40.

Reservations:
Bookings accepted without deposit on Alan Roger's booking form, although not usually necessary.

Mansle Town   *Charente River*   *Le Champion Camp Site*

1701 Camping Bois Soleil, St. Georges-de-Didonne, nr Royan
Large site with various amenities by sea south of Royan.

Bois Soleil is a site long patronised by the British, and English is spoken, although other nationalities also find it attractive. The site is in three separate parts. The two nearest to the beach, La Mer and Les Pins, consist entirely of 350 special pitches for caravans and some tents, for which one pays an all-in charge including electricity and water. The third and largest part (La Forêt), mainly for statics, is on the far side of the main road, some way from the beach and shops, although prices are lower. This can be used for both tents and caravans. Some pitches here are very sandy although they are now stabilised. The site has an hotel type reservation system for each caravan pitch and can be full mid-June - late August. The areas are well tended with pitches, all with names not numbers, cleared and raked between clients and there is good shade.

The sandy beach here is a wide public one with direct access from one of the caravan areas, and a very short distance from the other. It is sheltered from the Atlantic breakers but the sea goes out some way at low tide. The sanitary installations consist of 10 blocks of varying size, type and quality. They have been considerably improved recently and there are some hot showers, and hot water in some if not all washbasins, in all the blocks except one. Continental and British toilets. Individual basins in private cabins or cubicles and facilities for the disabled. 'Parc des jeux' with tennis, table tennis, children's playground (main season). Amusements and video games in a separate area. Launderette. Safe deposit. A busy little shopping area beside reception, an upstairs restaurant and bar with terrace and an excellent takeaway facility (all from 1/4) complete the provision. Doctor visits daily. No charcoal barbecues but gas ones can be hired by the evening. No dogs.

Directions: From Royan keep on coast road to south until you see camp signs.

Charges 1993:
-- Per unit with 3 persons: tent 82.00 - 88.00 Ffr (acc. to location of pitch), caravan 95.00 - 108.00; extra adult 19.00; child (2-7 yrs) 11.00, under 2 yrs 5.00.
-- Less outside July/Aug.
Open:
Easter/1 April - 30 Sept.
Address:
2 Ave.de Suzac - B.P. 85, 17110 St. Georges-de-Didonne.
Tel:
46.05.05.94.
FAX: 46.06.27.43.
Reservations:
Made with no min. stay with deposit (Ffr. 315) and fee (115).

1702 Airotel Le Puits de l'Auture, La Grande-Côte, nr Royan
Good seaside site to west of Royan and St Palais.

This popular region has a good, sunny climate and this camp is well situated with the sea right outside its gates just across the road, with a long sandy beach starting 400 m.away. The site is attractively laid out, with flower beds and shrubs giving it a well cared for look. The 400 pitches, which are of varied but sufficient size, are on flat ground largely covered by tall trees and most have some shade. They are numbered but not separated, with electrical connections in most areas. There are now 6 sanitary blocks, which should be a good provision, although they might be pressured in the busiest times. Some are more modern than others and they vary in type. Half British WCs, half continental; most basins are in private cabins and all have free hot water, as do showers and sinks. Most showers are pre-set. Facilities for babies and washing machines. There is a good self-service shop (probably open late May - early Sept) with delicatessen and butcher, takeaway food, bar, table tennis, volleyball, games room and children's play area. There are two excellent heated swimming pools, but they shelve quite rapidly (no shallow end for children). Doctor visits. A launderette and phone boxes are on site. Tennis, horse riding and 18 hole golf course nearby. Several good restaurants specialising in seafood are a few minutes walk away. No dogs are taken and barbecues are not permitted. The site is popular with British visitors and reservation is essential for main season. Mobile homes and large caravans for hire.

Directions: Site is 2 km.from St Palais and 8 km. from Royan. From north Royan take back road to St Palais, going past it following La Palmyre signs, then turn back left towards Grande Cote and St Palais at junction with D25.

Charges 1993:
-- Prices outside 17/6 - 1/9 in brackets.
-- Per unit incl. up to 3 persons Ffr.130.00 (100.00); with electricity (5A) 150.00 (125.00); with water/drainage also 180.00 (160.00); extra person (over 3 yrs) 28.00 (25.00); extra car 15.00; electricity (10A) 30.00 (29.00); plus local tax.
Open:
30 April - 30 Sept.
Address:
La Grande Côte, 17420 St. Palais sur Mer.
Tel:
46.23.20.31.
FAX: 46.23.26.38.
Reservations:
Made for min. 5 days with exact dates; deposit and fee required.

POITOU-CHARENTES - Charente-Maritime

1703 Camping L'Estanquet, Les Mathes, La Palmyre, nr Royan

Pleasant modern site a short drive from seaside town of La Palmyre.

This attractive site lies in beautifully wooded grounds approximately 5 km. from the sandy beaches of the `Côte Sauvage'. There are 420 good-sized individual pitches separated by small hedges, all of which have electricity and some 150 can be linked up to water. Set amongst tall pine trees the ground is flat and sandy, and almost all pitches have some shade. The sanitary installations are of good quality, providing plenty of hot water in basins, showers and sinks, which are thoroughly cleaned daily. The reception staff are friendly and helpful and, in the main season, speak good English. There is now a large swimming pool, small pool with water slide and a small children's pool, with paved surrounds for sunbathing. A card system involving a deposit is required for pool users. The bar/restaurant overlooks the pool. Shop. Takeaway. Tennis. Volleyball. Table tennis. Bicycle hire. Laundry facilities. Children's playground. 2 discos per week during July/Aug. Mobile homes to let. We notice that the site has become very popular with tour operators.

Directions: From the north and east follow D14 (Saujon-la Tremblade) road, turn south onto D141 at Arvert; turn east in Les Mathes, from where camp is signposted. From south take D25 from Royan, turn north at La Palmyre for Les Mathes and proceed as above.

Charges 1994:
-- Per pitch, incl. 2 persons Ffr. 110.00 (9/7-22/8) or incl. 3 persons 85.00 (other times); extra person 19.00; child (under 5) 10.00; electricity (6A) 19.00; extra car 19.00.

Open:
15 May - 15 Sept.

Address:
La Fouasse, 17570 Les Mathes-La Palmyre.

Tel:
46.22.47.32.
FAX: 46.22.51.46.

Reservations:
Made with 20% deposit and Ffr 120 fee; min. 1 wk.

see advertisement in previous colour section

1705 Camping L'Orée du Bois, La Fouasse, Les Mathes

Large, attractive site amidst beautiful pines and oaks of the Forêt de la Coubre.

L'Orée du Bois, near L'Estanquet, has 400 pitches of about 100 sq.m. in a spacious, pinewood setting, including 40 with individual sanitary facilities (shower, toilet, washbasin and washing up sink). Pitches are on flat, sandy ground, separated by trees and shrubbery and all have electrical connections (6A). The forest pines offer shade. There are 45 mobile homes (for hire) set apart and several tour operators use the site. The four large, sanitary blocks of modern construction, have free hot water to the controllable showers and the washbasins (in private cabins). Three of the blocks have a laundry room and washing up is under cover. All have fully equipped units for the disabled.

The excellent bar, restaurant and crêperie have terraces overlooking the swimming pool and children's paddling pool. Takeaway service available and very well stocked self service shop. Other amenities include a tennis court, boules, games room, TV lounge (with satellite), bicycle hire, 2 sand based children's play areas, volleyball, table tennis, twice weekly discos and children's entertainment are organised in July/Aug. Exchange facilities. Nearby are sandy beaches (lifguard in season); walking, riding and cycling in the 10,000 hectare forest; fishing; sailing and windsurfing; golf and the zoo at La Palmyre. Site rules are quite specific about total silence between 22.00 and 07.00 (except when entertainment is organised). Only gas barbecues are allowed due to the forest setting with 4 communal barbecue areas provided. There are extra fees for stays of less than 3 days or if you do not make a reservation, so this is probably a site for a planned family holiday.

Directions: From the north follow D14 (La Tremblade) and at Axvert turn onto D141 then east at Les Mathes. From the south, at Royan take D25 to La Palmyre, then in the direction of Les Mathes from where site is signed.

Charges 1993:
-- Per unit incl. 2 persons Ffr 90.00 - 130.00, with private sanitary facilities 140.00 - 210.00; extra person (over 3 yrs) 20.00; local tax 1.00 (child 4-10 yrs 0.50).
-- Extra charges for short or unreserved stays.

Open:
15 May - 15 September.

Address:
La Fouasse, 17570 Les Mathes.

Tel:
46.22.42.43.
FAX: 45.83.15.87.

Reservations:
Made with 30% deposit plus fee (Ffr 120).

134

1707 Camping de L'Océan, La Couarde-sur-Mer, Ile de Ré

Interesting site on the attractive Ile de Ré.

Now joined to the mainland at La Rochelle by a toll bridge (expensive - see below), the Ile de Ré is an attractive and understandably popular holiday area for the French although, as yet, largely unknown to the British. L'Océan is a somewhat unusual site offering a variety of pitches. Some are in long-established areas affording plenty of shade, others in newer areas without much shade. In total there are 330, all with electricity (3-10A). The site is situated some 100 m. from a sandy beach, quite near to the attractive old town and harbour of St. Martin-en-Ré. There are currently three sanitary blocks, of satisfactory rather than good quality (cleaning reported to be variable), with hot showers, basins in private cabins, and both British and continental WCs. A bar and restaurant complex with games and entertainment rooms and 2 attractively landscaped swimming pools, partly heated, were completed in 1993. Entertainment for children (free). Fishing lake (free in low season) planned. TV room. Small supermarket (mid-June - early-Sept). Tennis. Bicycle hire. Large children's play area.

Directions: Site is 3 km. beyond the town of La Couarde, towards Ars-en-Ré, just past the turning to Loix. (Toll bridge: car Ffr 110, car and caravan 220).

Charges guide:
-- Per unit incl. 3 persons in high season Ffr 105.00, in low season incl. 2 persons 60.00; electricity from 11.00.

Less 10% in low season on presentation of this 1994 guide

Open:
Easter - 15 Sept.

Address:
17670 La Couarde, Ile de Ré.

Tel:
46.29.87.70.
FAX: 46.29.92.13.

Reservations:
Necessary for July/Aug only - Ffr. 150 deposit.

★ ★ ★ ile de ré
CAMPING DE L'OCEAN
17670 LA COUARDE SUR MER
Tél: 46 29 87 70

Facing the sea and only 50m from one of the most beautiful blue flag beaches, this rurally situated campsite is well equipped to a very high standard. Very comfortable toilet facilities with baby changing room, washing machines, quality furnishings, mini-market, take-away, bar and restaurant.
As for the leisure facilities, they are numerous: tennis, table tennis, volley ball, boules, evening entertainment and games area. Landscaped swimming pool.
Mobile homes and bungalows to rent.

1708 Camping Les Chirats, Angoulins-sur-Mer, nr La Rochelle

Quiet site with first class amenities and swimming pool, near La Rochelle.

Good quality sites near large towns or cities are hard to find and so we were pleased to locate such a site near La Rochelle. Situated only 50 m. from the beach at Angoulins sur Mer (bathing only possible at high tide) and about 15 minutes drive from the centre of La Rochelle, this is a small site, with 146 marked pitches. Electricity (6A) is available. The site is relatively new but there is some shade now as the trees and hedges grow. The owners are continuing to improve the site and its facilities. Two sanitary blocks have British WCs, hot showers, washbasins in cabins and a washing machine in each block. There is a medium sized heated swimming pool with shallow end for children (open May-Sept). Snack restaurant, bar and takeaway in high season. Barbecues permitted. Children's play area on grass. A sauna and solarium may be added. Boules, games room and table tennis. Small shop. Entertainments programme in season. 8 wooden bungalows for hire. Watersports close by.

Directions: Site is situated off, and signposted from, the N137 La Rochelle - Rochefort road, shortly after passing or leaving La Rochelle.

Charges 1994:
-- Per pitch, incl. 2 persons Ffr 56.00 - 67.00, with electricity 70.00 - 81.00, with water and drainage also 73.00 - 89.00; extra adult 15.00 - 18.00; child (under 7 yrs) 12.00 - 14.00.

Open:
Easter - 30 Sept.

Address:
17690 Angoulins-sur-Mer.

Tel:
46.56.94.16.

Reservations:
Recommended for July/Aug. Write with Ffr. 500 deposit.

1706 Airotel Domaine de Montravail, Château (sur Ile) d'Oléron

Good quality site on the Ile d'Oléron with riding stables and swimming pool.

The Ile d'Oléron is an `island' onto which you drive across a long viaduct with a toll. The west side of the island has wide sandy beaches and Atlantic seas; the east side more like a tidal estuary with gentle safe sandy bathing at high tide and an expanse of mud flats at low tide. Fishing and boat trips available. The island has its share of mediocre sites, but Montravail is not one of them. It is a friendly camp of good quality with all you could want except perhaps that it is a bit back from the sea, but there is a new swimming pool (1/6-1/10). Quietly situated, it is 1 km. to the east side of the Château d'Oléron beach (5 km. to the west side). The site has 200 large pitches of about 100 sq.m., all marked out, with some mature trees and newer bushes and shrubs and many electrical connections. It can be full in high season but there may be odd vacancies; reservations are made for longer stays. American motorhomes accepted for minimum 5 days. Two good toilet blocks have British and continental toilets, individual basins with shelf and mirror, some in private cabins for ladies and free hot water in basins, sinks, and in the showers which have preset hot water that stops as soon as the hand-held cord is released. They should be sufficient in high season. Shop, self-service restaurant and takeaway (15/7-31/8) and bar. Children's playground. 2 tennis courts. Montravail particularly features equitation, having a good class riding establishment attached to the site (site entrance adjoins the stable yard), and it has something of a farm atmosphere, with a friendly welcome. Bungalows and rooms to let.

Directions: Turn right to Château d'Oléron immediately after the viaduct and follow camp signs at junctions.

Charges 1993:
-- Per unit incl. up to 3 persons 98.00 Ffr; extra person 26.00; local tax in July/Aug. 1.00 for over 14s, 0.50 for child; extra car 12.00; dog 10.00; electricity (6A) 22.00; water and drainaway 20.00.
-- Less 30% outside 15/6-15/9.

Open:
1 March - 30 Oct.

Address:
17480 Château d'Oléron.

Tel:
46.47.61.82.
FAX: 46.47.79.67.

Reservations:
Made for exact dates (min. about one week in Aug.) with deposit (Ffr. 470) and booking fee (130).

1704 Camping International Bonne Anse Plage, La Palmyre

Spacious, well organised site amongst shady pine trees with large pool.

Bonne Anse is a gently undulating site in a pine wood, 500 m. from the beach, with its own heated swimming pool (35 x 25m), with 2 water toboggans. The 860 pitches, of which 600 have electricity (6-8A), are clearly marked and are level and grassy, if a little sandy. On site facilities are neat and well kept. The sanitary blocks provide free hot water, a mixture of British and continental toilets, washbasins in cabins, hot and cold showers and facilities for the handicapped and babies. Covered washing up sinks and laundry facilities, including washing machines and dryers, are available. There is a pleasant bar/ restaurant with a terrace overlooking the boules area, and a shop complex. Takeaway. Organised activities, entertainment and dancing are arranged in the season. Children's playground. TV and children's room. Volleyball. Table tennis. Pétanque. Bicycle hire. Boating, tennis and horse riding available nearby. No dogs. Favoured by tour operators (over 20%), this is a busy site in an area popular with the British.

Directions: Site is 1 km. northwest of La Palmyre going towards the lighthouse on the D25 (Ronce-les-Bains road).

Charges 1993:
-- Per unit incl. 3 persons Ffr. 130.00; per unit incl. 1 or 2 persons 105.00; local tax 1.00 or child (4-10 yrs) 0.50; extra person (over 1 yr) 30.00; extra car 8.00; electricity (6A) 20.00.

Open:
22 May - 6 Sept.

Address:
La Palmyre,
17570 Les Mathes.

Tel:
46.22.40.90.

Reservations:
Not possible - write for information only.

LES MATHES 17570 CHARENTE MARITIME

Bonne Anse
PLAGE
★ ★ ★ ★

North of LA PALMYRE

17 ha. site for 2000 campers. Open Whitsun until beginning of September. Tel: 46 22 40 90. Reservations not possible. **No animals. We only accept campers with international Camping Carnet.** All sites are properly laid-out. Well shaded site with grass ground, particularly terraced. Electric for caravans and hot showers included in fees. Hot water in Wash Basins and for laundry. Restaurant, Food shop, Prepared meals, Cooling Ice, Camping Gas, Doctor, Ironing Room, Organised Leisure, Children's Playground, Cinema, TV, Dancing, Swimming Pool & Toboggans. Boating, Horse Riding and Tennis nearby.

7901 Camping Municipal de Noron, Niort

Reasonable, well kept municipal site convenient for southbound travellers.

A good example of the better type of municipal site, this well kept and agreeable camp should be perfectly satisfactory for overnight or a bit longer. On flat ground, in a quiet setting beside the river with mature trees and next to exhibition grounds, it has individual pitches over most of the site with a general meadow also. The modern, recently improved, sanitary block is of very fair standard, with free hot water throughout. British seatless toilets, many washbasins and plentiful free showers with pre-set hot water. No other facilities on site but town shops are a short drive. When visited a mobile takeaway service was working well.

Directions: Site is west of the town, adjacent to the ring road running between N148 and N11.

Charges 1994:
-- Per unit incl. 1 person Ffr 40.00, 2 persons 48.00, with electricity (5A) 60.00; extra person 17.00; child (under 8 yrs) 8.00.

Address:
Bd. Salvador Allende,
79000 Niort.

Tel:
49.79.05.06.

Reservations:
Write to site.

POITOU-CHARENTES - Vienne / PROVENCE

8601 Castel Camping Le Petit Trianon de St. Ustre, Ingrandes, nr Châtellerault

Family run site with swimming pool, close to main N10 between Tours and Poitiers.

Le Petit Trianon is much used by the British as an overnight stop as it lies close to the N10, one of the main routes to the southwest, but is well worth considering for a longer stay. The site consists of two large, slightly sloping fields and a wooded section only used in exceptional weather. The 90 pitches (70 with electricity and 5 `grand confort') are of a good size, partly shaded and separated by earth scrapings exposing bare chalk rather than hedges. Sanitary facilities are located in an old building close to the main house and are spacious and generous in their provision. Main rooms can be heated and have washbasins in private cubicles and British WCs, as well as showers. Elsewhere are rooms with showers and washbasins in the same cubicle, baby bathrooms and washing machines. A new block is to be added for 1994 with facilities for the disabled. Heated swimming and paddling pools (open at set hours) are located on the sunny side of a rather picturesque castled facade in which is a large, very cool reading room. Restaurant 50 m. with menu displayed on site. Shop - essentials and drinks kept; open till late. Takeaway. Children's playground. Table tennis, badminton, croquet, 4 bicycles for hire, volleyball and boules. TV room (satellite, eg. Sky Sport). Minigolf. Organised excursions. Some chalets and gite to let. This site has grown in popularity and reservation is advisable in high season. 15-20 pitches are given over to tour operators.

Directions: Turnings to site (E of N10) are marked north of Ingrandes, between Dangé and Châtellerault. From autoroute A10 use Châtellerault-Nord exit.

Charges 1994:
-- Per person Ffr. 31.00 - 32.00; child (under 7) 16.00 - 17.00; car 17.00 - 18.00; pitch 18.00; water and drainage for motorcaravan 17.00 - 18.00; electricity (6A) 20.00; dog 8.00; local tax (over 3 yrs) 0.50.

Open:
15 May - 1 Oct.

Address:
Ingrandes-sur-Vienne, 86220 Dangé-St. Romain.

Tel:
49.02.61.47.

Reservations:
Are made (min. 5 days in July/Aug).

PROVENCE

Haute-Alpes - Alpes-de-Haute-Provence - Var - Vaucluse
Bouches-du-Rhône

From the Alps to the Mediterranean, this large region seems to have everything. The often spectacularly beautiful (and sometimes spectacularly busy!) coastline includes famous resorts like St. Tropez and Fréjus. The distinctive cuisine, bright blue inland lakes, the breathtaking Gorges du Verdon, the majestic Alps, the impressive Vaucluse and fascinating historic towns such as Aix, Avignon and Arles provide a seemingly endless choice of attractions. If you are looking for the renowned peace and tranquility and the incomparable light that has made Provence so popular as a home for artists, it is still not difficult to find those `off the beaten track' places only a few miles inland from the busy coast.

1301 Camping Les Romarins, Maussane-les-Alpilles, nr Arles

Well tended site conveniently placed for sightseeing in Provence.

This is one of those neat, well kept and orderly municipal sites that one occasionally comes across, and readers who have reported have always been satisfied. Pitches, on flat ground adjoining made-up access roads, are of good size and enclosed by hedges, with electrical connections available everywhere. The three modern toilet blocks are good ones and should be large enough with continental and British seatless toilets; washbasins in cubicles with shelf, mirror, free hot water; free pre-set hot showers with chain operation which does not run on. On-site amenities are limited (2 tennis courts and a children's playground), but there are others only a short walk away; the municipal swimming pool very close, and shops and restaurants in town. Les Baux and St. Remy-de-Provence are just a short drive away. Les Romarins becomes full from 1 July - late August.

Charges 1993:
-- Per pitch, incl. 2 adults + 1 child Ffr 61.50; extra person 14.00 Ffr; child (under 12) 8.00; electricity 12.50 - 14.00, acc. to season.

Open:
15 March - 15 Oct.

Address:
13520 Maussane.

Tel:
90.54.33.60.

Reservations:
Made for any length with fee (Ffr. 50).

Directions: Site is within the little town of Maussane on the eastern edge.

1302 Camping Arc-en-Ciel, Aix-en-Provence

Well shaded site, with pool, within walking distance of the centre of Aix-en-Provence.

Family run, this site is a good base for discovering Aix, the centre of which is about a 20 min. walk away, or there is a bus service. Although close to a main road, there is not much traffic noise, as all the 65 pitches (all with electricity and water) are arranged amongst a variety of trees and shrubs. A small river, with ducks, runs alongside the site and helps to make it unusually attractive for a town site. Whilst many city sites are noisy, not only from traffic, but from groups of youngsters, this site caters particularly for families and does not accept groups. No bicycles are to be ridden after 7 pm. There is a heated swimming pool (electronically controlled), table tennis, table football and tennis and golf facilities are located nearby. The sanitary facilities, in two blocks, are good, with en-suite cabins with British WC, shower and washbasin. Although there is no shop or restaurant on the site, there is a supermarket nearby and numerous restaurants catering for all tastes and pockets. Bread available on site each morning. Washing machine. River walks and fishing. Golf and tennis near. Gates closed 8.30 pm. (electronic keys provided).

Directions: From the Paris - Nice autoroute, take the 3-Sautets exit onto the RN7 to Nice/Toulon (take RN7 also from Aix town centre), keep right and site is signed to the right after the Gendarmerie.

Charges 1993:
-- Per person Ffr 25.00; child (under 7 yrs) 14.00; local tax 1.00; pitch 25.00; electricity (6A) 15.00.

Open:
15 March - 1 Nov.

Address:
Pont des Trois Sautets, 13100 Aix-en-Provence.

Tel:
42.26.14.28.

Reservations:
Necessary for July/Aug. and made with no deposit.

1303 Camping Rio Camargue, Port St. Louis du Rhône

Recently developed site on southeastern edge of the Camargue.

Situated close to the Rhône estuary, this is a somewhat unusual site with a number of excellent features including a large swimming pool and a crèche. The buildings, recently constructed in Camargaise style, include a large bar/restaurant providing welcome relief from the sun, particularly as there is little shade and the 100 sq.m. pitches are mainly on gravel hardstanding, emphasising the heat. The site is divided into two main areas (one having the official 4 star grading, the other being 3 star). The 4 star pitches all have electricity and drainage points as do some of the 3 star ones. The two sanitary blocks, one in each area, are modern and functional rather than luxurious, clean when visited and provide hot showers, some washbasins in private cabins, British WCs and also WCs for children. Well equipped nursery with qualified staff (on payment). Other facilities include a café, shops, takeaway, laundry facilities, a fitness club, minigolf, tennis, table tennis, volleyball and basketball. Activities, excursions and entertainment programmes. Mobile homes and apartments for rent. This area of the Camargue is close to several industrial complexes, although it does make a very convenient base for exploring this interesting part of France. A large flat beach of hard sand (the Plage Napoleon) is 5 km. and the site provides cards giving free access to the beach car park. A typically `estuary type' beach, it does enjoy some good views and bathing is said to be clean and safe.

Directions: From the village of Port St. Louis du Rhône, drive through village one way system. Turn right after lifting bridge and site is on left by river.

Charges guide:
-- Per unit Ffr. 25.00 - 50.00, acc. to season; small tent 18.00 - 35.00; person 15.00 - 30.00; child (under 7 yrs) 10.00 - 20.00.

Open:
All year.

Address:
Route Napoleon, 13230 Port St. Louis du Rhône.

Tel:
42.86.06.06.
FAX: 42.86.33.13.

Reservations:
Write for booking form (deposit Ffr. 500).

PROVENCE - Alpes-de-Haute-Provence

0402 Castel Camping du Verdon, Castellane (see page 144)

0401 Hotel de Plein Air L'Hippocampe, Volonne, nr Sisteron

Attractive, friendly site with good pool complex and sports opportunities.

Haute-Provence is one of the most beautiful and unspoilt regions of France and the proprietor here has arranged access to some of the most intriguing ways of exploring the many canyons and mountains in easy reach from the site - guided rafting expeditions, the new sport of `canyonning', treks with pack mules. The famous Gorges du Verdon are not far away and there are more than 100 other canyons in the area. The site is well run and has a family atmosphere. There are tour operator tents but the vast majority of the 447 pitches are for touring units, 370 with electricity (6A). Pitches are numbered and well marked by trees and bushes. Some shade is available on most pitches from the olive and cherry trees that help make the site very attractive. Surrounded by rolling hills and old stone walls and with many flowers and shrubs, the site retains a Provencal ambience whilst having good facilities for visitors. Five toilet blocks, two larger and rather more modern, contain free hot water in showers and washbasin cabins; WCs are mostly British style (possibly under pressure in main season). Reasonably priced self-service restaurant and new pizzeria. Small shop. Takeaway. Friendly bar. Good sports facilities and some instruction is available (English spoken). The swimming pool complex is excellent, comprising a fairly deep swimming/diving pool, another large pool not quite so deep and a paddling pool for very young children. Tennis (free outside 3/7-21/8). Table tennis. Archery. Sound proof disco. Animation in season, aerobics sessions, some in water and mini-club for 7-12 year olds. Tourist information office with reservations service. Washing machines. Village 600 m. Mobile homes (with telephone and satellite TV) for rent. The site abuts a lake, really a wide stretch of the Durance, and pedaloes can be hired from the beach. A busy site, increasing in size, with lots going on for teenagers.

Directions: Appoaching from the north turn off N85 across river bridge to Volonne. Then right to site. From the south right on D4 1 km. before Château Arnoux.

Charges 1993:
-- Per unit with 2 persons Ffr. 57.00 - 99.00, acc. to season, with electricity 71.00 - 120.00, with water and drainage 71.00 - 133.00, large (140 sq.m. with all services 71.00 - 148.00; extra person (over 2 yrs) 8.00 - 16.00; extra car 10.00 - 12.00; local tax 0.50 - 1.00.

Open:
Easter - 30 Sept.

Address:
04290 Volonne.

Tel:
92.33.50.00.
FAX: 92.33.50.49.

Reservations:
Made with deposit and booking fee (Ffr. 120).

see advertisement in previous colour section

0403 Camping Lac du Moulin de Ventre, Niozelles, Forcalquier

Small, peaceful lakeside site, close to the Luberon.

Near Forcalquier, a busy French town, this is an attractive site situated beside a small lake offering opportunities for swimming (supervised in season) canoeing or for hiring a pedalo and 28 acres of wooded, hilly land available for walking. Trees and shrubs are labelled and the herbs of Provence can be found growing wild. A nature lover's delight - birds and butterflies abound. Some 75 of the total of 100 level, grassy pitches have electricity (6-10A) and there is some shade from the variety of trees; 8 tour operator tents. This is a family run site, providing an ambience which will appeal particularly to families with younger children. There is a bar, and during July and August, a restaurant serving both waiter service and takeaway meals. Pizzeria. Entertainment programme for children (July/Aug) and playground. Sanitary facilities are good, with hot showers, washbasins in cabins and some en-suite cubicles with showers and washbasins. There are facilities for the disabled, a baby bath, washing machines and fridges for hire. Shop for essentials; supermarket 5 km. Library. Fishing. Apartments and caravans to let.

Directions: From A51 autoroute take exit for village of Brillanne and follow N100 east for 3 km. Site is signposted near Forcalquier, 3 km. ESE of Niozelles.

Charges 1993:
-- Per unit, incl. 2 persons Ffr 80.00; extra person 23.00; child (under 4 yrs) 10.00; electricity 18.00.
-- Special offers, eg. 5th day free in low season, 3rd week free.

Open:
1 April - 25 September.

Address:
Niozelles, 04300 Forcalquier.

Tel:
92.78.63.31.
FAX: 92.79.86.92.

Reservations:
Made with deposit (30% of charge) and fee (Ffr. 90).

N0404 Domaine Naturist Castillon de Provence, Castellane

Very large naturist site with spectacular views.

One hundred pitches in 45 hectares of fairly wild Provencal countryside near the Gorges du Verdon (the French answer to the Grand Canyon and nearly as spectacular) make this a site for naturists who are also nature lovers. Quite apart from the size of the terrain, this is an unusual site and is perhaps of more interest to experienced naturist campers - the access road is narrow, steep and twisting - no problem for smaller caravans, trailer tents or small motorhomes, but probably rather daunting for larger units. The setting and the views are spectacular, and whilst the site has only a tiny pool for children, there is a large lake within hard walking distance (2 km. and hilly, but we did it!) where swimming and canoeing are possible from the naturist 'beach' (motor boats forbidden). The pitches are unmarked and scattered around the hilly terrain - they are really as large as you want - 2 or 3A electrical connections are available on over 30%; long cables may be required (the site operators offered to lend us one but our 50 m. cable was sufficient). You should be able to find a flat pitch even though a lot are not, although nobody seemed too bothered by this. The facilities are surprisingly extensive and include a bar/restaurant (with limited menu and take your own crockery/cutlery!), takeaway, shop and a quite varied range of activities including entertainment in the main season. The sanitary facilities were very clean and typically rural naturist site in style - mainly open shower and washbasins - hot showers in one block (on payment in high season) - but elsewhere only cold water. WCs of the French (Turkish) variety, apart from the one British type in the handicapped toilet and spotlessly clean when we visited on Bastille Day. There is nothing 'manicured' about this site, but if you like unspoiled and fairly wild (but not inhospitable) countryside and appreciate a warm welcome from the French owner and Dutch assistant, this could be a very attractive proposition.

Directions: From Castellane take the D955 before turning left onto the CD402 to the site. This is a very narrow road with few passing places and caravanners are asked to arrive **after** 14.00 hrs or to phone the site to check that no-one is about to travel in the opposite direction!

Charges 1994:
-- Per adult Ffr. 32.00; child 15.50; electricity 11.00.

Open:
Easter - end September.

Address:
La Grande Terre, La Baume, 04120 Castellane.

Tel:
92.83.64.24.

Reservations:
Made with deposit (Ffr. 700 paid by Eurocheque).

8303 Camping Val Fleury, Boulouris, nr Fréjus

Small camp of good quality catering for campers in all seasons.

At first glance Val Fleury may not appear anything very special but it has many regular visitors who like it a lot. It is a small, terraced site with 65 individual pitches closely spaced and some small or inaccessible to caravans. Most are well shaded and electricity is available. The site reports that new steps have been built between the terraces. It is close to the sea, but one has to cross the main road (best beach is 500 m. away, but nearest one 100 m.).

The sanitary block can be heated and has some individual washing cabins with free hot water, shelf and mirror as well as some communal units with cold, and free hot showers. British WCs. It is kept very clean. An attractive television room and separate reading room are also heated in winter. Restaurant (Easter - Oct.) and takeaway. Supermarket near. Laundry facilities. With space limited, reservation is advisable over a long season. Site accepts payment by credit card. Mobile homes and caravans for hire.

Directions: Easy - it is on the main coast road RN98 on the east side of Boulouris.

Charges 1993:
-- Per standard pitch with up to 4 persons 95.00 - 145.00 Ffr, large pitch 115.00 - 175.00, acc. to season; small tent pitch with up to 2 persons 70.00 - 90.00; extra person 30.00; extra child (under 5yrs) 20.00; dog 20.00; electricity 2A 18.00, 6A 23.00.

Open:
All year

Address:
83700 Boulouris.

Tel:
94.95.21.52.

Reservations:
Made with large deposit

8302 Castel Camping Caravaning Esterel, Agay, nr Fréjus

Attractive, good site in hills east of St. Raphaël with swimming pool, 3½ km. from sea.

Set among the hills at the back of Agay, in an attractive quiet situation with good views around, this site is 3½ km. from the sandy beach at Agay, where parking is perhaps a little easier than at most places on this coast. In addition to a section for permanent caravans, it has some 200 pitches for tourists, on which caravans of any type are taken but not tents. Pitches are on shallow terraces, attractively landscaped with some shade and a variety of flowering plants, giving a feeling of spaciousness and all with electricity connection and tap. There are 18 special ones which have their own individual washroom with WC, basin and shower (both with hot water) adjoining.

On-site amenities include two circular, heated swimming pools, one for adults and a smaller one for children, which are much used and open all season, a new disco, minigolf, 2 tennis courts and most unusual for France - a squash court. A pleasant courtyard area contains the shop, takeaway and bar/restaurant which overlooks the pools. Two toilet blocks plus one smaller one adjacent to the tourist section are very satisfactory which can be heated and have British WCs, most basins in private cabins or cubicles, and free hot water in all facilities, though the temperature varies a little at busy times. Facilities for the disabled and washing machines. Cleaning of these and dustbin emptying are very good. Organised events and entertainments in season. Riding. Children's playground. Good golf very close. Mobile homes with 2 bedrooms to let. A good site, well run and organized in a deservedly popular area. Some tour operators.

Charges guide:
-- Per unit incl. 2 persons Ffr 115.00; extra person 28.00 or child (under 7) 16.00; Special pitch with own washroom 25.00 extra; local tax 1.00.

Open:
Easter/1 April - 30 Sept.

Address:
Agay, 83700 St. Raphaël.

Tel:
94.82.03.28.
FAX: 94.82.87.37.

Reservations:
Necessary for high season and made for min. 1 week with large deposit and Ffr. 50 fee.

Directions: You can approach from St. Raphaël via Valescure but easiest way to find is to turn off coast road at Agay where there is good signposting. From the Fréjus exit from autoroute A8, follow signs for Valescure throughout, then for Agay, and you will come to site on left.

8301 Camping-Caravaning Les Pins Parasol, Fréjus

Family owned site with pool, 5 km. from sea; some pitches with individual sanitary units.

Not everyone likes very big sites, and Les Pins Parasol with its 189 pitches is of a size which is quite easy to walk around. Although on very slightly undulating ground, virtually all the plots are levelled or terraced and separated by hedges or bushes; shade only on some. They are of around 100 sq.m. and all with electricity. What is particularly interesting, as it is the most unusual feature of the camp, is that 48 pitches are equipped with a fully enclosed sanitary unit, consisting of British WC, washbasin, sink and hot shower, all quite close together. These naturally cost more but may well be of interest to those seeking extra comfort. The normal size toilet blocks, in three different places, are of good average quality and give a plentiful supply with British seatless WCs, washbasins in private cabins and free hot showers with preset hot water and pushbutton which does not run on. Facilities for disabled. On site is a swimming pool of 200 sq.m. with hard-surfaced terraced lying out area, a separate long slide with landing pool and a small children's pool. Small shop with reasonable stocks. Restaurant with takeaway (both from 1/5). General room with TV. Tennis. Tax free exchange facility. The nearest beach is the once very long Fréjus-Plage, now reduced a little by the new marina, which is 5½ km. and adjoins St. Raphaël. (See note on La Baume entry concerning traffic delays at the D4/N7 road junction.) Used by tour operators.

Charges 1994:
-- Per normal pitch with electricity incl. 2 persons Ffr 112.00; special pitch with sanitary unit incl. 2 persons 148.00; extra person 30.00; child (under 7 yrs) 20.00; car 9.00; dog 11.00.
-- Less 10% outside 16/6 - 31/8.

Open:
Easter/1 April - 30 Sept.

Address:
Route de Bagnols, 83600 Fréjus.

Tel:
94.40.88.43.

Reservations:
Made for 2 weeks min. for exact dates with large deposit but no fee.

Directions: From west on autoroute A8 take Fréjus-Ouest exit and turn right at roundabout. Right at junction and site is on right. From east take exit for Fréjus - St. Raphaël (a different one), right immediately on leaving pay booths on a small road which leads across to D4, where right again and under 1 km. to site.

8306 Camping-Caravaning de la Baume + La Palmeraie, Fréjus

Busy, large site back from sea with excellent pool complex and other amenities.

This large site has been well developed, with much money spent. It is about 5½ km. from the long sandy beach of Fréjus-Plage, but has such a fine and varied selection of swimming pools (4) that many people do not bother to make the trip. The two main pools are each about 300 sq.m., one quite deep for swimmers and the other shallower, with an annex to receive those coming down the very long slides which lead into it (including one of 48 m.) One pool (12½ x 6m.) can be fully covered for off-season and becomes quite warm. A paddling pool and jacuzzi complete the complex. The site has nearly 500 pitches of varying but quite adequate size with electricity, water and drainaway, with another 200 large ones with plumbing for mains sewerage to take mobile homes; separators to divide plots are being installed. Shade available over most of the terrain. Although tents are accepted, the site concentrates mainly on caravanning. The 7 toilet blocks are all similar and should be a satisfactory supply with British toilets with a few continental; washbasins in private cabins (H&C) and free hot showers and sinks for clothes and dishes, with hot water at preset temperature (which varied a little). Supermarket and several other shops. Bar with external terrace and TV. Restaurant and takeaway. Tennis courts. Organised events (sports, competitions, etc.), some evening entertainment partly in English. Cinema twice weekly. Amphitheatre for shows. Discos daily in high season. Riding from site. Site is likely to become full in season, but one section with unmarked pitches is unreserved and there is plenty of space off-peak. In one section there may be some road noise. Popular with tour operators.

Adjacent to La Baume is its sister site La Palmeraie, not for campers but for those who wish to hire self-catering accommodation. It has some 80 small chalet-type units for 4-6 persons. It also has its own landscaped swimming pool and provides some entertainments to supplement those at La Baume.

Directions: Site is 3 km. up D4 road, which leads north from N7 just west of Fréjus. From west on autoroute A8 take exit for Fréjus/St. Raphaël, turn towards them and after 4 km., turn left on D4. From east take exit for Fréjus/St. Raphaël (but it is quite a different one); after exit turn right immediately on small road marked `Musee' etc. which leads you to D4 where right again. (There should now be an exit for those coming from the east, which will be nearer).

Charges 1993:
-- Per unit incl. up to 3 persons on pitch with electricity, water and drainage Ffr 155.00 - 180.00, without services 132.00 - 155.00; extra person 28.00 - 32.00; child (under 7) 18.50 - 22.00; extra car or m/cycle 17.00 - 19.00; electricity 17.00 - 19.00; plus local tax in July/Aug.
-- Min. stay 3 nights.
-- For La Palmeraie charges apply to site.

Open:
Easter - 30 Sept.

Address:
Route de Bagnols, 83618 Fréjus Cedex.

Tel:
94.40.87.87 or 94.40.74.59.
FAX: 94.40.73.50.

Reservations:
Essential for high season, and made for exact dates with substantial deposit and fee (Ffr 180), from 1 January.

see colour advertisement
on back cover

Note: In peak season considerable traffic delays may be experienced at the D4/N7 junction if you wish to travel to Fréjus-Plage or to the nearest towns of Fréjus or St. Raphaël. To avoid these it is possible to turn off the D4 on a minor road (signpost `Zoo' and `Daniel Templon') leading past the easterly Fréjus/St. Raphaël motorway entrance, which can get you reasonably quickly to the motorway or the eastern part of St. Raphaël and areas east of that, but there can still be unwelcome delays in reaching Fréjus-Plage.

PROVENCE - Var

0402 Castel Camping du Verdon, Castellane (Alpes-de-Haute-Provence)
Good site with swimming pool close to 'Route des Alpes' and Gorges du Verdon.

Although it is an inland site, Camp du Verdon is in a popular holiday area and now has two heated swimming pools (both 19 x 7 m., one deeper than the other), open from mid-June to at least late Aug. In fact most visitors are here for a period, although it also has transit trade. It is very big and is sheltered, on flat ground which is part meadow and part wooded. The 400 pitches are numbered and vary in size and type, most with 6A electricity. The sanitary blocks, three fair-sized and two smaller, have been improved and are of very good quality. They have mostly continental toilets, individual basins with mirrors and shelves (cold water); free pre-set hot showers, free hot water for sinks and facilities for the disabled, kept spotless by resident cleaners. Traditional restaurant (very popular and good value) and separate fast food service in July/Aug. Pizzeria/ crêperie with terrace and takeaway. Bar and special room with fireplace for early season. Children's playgrounds. Volleyball. Football field. Games room. Minigolf. Lake for trout fishing; another for small boats; access to River Verdon at end of site with pebble beach and river pools. Rafting nearby. Horse riding. In July/Aug. organised sports in daytime; dancing/disco twice weekly. Washing machines, dryers and ironing facilities. Bureau de change. Ice boxes for hire. Mobile homes for hire. There is usually space except right at the peak, though not perhaps on the pitch that you would choose. Torches required at night. Used by main tour operators (5-10%). A busy but well run site.
Directions: From Castellane take D952 in direction of Gorges du Verdon and Moustiers.

Charges 1993:
-- Prices in brackets outside 15/6 - 1/9.
-- Per unit with up to 3 persons 110.00 - 160.00 Ffr (85.00 - 120.00) acc. to services and size of pitch; extra person 28.00; extra car, tent or caravan 12.00; dog 12.00; local tax 1.00 (adults) 0.50 (child 4-10).
Open:
15 May - 15 Sept.
Address:
Domaine de la Salaou, 04120 Castellane.
Tel:
92.83.61.29.
FAX: 92.83.69.37.
Reservations:
Made for any length with booking fee and deposit - details from site.

see colour advertisement opposite

8305 Camping-Caravaning des Aubrèdes, Fréjus
Smaller, family managed site with pool, 5 km. from sea.

This site has now become known and has its fair share of campers, though being just back from the sea, it may still have some space when others are full. It has a small swimming pool, open nearly all season, and is about 5 km. from the long beach at Fréjus-Plage and from St. Raphaël. Mainly on slightly sloping ground and quite close to the motorway (though not too much noise), the site has individual pitches without much to divide them. There are now about 30 special 'plateformes' - pitches with electricity, water and drainaway. Although the site has an open aspect, a reasonable amount of shade is available from tall trees over most of the site. Three sanitary blocks with free hot showers, British seatless and continental toilets; washbasins in cabins with cold water, hot water point for sinks; reasonable quality but only just enough. Shop. Bar/pizzeria with occasional dancing. Restaurant (open in main season but takeaway facility also. Tennis. Children's playground. Washing machine. Organised activities in season: sports competitions, shows, dancing etc. Caravans for hire.
Directions: Turn off N7 to north just east of Puget sur Argens autoroute entry and follow camp signs across motorway to site.

Charges 1994:
-- Per pitch with 2 persons 90.00 Ffr; extra person 20.00; child (under 7 yrs) 15.00; plateforme pitch with water and drainage 16.00 extra; electricity (8A) 18.00; extra car 8.00; animal 8.00; local tax 1.00.
-- Less in April/May (30%), June (10%) and Sept (20%) (not electricity).
Open:
Easter/1 April - 30 Sept.
Address:
83480 Puget-sur-Argens.
Tel:
94.45.51.46.
FAX: 94.45.28.92.
Reservations:
Made from December, for Sat. to Sat. (min. 1 week) with deposit (Ffr. 520) and fee (80.00).

HOTEL DE PLEIN AIR cat. 4 étoiles

CAMP DU VERDON

★ ★ ★ ★

DOMAINE DE LA SALAOU

Camping
Caravanning

Excellent site for family-holidays, right on the "Verdon"-River and the entry
to the famous "GORGES DU VERDON", the European Great Canyon.

**CASTELS
& CAMPING
CARAVANING**
★ ★ ★ ★

04120 CASTELLANE FRANCE
☎ 92.83.61.29   Fax: 92.83.69.37

Paris

Castellane

Caravaning
★★★★

l'Étoile d'Argens

TENNIS AND GOLF FREE LOW-SEASON

TEL: 94.81.01.41
83370 ST.AYGULF

8307 Camping-Caravaning L'Etoile d'Argens, St. Aygulf, nr Fréjus

Site between Fréjus and St. Aygulf, 2 km. from beach with access to sea by river.

L'Etoile d'Argens lies just back from the sea, a bit over 2 km. from the sandy beach at St. Aygulf. A river runs along one side of the camp which has direct access to the sea and on which moorings are available. There is also a boat which carries one free of charge to the beach at certain times. The main feature of the site is a large pool complex with three good swimming pools, not heated - one of 25 x 10m. for swimming, one 14 x 7m. less deep, and a small one for children - and a good lying-out area. The pool area extends to an attractively designed bar, ground and first floor terraces, restaurant/pizzeria and disco.

The site has 400 pitches on flat ground, fully marked out by tall trees and hedges in parallel bays. They are of good size (min. 100 sq.m) and 350 of them have electricity, water and drainaway. The 400 in the older part have good shade but there is little as yet in the newer section. Reservation for main season is most advisable. For each 20 to 30 units there is a small sanitary unit with 2 British WCs, 5 washbasins in cubicles with shelf (with hot and cold water), 2 good controllable free hot showers, and 2 cabins with WC and shower. Their sufficiency is difficult to assess but the site does report the addition of further facilities for 1994. Self-service shop. 4 tennis courts, one with multi-sport markings. Golf practice net. Minigolf. Table tennis. Football pitch. Children's playground. Washing machines. Free water-bus service to beach between 20/6 - 20/9. Barbeques not permitted. Several British tour operators use the site, which is busy with much activity in the main season. Mobile homes to let.

Directions: Site lies 4½ km. NNW of St. Aygulf, where camp signposts are not easy to find. You can also approach by turning off the N98 coast road midway between St. Aygulf and Fréjus, or from the N7 just outside Fréjus to west, taking a turning to south over a level crossing, and left after 3½ km.

Charges 1994:
-- (Provisional) Per `comfort' pitch (100 sq.m.), incl. 3 persons, water/drainage and electricity (10A) Ffr 196.00; extra person 35.00; child (under 7) 23.00.
-- Less in low seasons.

Open:
Easter - 30 Sept, with all services.

Address:
83370 St. Aygulf.

Tel.
94.81.01.41.
FAX: 94.81.21.45.

Reservations:
Made for any period with substantial deposit and fee.

see colour
advertisement opposite

8311 Camping de la Baie, Cavalaire

Busy site, with pool, within the resort of Cavalaire and only a short way from the beach.

This site is only a short walk from the beach and from the main street of a pleasant little holiday resort where there is a new harbour and restaurants and shops. A long, sandy beach runs right round the bay and there are plenty of watersports activities nearby. The site has an attractive, free, kidney-shaped swimming pool with sunbathing terrace (open Easter - end Sept.) and a small children's pool.

Pitches are individual ones on slightly sloping ground with terracing and access roads, nearly all with electricity. Trees have grown well to give plenty of shade. There are four main toilet blocks, with free hot showers, and with washbasins in tiled private cabins and four smaller units with toilets and open washbasins behind. British toilets, with some continental. Small shop with baker on site; town shops are close. Restaurant (all season) and bar, with takeaway. 'Animation' with dance evenings. Full launderette. Children's playground. Table tennis. TV room. Exchange facilities. Doctor at 150 m. Mobile homes for hire - details from site. English spoken.

Directions: Site is signposted from main street of Cavalaire, in the direction of the harbour.

Charges 1993:
-- Per unit with up to 3 persons 120.00 Ffr, (with small tent 70.00 for 2 persons); extra person 27.00; child (under 7) 13.50; extra car or boat 19.00; local tax 1.00 per person; electricity 25.00.
-- Less 20% outside 19/6 - 4/9 or 30% before 15/5 or after 18/9.

Open:
15 March - 15 Oct.

Address:
Bd. Pasteur, BP.12, 83240 Cavalaire/s/mer.

Tel:
94.64.08.15 or 94.64.08.10.

Reservations:
Recommended for 15/6-15/9 and made from 1 Jan. (min. 1 week, Sat. to Sat) with deposit (Ffr. 1,000 incl. fee 200).

8312 Camp du Domaine, La Favière, Le Lavandou

Site by a sandy beach which gives you plenty of space, 3 km. south of town.

For a seaside camping site, the individual pitches which the Domaine provides are in most parts large. There are some on sandy ground very near to the beach, and some specially large ones on a level hard surface a little further back, both of which have some artificial shade and electricity available. There is also a large number of levelled plots throughout the vast wooded estate which covers most of the site: some not so large, and maybe more suitable for tents. Those at the back can be up to 700 m. from beach and shop. Very early reservation is necessary over a long season - say late June to early Sept. - as regular clients book from year to year. The site is entirely for tourists and has no hire units.

The second main asset of the Domaine is the sea, for the site has direct access to a good beach of considerable length. This has become narrower following the major construction of the La Favière marina but it offers good bathing and is cleaned by the site. The sanitary blocks have undergone some extensive renovation in recent years, and 8 of the 10 are now in modern style, with private washing cabins, though some still have individual, open washbasins. All blocks have WCs virtually all of the Turkish type, in which the site firmly believes. Free hot water, mostly premixed, throughout. Facilities for the disabled. Washing machine. Self-service supermarket with good stocks and restaurant serving simple fare, either to eat there or take away (both June - late Sept). Pleasant separate bar with pizzeria. Sports field. Animation for children and adults in season. Boats and pedaloes for hire. 6 tennis courts. Doctors will call. American motorhomes not accepted. Site is strict in forbidding all barbecues.

Charges 1993:
-- Per person Ffr. 22.00 plus local tax 1.00; child (under 7) 11.00 plus local tax 0.50; pitch incl. car + tent/caravan 29.00; special pitch with electricity, water and drainaway, near beach 65.00; extra car 7.00.
-- Less outside high season.

Open:
April - mid-Oct.

Address:
La Favière, 83230 Bormes.

Tel:
94.71.03.12.

Reservations:
Made Sun.- Sun. only, by letter from Jan.- March, with booking fee (Ffr. 150). Regular clients have the right to re-book for following year.

Directions: Just outside and to west of Le Lavandou, at roundabout, turn off N559 towards sea on road signed 'Favière, Bénat'. After 2 km. turn left to site.

CAMP DU DOMAINE
★ ★ ★ ★
83230 BORMES-LES-MIMOSAS
Côte d'Azur
Tel: 94.71.03.12

● Right beside the sea, with direct access to a sandy beach. 4 km from Le Lavandou.

● A very spacious site set in the green countryside. Many pitches in a vast pinewood, from where dust-free roads lead down to the beach

● It is particularly attractive here in May, June and September

8308 Au Paradis des Campeurs, La Gaillarde Plage, nr Fréjus

Agreeable small site with direct access to beach.

Just across the coast road from a sandy beach with direct access by an underpass for pedestrians, this well kept little site in an attractive and popular area is family owned and run. It has 130 pitches (all with electricity) of varying but satisfactory size and shape (they have made the most of the space), 70 of which have their own water tap and drainaway as well. Some shade on most pitches. The two toilet blocks, of good size for the site and found very clean, have WCs of various types, washbasins with hot water mainly in cabins or cubicles, and free hot showers at pre-set temperature. Shop and full restaurant with takeaway service; both front onto main road but separate dining room for campers. TV room. Washing machines. Children's playground. Caravans and bungalows to let. Some road noise possible in the front part of the camp.

Directions: Site is signposted from N98 coast road at La Gaillarde, 2 km. south of St. Aygulf.

Charges 1993:
-- Per unit incl. 3 persons Ffr. 107.00 - 130.00 (73.00 - 89.00 outside July/Aug); extra person 22.00; electricity 14.00.
-- Less 40% outside 26/6-25/8.

Open:
15 March - 30 Sept.

Address:
La Gaillarde Plage, 83370 St Aygulf.

Tel:
94.96.93.55

Reservations:
Advised for main season

AU PARADIS DES CAMPEURS ★★★★NN
LA GAILLARDE PLAGE (RN98)
83 370 SAINT AYGULF.   Tél: 94 96 93 55

- Friendly ambiance
- Direct access to beach (50m)
- Sandy beach with life guards
- Hot water – electricity
- 75 individual pitches
- Self service restaurant and bar
- 40% reduction before 25 June and after 1st Sept.
- Reservation advised for main season

8310 Camping de la Plage, Grimaud, nr St. Tropez

Popular site by a sandy beach opposite St. Tropez.

This camp near Ste. Maxime is situated right by the sea with its own sandy beach, which can become crowded. The site is divided into two parts by a main road (N98), but there is now a pedestrian underpass which avoids the rather dangerous crossing of the N98. All pitches in both parts of the camp are numbered and all can be reserved. Except perhaps for those bordering the beach, they are of good size, and many are pleasantly grassed and shaded. Electrical connections available (2, 4, 6 or 10A). There are three sanitary blocks in the part near the sea and two on the far side. They have mixed British and continental WCs, washbasins with free hot water (some in private cabins), and free hot showers - a satisfactory supply. Supermarket, bar and restaurant, with takeaway also (none all season). Volleyball. Children's playground. Tennis. Mobile bank. Doctor calls daily up to 15 Sept. Boat service to St. Tropez all season and boat hire from close to site.

Directions: Easy: it is on the main coast road (N98) about 6 km. southwest of Ste. Maxime. Take care - this road is very busy in main season.

Charges 1993:
-- Per unit with 2 persons Ffr 90.00; extra person 24.00 plus local tax 2.00; child (under 7) 12.00; electricity 14.50 - 30.00, acc. to amps.

Open:
Easter/1 April to 30 Sept.

Address:
83360 Grimaud.

Tel:
94.56.31.15.

Reservations:
Bookings taken for exact dates with booking fee (Ffr. 140) from Oct.- March only.

PROVENCE - Var

8314 Castel Camping Les Lacs du Verdon, Regusse

Conveniently situated site for touring Provence.

This site is in beautiful countryside, within easy reach of the Grand Canyon du Verdon and the nearby lakes (with sailing and windsurfing facilities), yet is only about 90 minutes by road from Cannes or St. Tropez; it is now under new ownership. In a 30 acre wooded park, the site is in two parts, on either side of a minor road. On one side the pitches are quite formally arranged (mainly for caravans), on the other side less so, giving a more natural appearance. In total there are 400 level, marked pitches on rather stony ground, mostly over 100 sq.m. in size and 270 with 6 or 10A electricity. There is a bar/restaurant with takeaway and terrace (open June-Aug.) and separate pizzeria with outdoor terrace. Small shop and facilities for various sports including tennis, volleyball, sailing and windsurfing at the site's club at Saint-Croix, bicycle hire, guided walks, minigolf, table tennis and pétanque. There is a good sized swimming pool with paved sunbathing area and rafting, climbing and riding nearby. Small disco/games room with table tennis for teenagers - although not completely sound-proofed, we understand that the disco finishes at 11.30 pm, half an hour before the bar (some 50 m. away) closes. Barbecues restricted.

The sanitary facilities, in four blocks of similar design and one new modern block (mixed M&F), provide hot showers with separators and some washbasins in private cabins. Laundry facilities. Caravans and mobile homes for hire. Tour operator tents. This site is well situated for touring Provence and offers much for the family with older children in terms of suitable activities.

Directions: From St. Maximin go via the D560 north-eastward to Barjols. Turn off at Barjols onto the D71 to Montmeyan where you turn right onto the D30 to Regusse and follow the site signs.

Charges 1993:
-- Per pitch with electricity, water and drainage, incl. 2 persons Ffr 103.00; pitch with electricity only, incl. 2 persons 93.00; extra person 29.50; child (2-7 yrs) 22.00; electricity (6A) 16.00, (10A) 22.00; local tax 1.00.
-- Less 25% outside 15/6-31/8.

Open:
10 April - 30 Sept.

Address:
Domaine de Roquelande, 83630 Regusse.

Tel:
94.70.17.95.
FAX: 94.70.51.79.

Reservations:
Write to site.

8315 Camping International de la Sainte-Baume, Nans-les-Pins

Holiday style site with excellent swimming pools.

This is a family orientated 'holiday' site in Provencal countryside some 30 minutes by car from the coast at Cassis. Somewhat smaller than other sites of this type, there are some 200 good sized pitches (150 with 6 or 10A electricity) on mainly level, rather stony ground, with variable shade. There is an attractive large new complex with 3 swimming pools (1 for children) and jacuzzi, surrounded by ample paved sunbathing area with some shade from palm trees. Other amenities include a small (limited menu) restaurant overlooking the pools, takeaway, small shop, bar, disco and TV room. Sporting facilities include tennis, table tennis, volleyball and boules. Entertainment programme in July/August with children's mini-club.

The 2 main sanitary blocks, including one new super de-luxe, are of a good standard with free hot showers with dressing area, washbasins in private cabins and British WCs, dishwashing and laundry. Although having all the facilities, activities and entertainment expected of a holiday site, the atmosphere is very relaxed and much less frenzied than some other similar sites.

Directions: Take St. Maximin exit from A8 and head for Auriol on the N560, turning after 9 km. for Nans-les-Pins (D80); site on left just before this village.

Charges 1993:
-- Per unit incl. 2 persons Ffr. 70.00 - 95.00; extra person 19.00 - 25.00; child (under 7) 15.00 - 20.00; electricity 18.00 (6A), 26.00 (10A); drainage and water or extra vehicle 15.00.

Open:
Easter - first Sat. in Oct.

Address:
83860 Nans-les-Pins.

Tel:
94.78.92.68.
FAX: 94.78.67.37.

Reservations:
Made with deposit (Ffr. 300, over 7 nights 600) and fee (90).

8401 Parc Municipal du Pont St. Bénézet, Avignon

Neat and well kept site within 15 minutes walk of town centre.

This site, now run by the municipality, has an excellent situation with fine views across the river Rhône to the Pope's palace and the famous 'Pont d'Avignon', which is in fact the Pont St. Bénézet. On flat, well tended grass, it has separate sections for caravans - with good-sized marked out pitches with electricity, mainly with hedges to separate them and good shade - and for tents a more open area. The five sanitary blocks were satisfactory and clean though, as often in France, lavatories seemed fewer than the other facilities and were only of continental type for men. Individual basins in cubicles, no shelf, all with hot water, free pre-set hot showers, hot water for laundry sinks and facilities for the disabled. Shop (Whitsun - late Sept.). Bar with bar meals or takeaway food. Children's playground. Table tennis. Tennis with racquets for hire. Bicycle hire. Activities organised. Swimming pool nearby. The site normally becomes full from about 10/7-2/8 when the festival of Avignon is held, and reservation is then advisable for longer stays.

Directions: Site is northwest of town on an 'island' which is crossed by the D100 Nîmes road. It is signposted but the access roads to get onto the bridge need attention.

Charges 1993:
-- Per person 17.00 Ffr; child (under 7) 8.50; caravan/car 20.00; tent/car 14.00; motorcaravan 20.00; electricity (6A) 14.00.

Open:
March - 31 Oct. but best to phone to check.

Address:
84000 Avignon.

Tel:
90.82.63.50.

Reservations:
Made for min. 2 weeks with deposit.

8403 Camping Le Brégoux en Provence, Aubignan, nr Carpentras

Strategically situated municipal site near Mont Ventoux.

Near Mont Ventoux – giant of Provence at the heart of the Comtat Venaissin region.

The **Bregoux Camp Site** at Aubignan (Vancluse) welcomes you from 15 March to 31 October.

Peaceful, comfortable, shady pitches, pleasant walks, all services

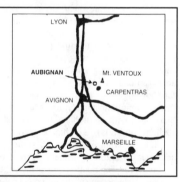

Generally speaking, reasonably priced sites of a good standard in this area are few and far between. This attractive municipal site is an exception and well worth considering as a base for exploring this region, being conveniently situated for visiting Mont Ventoux and the Dentelles de Montmirail, Orange, Carpentras, Vaison la Romaine, Avignon and even Aix-en-Provence. The site itself is about 10 minutes walk from the town, is on level grass and fairly well shaded. The 200 or so pitches, most with electrical connections, are of a reasonable size and are partially separated. Sanitary facilities, in three blocks, include pre-set hot showers, with dressing area, some washbasins in private cabins, covered washing up areas, and two washing machines, all very clean when inspected in July.

Directions: Site is situated on the southern outskirts of the small town of Aubignan, 6 km. north of Carpentras via the D7. Site is signed in Aubignan.

Charges 1993:
-- Per person Ffr. 12.00; child (under 7) 6.00; pitch 10.00; extra car 10.00; electricity 9.70; dog 4.60.
-- Less 10-20% on person charges in low seasons.

Open:
15 March - 31 October.

Address:
Mairie, 84810 Aubignan.

Tel:
(Reservations) 90.62.62.50.

Reservations:
Telephone or write.

PROVENCE - Vaucluse

N8402 Domaine Naturiste de Bélezy, Bédoin, nr Carpentras

Excellent naturist site with enormous range of amenities and activities.

By any standards, this is an excellent site and the extent to which the owners
have created a site in harmony with the Provencal countryside is remarkable.
The ambience is essentially relaxed and comfortable. English is spoken widely
amongst the staff and customers. The site has been developed to provide an
area in which to stay and an area in which to 'play', joined by a short pedestrian
tunnel. There are 25 marked and numbered pitches, but the majority of the 200
pitches are unmarked and informally arranged - you simply find a place
amongst the many varieties of trees and shrubs - oaks, olives, pines, acacias,
broom, lavender, etc. Electrical points (12A) are plentiful but you may need a
long cable. The emphasis is on informality and concern for the environment,
and during the high season, cars (and pets) are banned from the camping area -
there is ample parking nearby, mostly shaded - and this provides not only an air
of tranquillity, but safety for children.

So far as naturism is ·concerned, the emphasis is on personal choice (and
weather conditions!), the only stipulation being the requirement for complete
nudity in the pool and pool area. The facilities in general are what you would
expect from a four-star site, although some of the sanitary blocks are a little
'different'. The newer ones are of a standard type and excellent quality, with
free hot showers in cubicles with separators, washbasins (H&C) in private
cabins and British WCs. Older ones are well maintained and different in that
the hot showers are open air, separated by natural stone dividers. Numerous
washing up areas, with H&C, again mostly open air. Laundry facilities.

The leisure park includes numerous sports facilities, including two good tennis
courts and three swimming pools (one is open and heated April - Oct.). The
largest is for swimming/relaxation, the smaller one for watersports and the
smallest for young children and there are ample, very attractive sunbathing
areas around the pools. Apart from the pools, the old Mas (Provencal
farmhouse) houses many activities including a virtually sound-proof disco and
the restaurant/bar and terrace. The leisure park is an unspoiled area of natural
'parkland', with an orchard, fishpond and woodland (with many small animals
such as squirrels), and blends well with the surrounding countryside. It is
possible to walk into Bédoin - the market is fascinating. The variety of
activities available at Bélezy is one of the most extensive we have ever
encountered. To mention but a few, they include painting courses, language
lessons, archery, music (bring your own instrument), a sauna and guided walks
with a guide. There is also a (little used) TV room and of course the usual
boules, table tennis and large scale chess set. A Hydrotherapy centre offers
courses of massages, steam baths, acupuncture and a variety of other treatments
including osteopathy and Chinese medicine (on payment). You can use your
holiday to tone up and revitalise, with qualified diagnosis. There is a reasonably
priced shop and a small boutique selling a range of good quality souvenirs and
even clothes! The restaurant, with bar/terrace, provides both waiter service and
takeaway meals again at reasonable prices. Child minding. Mobile homes,
bungalows, etc. to let. All in all, we continue to be impressed both with the site
itself and with the French approach to naturism and the environment.

Directions: From the A7 autoroute or the RN7 at Orange, take the D950
southeast to Carpentras, then northeast via the D974 to Bédoin. The site is
signposted in Bédoin, being about 2 km. northeast of the village.

Charges 1993:
-- Per person Ffr 42.00 -
53.00, acc. to season; child
(3-7 yrs) half price;
electricity 17.50; pitch with
water, drainage and sink +
14.00. Recreation fee (high
season) 3.80 per night, per
person (child 1.90).

Open:
April - October.

Address:
B.P. 3, 84410 Bédoin.

Tel:
90.65.60.18.
FAX: 90.65.94.45.

Reservations:
Write with deposit of 25%
of total charge (includes
fee of Ffr. 20 and
cancellation insurance 120)

RHÔNE VALLEY
Ain - Rhône - Drôme - Ardèche - Loire

The Rhône Valley is one of Europe's main arteries - this traditional route carries millions of travellers and millions of tons of freight - by rail (TGV), by Autoroute and by water - to the Mediterranean area. However, either side of this busy corridor are areas of great interest and natural beauty; the sun-baked Drôme, with its ever changing landscapes, culminating in the isolated mountains of the Vercors, the spectacularly beautiful Ardèche, with its gorges, the Doubes ornothological reserve, with its rare waterbirds, and Lyons. They just touch the surface of what is available to the visitor. The Rhône Valley enjoys a very high reputation for food and wine, and first rate meals can be had at simple country auberges, as well as at first-class restaurants. Take a break from the stress of driving the RN7 or A7 and enjoy what the Rhône Valley has to offer.

0702 Camping-Caravaning L'Ardechois, St. Sauveur-de-Montagut
Well equipped site in spectacular setting.

This site is quite a way off the beaten track with a steep and windy approach (now improved). It is worth the effort, however, to find such an attractive hillside site offering first class amenities and a variety of different types of pitch. All 95 pitches have electricity (3, 6, 10 or 15A) and are said to be 100 sq.m. Some are situated alongside the small fast-flowing river, while the rest (60%) are on higher, sloping ground nearer the restaurant/bar with steep, gravelled access roads which are not so good for large units. Many are separated by trees and plants. The main sanitary block, bar/restaurant, shop and `salle de jeux' (more or less sound-proof!) have been created by the careful conversion of old buildings and provide modern amenities in an attractive style. (Shop, bar and takeaway open 10/6, restaurant (15/5-end Sept). TV. Table tennis. Heated swimming pool, open from end of May, with bar, snack bar and terrace. The sanitary facilities are good, providing British toilets, hot showers, washbasins in private cabins, etc, and dishwashing and laundry facilities. A new block of equal quality has been added near to the riverside pitches with facilities for the handicapped and a laundry. Chalets and mobile homes for hire. The owners have developed an extensive and unusual excursion programme for exploring this attractive area on foot or by car. Used by tour operators.

Directions: From the north, follow N86 south from Valence for 12 km. Turn right onto D120 to St. Sauveur de Montagut, then D102 (alongside which site is situated) in direction of Mezilhac. This was very narrow and twisting alongside the river, needing care, but it has now been much improved.

Charges 1994:
-- Per unit incl. 2 persons Ffr 85.00, with electricity 100.00; extra person (incl. children) 20.00; pet 10.00.
-- Less outside July/August and for longer stays.

Open:
Easter - 30 Sept.

Address:
07190 St. Sauveur-de-Montagut.

Tel:
75.66.61.87. (winter: 72.02.11.79). FAX: 78.90.84.38.

Reservations:
Write with deposit (Ffr. 400) and fee (100).

RHONE VALLEY - Ardèche

0703 Camping Soleil Vivarais, Sampzon, nr Ruoms

Attractively situated site beside the Ardèche river, with good swimming pools.

Although in a rural setting, this site offers a range of activities and facilities which will appeal to families with teenage children. These include a large modern swimming pool (22½ x 10½ m.) and smaller children's pool, with ample sunbathing areas. A feature of the site is its very modern and attractive bar/restaurant with several terraces, offering a wide range of meals including takeaway meals, pizzas, etc. There is also a quite large disco (soundproofed we understand) adjacent to the bar/restaurant.

The site provides some 200 pitches, including several `double' pitches for two families travelling together. The majority have electricity (6-10A) and 33 are serviced. There are 4 sanitary blocks, two modern and of high quality with facilities for the disabled, excellent babies room, dishwashing (H&C) and 2 washing machines. The other blocks are older, but with washbasins in cubicles and free hot water. One block (including the babies' room) is heated for Easter. In addition to the disco, the site provides an `animation' programme, mountain biking, climbing, pot holing and canoeing and rafting on the river. Large shop. Sports available include tennis, archery, handball, water polo, minigolf, table tennis, volleyball, basketball, badminton and petanque. Children's playground and child minding. Games room. TV. Bicycle hire. Riding, fishing and golf near. Chalets, mobile homes and tents to hire. Motorcaravan service point.

Directions: At St. Just on the RN86 (west side of the Rhône south of Montélimar) take the D290 westward to Vallon Pont d'Arc, then via the D579 towards Ruoms, turning left to site across the river. Alternatively via Villeneuve-de-Berg take N102 and D579 to Ruoms.

Charges 1994:
-- Per pitch incl. 2 persons and car Ffr. 80.00 - 120.00; extra person 18.00 - 24.00; child (under 7 yrs) free - 12.00; electricity 17.00; local tax 1.00.
-- Less outside 24/6 - 25/8.

Open:
Easter - 30 Sept.

Address:
Sampzon, 07120 Ruoms.

Tel:
75.39.67.56.
FAX: 75.93.97.10.

Reservations:
Write to site with deposit (Ffr 500) and fee (80).

EXCELLENT SITE FOR FAMILIES WITH TEENAGERS

★ ★ ★ ★

- Animation programme with six animators
- Canoeing, Rafting, Climbing
- Mountain biking, Pot holing
- Tennis, Table tennis, Mini golf
- Volleyball, Basketball, Handball
- Archery, Waterpolo, Petanque

Chalets, Mobile Homes and Tents to Hire
For information or reservation Tel. 75 39 67 56.
Camping Soleil Vivarais, Sampzon, 07120 Ruoms

Please show reception staff this Guide when you arrive at a site

- it helps them, us and eventually you too

0704 Camping La Rouveyrolle, Casteljau, nr Les Vans

Attractive, family run site in peaceful surroundings beside the Chassezac river gorge.

Family run and aimed at families, this is a very tranquil site by the river in attractive countryside with vineyards and orchards. There are 100 good sized pitches here, all with electricity (3 or 5 A), on flat grass, some with ample shade and others with less for those preferring the sun. The site has a relaxed atmosphere and provides good facilities for families, including an attractively shaped swimming pool, positioned to catch the sun all day. It was built by the site in 1990 after the water level in the river dropped following the building of a dam upstream. The site offers a pleasant bar/restaurant serving a range of meals including takeaway. The sanitary facilities are situated in two modern blocks providing free hot showers in cubicles with separator, and some seatless WCs although the majority are French type. There are part covered washing up and laundry areas, including a washing machine, a shop, tennis courts and a children's playground. River beach (100 m.) with swimming and canoeing if water level permits. Near Cévennes and the Gorges of the Ardèche (20 km). Riding and pot-holing near. Mobile homes, tents and caravans for hire.

Directions: From the A7 at Montélimar, take the D102 west to Aubenas, then the D104, south through Joyeuse and the hamlet of Chandolas. Turn right just after the bridge over the Chassezac and right again to site.

Charges 1993:
-- Per unit incl. 2 persons Ffr 49.00 - 90.00, acc. to season; extra person 14.00 - 25.00; child (under 7 yrs) free, (7-16 yrs) 11.00 - 20.00; electricity 15.00.

Open:
1 April - 30 Sept.

Address:
Casteljau,
07460 Berrias et Casteljau.

Tel:
75.39.00.67.
FAX: 75.39.07.28.

Reservations:
Write to site.

0705 Camping-Caravaning Ranc Davaine, St. Alban Auriolles, Ruoms

'Lively but tasteful' - family orientated site in southern Ardèche.

This is a quite large site with an extensive programme of entertainments, especially for families with small children. Although lively, there is nothing 'tacky' about it - even the background music in the attractive partly open air restaurant beside the pool was Baroque, and listening to Bach, Handel and Vivaldi makes a change from Johnny Halliday. The 300 pitches, all of at least reasonable size, are all supplied with electricity (3, 6 or 10A.) and are situated on fairly flat, rather stony, ground under a variety of trees giving plenty of shade. There is an attractive, large, irregularly shaped swimming pool overlooked by terraces and the bar/restaurant which serves a good range of meals in very pleasant surroundings, made more attractive in the evenings by the lighting and floodlighting. The entertainment programme (July/Aug) is extensive and varied with a particular emphasis on the participation by younger children in a quite imaginative way.

The five sanitary blocks are all of a good standard, with British seatless WCs, hot showers with dividers and many washbasins in private cabins. Washing machines, dryer and irons. Amenities include a takeaway, pizzeria, large shop, children's play area, tennis, table tennis, archery, minigolf and an extensive programme of watersports and excursions on and to the river Ardèche.

Directions: Continue south on D111 after Ruoms. Turn left just before Grospierres on D246, across bridge and then left in the direction of Chandolas to site.

Charges 1993:
-- Per unit incl. 2 persons Ffr. 80.00 - 120.00; extra adult, 22.00 - 26.00: child, 16.00 - 20.00; electricity 17.00.

Open:
1 April - 30 September.

Address:
St. Alban Auriolles,
07120 Ruoms.

Tel:
75.39.60.55.
FAX: 75.39.38.50.

Reservations:
Made with deposit (Ffr 600) and fee (120). Write or FAX site.

6901 Camping International de Lyon, Lyon

Modern overnight site just off autoroute A6 with swimming pool.

Camping International is kept busy with overnight trade and reception and the café (in main season) are open until quite late. There are 150 separate numbered plots with electricity in most parts. Those for caravans are mostly on hardstandings on a slight slope, with another small grassy part, while those for tents are on a flatter area of grass. The 3 sanitary blocks are good, with free hot water (solar heated) in all basins, good showers and sinks; in most blocks basins are in cabins. Amenities on site include a TV room, table tennis, a children's playground, medical service and a smallish swimming pool. Some basic provisions are kept in the café, but a very large commercial centre has been developed just outside the site, with 8 hotels, restaurants, supermarket, petrol station, etc.

Directions: Do not take new A46 motorway around Lyon, but continue on A6 autoroute and take exit marked 'Limonest, Dardilly, Porte de Lyon' about 8 km. north of the Lyon tunnel; at once turn left for Porte de Lyon.

Charges 1994:
-- Per person Ffr. 16.00; child (7-15 yrs) 10.00, under 7 free; tent pitch 32.00; motorcaravan 40.00; caravan: 1 axle 40.00, 2 axles 80.00; extra car 50.00; electricity 11.00; local tax 1.00 (child 0.50).
Open:
1 March - 31 Oct.
Address:
Porte de Lyon,
69570 Dardilly.
Tel:
78.35.64.55.
Reservations:
Made if you write, but there is usually space.

2603 Camping Le Grand Lierne, Chabeuil, nr Valence

Conveniently and attractively situated family site on the route south.

In addition to its obvious attraction as an overnight stop, convenient to the A7 autoroute, this site provides a pleasant situation to explore this little known area between the Ardèche and the Vercors mountains and the Côte du Rhône wine area . The site has 134 marked pitches, mainly separated by hedges or oak trees, with good shade. They are set on flat grass and all have electricity (4-10A). There is a feeling of spaciousness and the site offers good views to the mountains on either side of the valley. A varied entertainment programme has a particular emphasis on activities for children, with the possibility of various excursions, both organised and informal. A disco for teenagers is organised by the owner's sons but is well managed to avoid noise. Two heated swimming pools, one covered in low season (no bermuda shorts allowed in pool) and children's pool. A bar/snack bar with terrace provides both 'eating in' and takeaway service including pizzas (facilities open all season).

The two modern sanitary blocks provide hot showers, with separators and hooks, seatless WCs and washbasins in private cabins with warm water, razor points, etc. Facilities for the handicapped and even a tiny WC for small children. Partly under cover dishwashing area (H&C). Washing machines and dryer. Other amenities include a shop, tennis, children's playgrounds and trampoline, minigolf, table tennis, volleyball, a football field, small climbing wall and bicycles for hire. Library. Bureau de change. Fridge rental. Golf, archery, riding and hang gliding near. American motorhomes not accepted. Bungalows, chalets and tents for hire. No pets allowed. The site is used by an international tour operator and the owners wish to keep a balance between nationalities and are also keen to encourage rallies and will arrange visit programmes. English spoken.

Directions: Site is signposted in Chabeuil about 11 km. east of Valence (18 km. from autoroute). It is best to approach Chabeuil from the south side of Valence via the Valence ring road, thence onto the D68 to Chabeuil itself.

Charges 1994:
-- Prices outside July/Aug. in brackets.
-- Per unit, incl. 2 persons and electricity (4A) Ffr 115.00 (92.00); extra person 29.00; child (under 7 yrs) 20.00 (free); electricity (10A) 15.00; water/drainage 15.00.
Open:
12 May - 25 Sept.
Address:
BP.8, 26120 Chabeuil.
Tel:
75.59.83.14.
FAX: 75.59.87.95.
Reservations:
Accepted with deposit (Ffr. 500) and fee (100).

2602 Castel Camping du Château de Sénaud, Albon, nr Tournon

Night stop with swimming pool, near N7 south of Vienne.

Château du Sénaud makes a satisfactory stopover on the way to the Riviera. It has a fair number of permanent caravans used at weekends, but there are also some 140 pitches in tourist parts with their own toilet blocks, and you should find space. Shade and electrical connections are available. There is a swimming pool, (open perhaps late June - Sept., depending on weather) and a tennis court. Five small, somewhat elderly sanitary blocks have constant hot water in basins, showers and sinks, British and continental toilets and washbasins in private cabins. Provision shop (late June - mid-Sept). Bar and takeaway (July/Aug). Table tennis. Bowling alley. Minigolf. Golf course adjacent. Simple general room. Possibly some noise from the autoroute.

Directions: Leave autoroute at Chanas exit, proceed south along N7 for 8 km. then east near Le Creux de la Thine to camp. From south you should leave autoroute at Tain-Tournon exit and proceed north, approaching camp on D122 through St. Vallier then take D172 towards Anneyron to camp entrance.

Charges guide:
-- Per person 18.50 Ffr; child (under 7) 10.00; pitch 27.00; electricity 14.00.

Open:
1 March - 31 Oct.

Address:
26140 Albon.

Tel:
75.03.11.31.

Reservations:
Made with deposit for min. 3 nights.

Camping - Caravanning
"Château de Senaud"
ALBON (Drôme)
Your night stop or holiday centre in the Rhone Valley

The famous Senaud castle, between Lyon and Valence, has been placed at the disposal of campers and caravanners by the Comtesse d'Armagnac.

In the huge century-old park you can go for wonderful walks. There is a swimming pool for your relaxation, a tennis court, fishing in the lake. The sanitary installations are modern, of course, with showers and hot water.

Only 2 km. from the RN7, the Château de Senaud offers you complete quiet and repose and very good amenities

LARGE NEW PART OF CAMP RESERVED FOR FOREIGN TOURISTS

Please make us aware of your experiences at these or other sites.

See Readers' Reports on page 181

SAVOY - Haute-Savoie

SAVOY
Savoie - Haute-Savoie

The Savoy Region, of which the Savoyards are justly proud, has been called 'the ceiling of Europe' and many of its snow-capped peaks are more than 4,000 metres above sea-level, with Mont Blanc, at 4807m, Europe's highest mountain. It is an area of pine and larch forests, fast running streams and high glaciers, clean air and lovely lakes. Not only is there snow skiing for much of the year, there are many other outdoor activities available. Within the region are many old and interesting towns such as Annecy, Aix-les-Bains, Evian and Chambery, as well as purpose built resorts for both winter and summer visitors. Italy and Switzerland are both within easy reach for day excursions.

7401 Camping Les Deux Glaciers, Les Bossons, nr Chamonix
Well kept mountain site close to well known resort.

A pleasant little summer or winter site, Les Deux Glaciers has about 100 individual pitches on terraces or single plots, levelled out of quite steeply rising ground, with electricity available in all areas. Well laid out with different trees - and floral displays in their season - it is well tended and maintained. It is quietly situated with fine views of the high mountains around but, being a northern slope, it loses the sun a little early. The two small sanitary blocks, both heated in cool weather, should suffice. They have British toilets, at least half the washbasins in private cabin with shelf and mirror, and free hot water in all basins and showers and most of sinks. The site reports a new snack restaurant (11/6-15/9). Mobile traders call in season, otherwise 500 m. to shop. On site is a general room, table tennis and a washing machine and drying room. The site becomes full for much of July/Aug. and is not keen on reservations but could make some for Britons, so try. If not reserved, in season arrive early.

Directions: From west take 2nd road leading off main N506 to right for Les Bossons, which takes you direct to site. From east turn right at sign for 'Les Bossons', then left at T-junction, and on to camp.

Charges 1994:
-- Per unit with 2 persons Ffr. 57.00; extra person 19.00; child (under 7) 9.50; local tax 1.00; electricity 10.00 (2A).
-- Less in low seasons, slightly higher in winter.

Open:
All year except 15/11 - 15/12.

Address:
Les Bossons 74400 Chamonix.

Tel:
50.53.15.84.

Reservations:
May be possible - see text.

7403 Camping Le Belvedere, Annecy
Hillside camp with good views over lake, in lovely area.

Annecy is a attractive town in a beautiful setting at the head of the lake of the same name. The old centre is intersected by flower decked canals and also has historical interest. There is much to see and do in this region in both summer and winter with Geneva and the high Alps nearby. Le Belvedere, as its name implies, overlooks the lake and is the nearest camp to the town. It is now under private management on lease from the town authorities. There are hardstanding terraces for caravans (all pitches have electricity) and grass areas for tents. One small area is reserved for groups. Tall pines and steep hillside back the site on the west and small trees decorate the site without giving much shade. The three modern sanitary blocks are around the camp, one heated in cold weather and with a washroom for the disabled. There is a room for games with pool, table tennis, a good children's playground and one may swim in the lake. In July and August, singers and clowns amuse the children. This is a neat and tidy camp which is ideally placed for visiting Annecy.

Directions: From the town centre follow signs for 'Camping Municipal' towards Albertville on road N508. Turn right to follow sign for 'Hopital' up hill and take first left after passing this towards Semnoz and camp.

Charges 1993:
-- Per person Ffr. 20.00; child (under 7 yrs) 10.00; car 5.70; large tent, caravan or motorcaravan 31.00; small tent 20.00; dog 5.00; extra car 10.00; electricity 20.00; local tax (1/6-31/8) 1.00.

Open:
Easter - 30 Oct.

Address:
Rte. de Semnoz, 74000 Annecy.

Tel:
50.45.48.30.
FAX: 50.45.55.56.

Reservations:
Necessary for July/Aug. - write to site.

7301 Camping Le Bois Joli, La Chambre, nr St. Martin-sur-la-Chambre

Very pleasant rural site in mountain area.

If you are looking for somewhere different, off the beaten track or happen to be passing on the N90 from Albertville to Modane and the Frejus tunnel to Italy, this might well be a good stopping place. Le Bois Joli (roughly speaking `pretty woodland' - which it certainly is) is in wooded country in a most peaceful situation. There are 70 grass pitches, all with electrical connections, in small terraced clearings and the site is divided by a minor road. Every effort has been made to disturb the natural habitat as little as possible and, although the camping area could be increased to accommodate more people, the owners like it as it is and will not do this. There are two sanitary blocks, one older one (which has been refurbished) near the swimming pool (free) and a new, pre-fabricated one in the other section. British and continental toilets. Laundry and dishwashing sinks. There is a kiosk with a terrace for drinks, takeaway food and basic food supplies and a bar with rest room which may become a restaurant in time. Two children's play areas and table tennis. This is a delightful site run by a very helpful and pleasant family. They organise guided walks by a qualified guide and games for children in high season.

Directions: From N90 take road D75 at Le Chambre and follow signs to camp, 1 km. northeast of St. Avre.

Charges 1994:
-- Per unit incl. 2 persons Ffr. 50.00; extra person 20.00; child (under 7 yrs) 12.00; electricity 12.00 - 18.00, acc. to amps.

Open:
1 June - 15 Sept.

Address:
73130 St. Avre-la-Chambre.

Tel:
79.59.42.30 or 79.56.21.28.

Reservations:
Write to site.

7302 Camping-Caravaneige Le Versoyen, Bourg-St. Maurice, Les Arcs

Good quality mountain site open all year.

Bourg-St. Maurice is situated on a small, level plain at an altitude of 830 m. on the River L'Isère, surrounded by high mountains. For many years a winter ski-ing resort, it now caters for visitors all year round. The Parc National de la Vanoise is near, along with a wealth of interesting places. Le Versoyen attracts visitors all year round except for October when they close. Trees usually seen at this altitude give shade in some parts. The flat, grass pitches, divided by young trees and numbered by stones, are on either side of tarmac roads. Duckboards are provided for snow and wet weather and hardstandings for motorcaravans (also service area). Some 75% of the pitches have electrical connections. The two sanitary blocks, acceptable but not luxurious, are in separate places on the camp and the provision may be hard pressed in high season. They have mixed British seatless and continental WCs. There is a heated rest room with TV and laundry facilities. Restaurants and shops are 1½ km, tennis and swimming pool 300 m. and there is a park for walking. The site makes a good base for winter ski-ing and summer walking, climbing and car excursions.

Directions: Site is 1½ km. east of Bourg-St. Maurice on CD119 Les Arcs road.

Charges 1994:
-- Per person Ffr. 20.00; child (2-7 yrs) 12.00; caravan or motorcaravan 18.00; small tent 10.00; electricity 21.00 - 44.00, acc. to amps.

Open:
All year except Oct.

Address:
73700 Bourg-St. Maurice.

Tel:
79.07.03.45.

Reservations:
Write to site.

All the sites featured in this Guide are regularly inspected by our team of experienced site assessors

WESTERN LOIRE
Mayenne - Sarthe - Maine-et-Loire - Vendée - Loire-Atlantique

The Western Loire region's five dèpartements, to the south of Brittany, have become increasingly popular with British visitors, involving no more than a day's drive from the Channel ports. The region includes a wide range of attractions, including the beaches of the Vendée, châteaux on the Loire, Le Mans 24 hour sports car race and the Parc Regional de Brière, north of St. Nazaire. The coastline extends from the sophisticated resort of La Baule in the north to La Tranche in the south. Inland areas are less well known, but well worth a visit.

4404 Castel Camping Parc Sainte-Brigitte, La Turballe, nr La Baule
Well established site in the grounds of a manor house, 3 km. from beaches.

A fairly small site, Ste. Brigitte has about 200 individual pitches, which are of good size. Some are in a park-like setting near the entrance, about 25 with electricity and water connections. A further 25 are in a wooded area under tall trees, with the remainder on more open grass, with an un-marked area in addition near the pool. One can walk around much of the areas of the estate not used for camping and there is a TV/sitting room next to the manor house. The main sanitary block has free hot water in all facilities and is of fair quality. It offers British toilets, washbasins in private cabins, with bidets for women; free hot water in basins, fully controllable showers, and sinks. Water taps around. Washing machines and dryer (no washing to be hung out on pitches - lines provided). Children's playground and table tennis. Swimming pool, solar heated, with children's pool also (open from mid-June), shop (July/Aug. only but baker calls also) and restaurant/bar with takeaway (mid June - early Sept). A quiet place to stay outside the main season, with few facilities open; in high season, however, it is mainly used by families with its full share of British visitors and can become very busy. Facilities then are put under considerable pressure. Inland from the main road, it is a little under 3 km. from the nearest beach; variety of sandy ones near with safe bathing. It has a comprehensive reservation system and advance booking normally required for July/Aug.

Directions: Entrance is off the La Turballe-Guérande road D99, 3 km. east of La Turballe.

Charges 1993:
-- Per person Ffr 22.00 plus 1.00 tax; child (under 7) 15.00; pitch 23.00; with water and electricity 47.00; car 12.00; dog 6.00.

Open:
1 April - 30 Sept.

Address:
44420 La Turballe.

Tel:
40.23.30.42.

Reservations:
Made for any length with exact dates and recommended for July/Aug, with deposit (Ffr. 310) plus fee (90).

4401 Camping du Val du Cens, Nantes

Well kept town site providing good night halt and equipped for all year caravanning.

This modern municipal site, which is within the town limits, is well maintained and of good quality. It has some 122 flat good-sized hardstandings for caravans, all with electricity, water and drainaway. From Easter - 30 Sept. it also takes about 80 tents on separate meadows. At certain times the caravan pitches become full with those working in the town or visiting for commercial reasons; however, in the holiday season, it is said that about half are available for tourists and one should usually find a space.

The four sanitary blocks are good, with British toilets, individual basins in cubicles or cabins with shelf and light, and free hot water throughout including the showers. Facilities for disabled. Amenities on site include a shop (high season only), a launderette, TV room, children's play area and football pitches on the nearby Hippodrome can be used for play areas. A swimming pool, ice rink, bowling alley and café are very close. Golf near. A reader reports that public transport within the town is cheap and reliable and the site is easily reached by bus from the railway station.

Directions: Site is on the northern edge of the town on the Bvd. Petit Port, near the university (ring road east).

Charges 1994:
-- Per caravan incl. car or motorcaravan Ffr 40.00; tent plus car 30.00, without car 20.00; per person 15.00; child (under 7) 10.00; electricity (6A) 10.00 (summer) - 15.00 (winter).

Open: All year.

Tel: 40.74.47.94. FAX: 40.73.44.19.

Reservations: Not made, but you could phone the previous day.

NANTES CAMPING-CARAVANNING

VAL DU CENS
★★★★
21, bd du Petit port
44300 NANTES
Tél. 40 74 47 94
Fax. 40 73 44 19

Close to
The Leisure Centre of Petit Port with:
☆ Swimming ☆ Skating ☆ Bowling
☆ Billiards ☆ Restaurant

NANTES-ERDRE Golf Course and town centre (tramway)

200 tourist pitches equipped with all services including drainage.

OPEN ALL YEAR

4402 Camping de l'Eve, St. Nazaire

Satisfactory, large site close to beach between St. Nazaire and La Baule.

Formerly a municipal site, Camping de l'Eve is an orderly site almost on the edge of the sea which would satisfy the requirements of most campers (without perhaps being really exceptional). It offers about 400 individual marked-out pitches (many with electricity) which are separated by means of low hedges and accessible by tarmac roads, giving a neat, cared-for appearance. A sandy beach, supervised by lifeguards during the main season, is on the other side of the road, with direct access through an underground passage in one corner of the site. The six sanitary blocks, probably adequate except maybe right at the peak, are not luxurious and not always impeccable. British and continental toilets; washbasins with cold water in small groups or private cabins; free hot showers, mostly in a large separate block. At the entrance is a shopping centre with provisions and a takeaway (all from 15/6). Watersports and fishing nearby and a bus service stops outside the site. A popular site, it is mostly full from late June to late Aug. Reservations are not made, so it clearly pays to arrive early.

Directions: Site is west of St. Nazaire close to St. Marc-sur-Mer. From D92 La Baule - St. Nazaire road, follow signs to St. Marc-sur-Mer (D292 or D492) and site is E of village on coast road.

Charges guide:
-- Per pitch, incl. 3 persons 54.00 Ffr; extra person 12.00; child (under 7 yrs) 7.00; electricity 16.00.

Open: 18 May - 15 Sept

Tel: 40.91.90.65.

Reservations: Not made.

4403 Castel Camping Le Pré du Château, La Baule

Select, quiet, little camp for caravans and motorcaravans only.

In the grounds of the Château de Careil (a building dating from the 14th century which may be visited) this attractive small site, shaded by mature trees contains less than 50 good-sized individual pitches, all equipped with electricity, water and drainaway. Strictly speaking, it is only open to caravans or motorcaravans, though children's tents beside caravans are permitted and they MAY accept tents outside the main season. It is a simple site with a quiet atmosphere. Some essential provisions are kept (supermarket near). Cooked dishes to order in high season. Children's playground. Washing machine - laundry service at times. TV Room. Volleyball. The sanitary facilities, in converted outbuildings, are small with British toilets, cubicles for washing, and free hot water everywhere. New facilities have been added for the disabled. There is a small heated swimming pool (11 x 5m.) and a sauna on site.

Directions: Take D92 road from Guérande to La Baule and turn east to Careil before the town. From the D99 Guérande - St. Nazaire road, turn on to D92, following signs to `Intermarche'. Site is signposted after store.

Charges 1994:
-- Per unit all-inclusive with 2 persons Ffr 110.00, extra person 25.00; local tax 1.00.

Open:
Easter - 30 Sept.

Address:
Careil, 44350 Guérande.

Tel:
40.60.22.99.

Reservations:
Necessary for July/Aug. and made for min. 1 week, with deposit and fee.

LE PRÉ DU CHATEAU DE CAREIL

Small luxury camping site with sanitary installations
comparable to those of a hotel.
Close to the marvellous free sandy beach of La Baule, and to many other
good beaches and attractive places such as the old town of Guérande (5 km.)
Heated swimming pool.

Particularly agreeable in spring, when climate is good and prices lower

4406 Hotel de Plein Air Camping de Pouldroit, Piriac-sur-Mer

Pleasant campsite on the outskirts of small, unspoilt fishing and yachting port of Piriac.

With the medieval town of Guérande and the popular seaside resort of La Baule only a few miles away, Pouldroit, within walking distance of the beaches, offers an attractive base for this area. The site gives a sense of spaciousness, with 280 clearly marked, level pitches, either open or shady, in a series of connecting fields with some shade. Electricity is available on about half of them. There is a heated swimming pool at the far end of the site with a snack bar area and new games and TV room overlooking. The site prides itself on its many sporting activities (high season) of which archery is the most unusual. Free, professional instruction for beginners to Olympic standard available. Also children's play area, a shop, 2 tennis courts, volleyball, billiards and table tennis, Bicycle hire in village (600 m.). Sailing, windsurfing, fishing and horse riding nearby. The sanitary installations are of good standard, with British WCs, free hot water everywhere, including washing up and laundry sinks. Washing machine and dryer. A well maintained site, which is supervised by friendly staff.

Directions: Site signposted north of Piriac town, on the D52 road to Mesquer.

Charges 1994:
-- Per person Ffr. 24.00; child (under 7) 14.00; pitch 21.00; car 19.00; electricity 4A 20.00, 10A 32.00; water and drainage 20.00; local tax (Jul/Aug) 1.00. -- Less 10% outside 15/6-26/8.

Open:
1 April - 30 Sept.

Address:
44420 Piriac-sur-Mer.

Tel:
40.23.50.91.
FAX: 40.23.69.12.

Reservations:
Made with deposit (Ffr. 300) and fee (120).

OR CARAVANNING IN EUROPE...

Let Eurocamp Independent handle all your camping and caravanning holiday arrangements. We'll book your ferries and sites, arrange insurance and even supply your route directions. All this is backed by 20 years' experience of providing trouble-free holidays.

Be as flexible as you want to be, choosing from 180 superb sites in 9 countries. Our prices are such good value, you'll find it always pays to go with Eurocamp Independent.

Phone now for your free Eurocamp Independent brochure.

☎ 0565 625544

Eurocamp Independent

SITE AND FERRY RESERVATION SERVICE

EUROCAMP INDEPENDENT
PRINCESS STREET, KNUTSFORD, CHESHIRE WA16 6BN

ABTA

NO
STAMP
REQUIRED

Eurocamp Independent
FREEPOST,
KNUTSFORD,
Cheshire
WA16 67BR

Will you book a holiday independently?

Go to town to buy books on Europe and recommended sites.

Decide on an area and choose a site.

Write or phone abroad to book a site.

Site full. Start again!

Await information.

Pay site in foreign currency.

You've found a site, now decide on a ferry crossing.

Ring ferry operator, or visit travel agent to book crossing.

Nothing suitable – ring other operators.

Pay now for ferry.

Write to foreign tourist office for local information.

Arrange personal and car breakdown insurance.

Pay now for insurances.

Go to shops to buy road atlas and local maps.

Work out a route plan.

Pay site for electricity etc in foreign currency.

Problems on holiday? Who's there to help?

Don't you wish you'd booked with Eurocamp Independent?

Or will you book Eurocamp Independent?

Send off for our brochure.

Choose a site from 180 of Europe's very best.

Choose a ferry crossing from the widest choice of routes.

Telephone Eurocamp Independent and book everything with just one call.

Pay in sterling 10 weeks prior to departure.

Receive free comprehensive maps, guides and route plan before you leave.

Sit back and enjoy a trouble-free holiday!

Please send me a copy of your free colour brochure   GCf01

Name Mr/Mrs/Miss _____

Address _____

_____

_____   Postcode _____

Age range of children living at home _____

In which month are you planning to take holiday _____

Do you have: tent ☐   trailer tent ☐   caravan ☐   motorhome ☐

☐ Tick if you do not wish to receive direct mail from other carefully screened companies whose products or services we feel may be of interest.

SITE AND FERRY RESERVATION SERVICE

4405 Camping La Falaise, La Turballe, nr La Baule

Site beside beach and a short walk from resort centre.

This camp is unusually situated right by the edge of the sea with direct access to a beach of sand and rocks and it is also a walk of only some 600 m. to the centre of the village of La Turballe. It may therefore appeal to many. There is good bathing from a beach just along from the site, especially at high tide. The 150 pitches, on flat sandy/grassy ground with very little shade, are individual ones in rows separated mainly by low hedges but some by stones on frontage. They vary a bit in size but are mostly near 100 sq.m.; about 120 have water taps and 80 electricity. The central toilet block is of good size and fair quality, with mixed continental and British WCs, washbasins not in cabins but with free hot water, and good fully controllable free hot showers. Washing machine and dishwasher. Only bread, milk etc. are kept on site and there is a limited takeaway and drinks service in season. TV room. Exchange facilities. There are few other special on-site amenities as the village, with a supermarket (100 m.) and restaurants, is so near. No tour operators but a few mobile homes to let.

Directions: Site is where the main D99 road joins the western exit road from La Turballe.

Charges guide:
-- Per unit, up to 3 persons with water 117.00 Ffr; with electricity (4A) also 136.00; extra person 19.00; child (up to 4 years) free; visitor 19.00; extra car 9.50; local tax 1.00 per day 15/6-31/8.

Open:
25 March - 31 Oct.

Address:
1 Bvd. de Belmont, 44420 La Turballe.

Tel:
40.23.32.53.

Reservations:
Accepted for min. 7 days, Sat. - Sat. only with fee payable.

WESTERN LOIRE - Loire Atlantique

4407 Parc du Guibel, Piriac-sur-Mer

Unusual site in mature parkland, with swimming pool.

Parc du Guibel has spacious grassy pitches, naturally developed with good shade. There is bird life in abundance, varied species of trees and even red squirrels. It is situated 1 km from the beach and 3½ km. from Piriac. The site is divided by a minor road, one part being more mature and containing reception and a heated pool (l0 x 20 m.) with two smaller children's pools joined by a small slide. This area has been redeveloped to provide a snack bar and takeaway with a terrace around the pool and a shop. The other part of the site has a more open aspect. In total there are 321 pitches of which 250 have electricity. There are also pitches with all services.

There are four toilet blocks, all of slightly different design, with facilities for the handicapped in one. They have British toilets and free hot water and should be an adequate provision with laundry facilities also. Amenities include minigolf, bicycle hire, petanque, volleyball, table tennis and entertainment is organised in season. Mobile homes for rent.

Directions: Take the D52 road from Piriac towards Mesquer and site is signposted; also from D452 in the direction of Kerdien.

Charges 1994:
-- Per person Ffr 22.00; child (under 7) 12.50; pitch 21.00; car 14.00; local tax (15/6-15/9) 3.00 or 1.50 (child); electricity (3-12A) l7.00 - 24.00.
-- Less 20% before 26/4, 10% outside 29/6-30/8.

Open:
Easter - 30 Sept.

Address:
44420 Piriac-sur-Mer.

Tel:
40.23.52.67.

Reservations:
Made with deposit (Ffr. 320) and booking fee (80).

4409 Castel Camping Château de Deffay, Pontchâteau

Quiet, family managed site, near the Côte Armor and Brière Regional Natural Park.

Château de Deffay has a rural setting and has been developed to blend into the natural environment of the estate. The 70 large pitches (150 sq.m) are either wooded and terraced or open, with views of the lake or farm land, most with electricity (6A), some fully serviced. The natural wild life and old farm buildings combine to produce a quiet relaxed atmosphere.

The main sanitary block has been designed to be unobtrusive, in an old barn, but is well equipped with modern free controllable hot showers, British type toilets, washbasins in cabins with hooks and shelves. Provision for the handicapped and a baby bathroom have now been added and there are washing machines, dryer and a dishwasher. Extra facilities are available in the old courtyard area of the smaller château (dating back to before 1400) which is also where the bar/restaurant (with takeaway), well stocked shop and solar heated swimming pool and paddling pool are located. The larger château (built in 1880) and another lake stand away from this area providing pleasant walking and there are weekly dinners in the château. The reception has been built separately to contain the camping area. There is a play area for children on grass, a TV room with table tennis, `animation' in season, tennis and swimming, paddle boating and fishing in the lake. Riding. Golf (5 km.). The Guérande Peninsula, La Baule Bay and the natural wilderness of the `Grande Brière' are all nearby. Ten alpine type chalets for letting have been built overlooking the lake and fit well with the environment.

Directions: Site is signposted from the D33 Pontchâteau to Herbignac road near Ste. Reine.

Charges 1994:
-- Per pitch simple Ffr 49.00, with electricity (4A) 68.00; with 3 services 85.00; per adult 20.00; child (3-12 yrs) 13.00.
-- Less outside high season.

Open:
15 May - 15 Sept.

Address:
Ste. Reine, 44160 Pontchâteau.

Tel:
40.88.00.57. (winter: 40.01.63.84) FAX: 40.01.66.55.

Reservations:
Accepted for a min. period of 6 nights with deposit (Ffr. 300) and fee (80).

4901 Castel Camping L'Etang de la Brèche, Varennes-sur-Loire, nr Saumur

Peaceful, spacious family site with swimming pool, adjacent to the Loire.

Towards the western end of the Loire Valley, about 6 km from Saumur, L'Etang de la Brèche provides an ideal base from which to explore the châteaux for which the region is famous and also its abbeys, wine cellars, mushroom caves and Troglodyte villages. Developed within a 12 ha. estate on the edge of the Loire, the site has a feeling of spaciousness and provides 175 large, level pitches with shade from tall trees, facing central grass areas used for recreation and less shaded. Electrical connections to most pitches, water and drainaway on some. The three toilet blocks have all been modernised to a high standard, providing showers with washbasins, hooks, mirrors, and dividers, and separate British WCs. Good hot water supply to washing up sinks, laundry, baby facilities and there are 2 units for the handicapped.

A newly extended restaurant (used by locals as well) blends well with the existing architecture and, together with the bar area, provides a social base to the site and is probably one of the reasons why the site is popular with British tour operators. The site includes a small lake (used for fishing) and wooded area ensuring a quiet, relaxed and rural atmosphere. The enlarged swimming pool complex provides 3 heated pools for youngsters of all ages and there is a well organised entertainment programme. There is a shop, an epicerie, takeaway, pizzeria, general, games and TV rooms. Tennis, field for football, BMX track and child minding is arranged in the afternoons. Torches required at night.

Directions: Site lies 100 m. north off the main N152, about 5 km. southeast of Saumur on the north bank of the Loire.

Charges 1994:
-- Per unit incl. 2 persons Ffr 115.00, 3 persons 126.00; extra adult 22.00; extra child (2-7 yrs) 11.00; electricity 14.00; extra car 20.00.
-- Less in low season.

Open:
15 May - 15 Sept.

Address:
49730 Varennes-sur-Loire.

Tel:
41.51.22.92.
FAX: 41.51.27.24.

Reservations:
Made for min. 7 days with deposit and fee.

4902 Camping de Chantepie, St. Hilaire-St. Florent, Saumur

New, caring site with swimming pools, close to Saumur with lovely views over the Loire.

This medium sized site, created from open, flattish meadows on a high terrace with a panoramic view over the Loire, offers a choice of sunny or more shady pitches as the many trees planted grow to maturity and could provide a good base from which to visit the attractions of the western Loire. The Vendée coast is possible for a day's run. The 193 spacious, grassy pitches, 165 with electrical connections, on one field are well marked and separated by a variety of well chosen flowers and shrubs, with gravel tracks linking them. About a fifth of the pitches are taken by tour operators.

The sanitary provision is exceptionally good in both quantity and quality - if a little scattered between buildings. Hot water is free to washbasins in private cubicles and the many showers of the pushbutton, pre-mixed type. Facilities for the handicapped are particularly noteworthy, with 3 washbasin/shower rooms and at least 2 toilets - the site in fact actively welcomes custom from either institutions caring for, or families with one or more handicapped persons. Other facilities on site include 3 pools (not heated), a bar/restaurant which also serves takeaway food and icecreams, and a small shop. Leisure activities for all ages are well organised with daily entertainment for children and adults in high season. Activities include mountain biking, table tennis, pony rides, donkey or horse and cart rides and an organised family barbecue each week. There are TV, games, video games and reading rooms, a picturesque minigolf, volleyball, well equipped children's play area, BMX bicycles to hire and track, a football field and table tennis. Bureau de change. Fishing permits obtainable

Directions: Site is about 4 km. from Saumur and downstream (NW) of St. Hilaire-St. Florent. From the traffic lights at the southern end of the N147 bypass bridge in Saumur, follow signs to St. Hilaire-St. Florent. Continue northwest, beyond the village limits on D751 and the site is signposted off this road soon after. A further 2 km. to site.

Charges 1994:
-- Per adult Ffr 20.90; child (under 7 yrs) 10.20; pitch incl. car 53.50; electricity 16.00.
-- less 10% in May.

Open:
15 May - 15 Sept.

Address:
St. Hilaire-St. Florent, 49400 Saumur.

Tel:
41.67.95.34.
FAX: 41.67.95.85.

Reservations:
Made for min. 3 nights with Ffr. 300 deposit.

see advertisement opposite

4903 Camping Caravaning Le Val de Loire, Les Rosiers-sur-Loire

Select, quiet site midway between Angers and Saumur.

This is an attractive, well managed site which is ideally situated for exploring many of the Loire châteaux and the Troglodyte villages of the area. The 100 tourist pitches, all over 100 sq.m. and with water, electricity and drainage, are level, grassy and divided by hedges or cordon apple trees providing some shade. Motorhome facilities are very good. The three sanitary blocks have British toilets and the first-class fittings include washbasins in private cabins with hot water, razor points, shelves and mirrors. Showers are pre-set, pushbutton type and each has a dressing area with hooks. There are excellent facilities for the disabled. Washing machines, dryers, iron and ironing board are provided. There is no shop, but milk and bread are delivered daily in July/August and a small supermarket is 400 m. away. No bar or restaurant either - the nearest are at Gennes and Les Rosiers. There is a children's play area, 2 adjoining swimming pools (1 adult, 1 children), table tennis, volleyball, tennis, boules and crazy golf. Extensive water sport facilities may be found on the Loire nearby. TV room with books. A few 'bungalow' tents and mobile homes for hire.

Directions: From Saumur cross the Loire to northern side and take the D952 (signposted Angers) to Les Rosiers. In Les Rosiers turn left (north) onto D59 (signposted Beaufort en Vallée, Longue). Site is a few hundred metres on left and is well signposted.

Charges 1993:
-- Per pitch incl. 3 persons Ffr. 90.00; extra adult or child over 1 yr 24.00; electricity (10A) 9.00.

Open:
1 May - 30 Sept.

Address:
49350 Les Rosiers s. Loire

Tel:
41.51.94.33.

Reservations:
Made with deposit and Ffr. 50 booking fee; no min. length.

CAMPING ★★★★
DE CHANTEPIE

Saint-Hilaire Saint-Florent
49400 Saumur sur la CD751
Tel. 41.67.95.34 Direction Gennes
Open 1st May to 15th September
Panoramic views of the Loire. SWIMMING POOL.
Very beautiful site. Snack restaurant. Bar. Ice Creams.
Shop. Children's Entertainment. Mini Golf.
NEAR BY: Loire Châteaux National Riding School. Mushroom museum. Visit wine cellars.
Canoe or fish on the Loire. Play tennis …

5300 Camping Municipal de Mayenne, Mayenne
Small site next to swimming pool, with many local attractions.

The old port town of Mayenne, 200 km. from Cherbourg, is built on the steep banks of the river of the same name and this small municipal site could make a very pleasant night stop or possible base for visiting the Le Mans 24 hour race (70 km.). Mayenne itself has a cathedral and castle - river cruises are available. The site is also known as Camping M. Raymond Fauque. The 100 pitches are on fairly level grass and include a number right by the river. Most have electrical connections (5 or 10A). There is a fair amount of shade from the many tall, but 'narrow' trees. The river is used for fishing but could be dangerous for young children. The substantially constructed sanitary block, tiled throughout, has hot showers, with dividers, British seatless WCs and (in the ladies section) some washbasins in private cabins. Amenities include a children's play area, small shop/café and a salle de jeux. The town, with all its amenities, is just 800 m. away. There is a large municipal swimming pool right by the site (open July/Aug. - another pool in the town is open at other times), which is used by the community, including school parties.

Directions: Site is situated 0.8 km. north of Mayenne, just off the D23 to Caen, and is signposted from the town.

Charges 1993:
-- Pr unit incl. 3 persons Ffr. 26.00 - 38.00 with pool entry, 25.00 without; electricity (10A) 8.00.

Open:
15 March - 30 September.

Address:
Rte de Brives,
53100 Mayenne.

Tel:
43.04.57.14.

Reservations:
Write to site.

7201 Camping La Route d'Or, La Flèche
Agreeable municipal camp on much used through routes.

This is a useful site to know as La Flèche lies at the junction of the Le Mans-Angers and Laval-Saumur roads, along which Britons frequently travel. Readers report a very friendly welcome and reasonable charges. The site lies on the south bank of the Loir, only a short walk from the town centre where there are plenty of shops and restaurants (neither on site). There are about 300 pitches on flat grass, many in excess of 100 sq.m. and these may now be fully marked out. Electrical connections in all parts but long leads needed in certain places.

The two, adequate sanitary blocks have continental and some British WCs, washbasins with shelf, mirror, and free hot water, which for ladies are all in cabins with light, and for men also in one block, and more limited free hot showers with pre-set water and pushbutton which runs on a bit. Water points around. Hot tap to draw from for sinks. The site also has a very good, separate sanitary block for the disabled. Amenities on site include tennis, boules, a children's playground, pedaloes and canoes for hire on the river, bicycle hire and a laundry room. Caravans and bungalows for hire.

Directions: Site lies in southwest outskirts of town just off D938 road to Saumur and is signposted from a junction on the bypass.

Charges 1993:
-- Per person Ffr. 14.60; child (under 7) 7.30; car 3.90; tent 4.30; caravan 6.30; motorcaravan 14.00; electricity 13.80 - 16.00; local tax 1/6-31/8 1.00. (1994 + 4%)'

Open:
All year.

Address:
Allée de la Providence,
72200 La Flèche.

Tel:
43.94.55.90.

Reservations:
Made without deposit but space is usually available.

WESTERN LOIRE - Sarthe / Vendée

7202 Camping Municipal du Lac, St. Calais
Small municipal site convenient for Le Mans.

St. Calais is a small town some 37 km. east of Le Mans with a small municipal site. Camping du Lac has some 60 marked pitches, all with electricity, on level grass and close to a lake and river. It offers very good value in terms of price. There is a swimming pool adjacent and the site is within walking distance of the town and restaurants. There are two sanitary blocks with British WCs, large hot showers with dividers and some washbasins in private cabins. There are few 'on-site' facilities, but being so close to the town centre this hardly matters. Reception is very welcoming, the value is excellent and this would make a good night stop or base for visiting the Le Mans 24 hour race.

Directions: Signed from N157, site is beside lake north of town, near station.

Charges 1993:
-- Per pitch Ffr. 3.70; adult 6.00; child (under 10 yrs) 3.60; car 3.50; electricity 10.00 (6A), 6.20 (3A).

Open:
1 April - 15 October.

Address:
72120 St. Calais,

Tel:
43.35.04.81.

Reservations:
Write to site.

7203 Castel Camping de Chanteloup, Sillé-le-Philippe, Savigne l'Eveque
Pleasant site 15 km. from Le Mans from which to explore La Sarthe.

Situated in the park of an old château in the heart of the Sarthe countryside, this site has a somewhat faded elegance. There are 100 pitches, some well wooded, some on the lawn and completely open, plus some overlooking the lake, so the degree of shade varies. All are more than 100 sq.m. and about 50% have electricity. There is no special facility for motorhomes, no statics and very little tour operator presence. There are three sanitary blocks formed in the château outbuildings, some in the process of being tiled, but all with good facilities. All toilets are British and washbasins are in private cabins with hot water, razor points and mirrors. Some showers are push button, some operate by chain and all have dressing areas with hooks and shelf. There are undercover dishwashing facilities and a washing machine. A small shop sells only necessities (baker calls daily) and takeaway chicken and chips are available. There is a pleasant bar with terrace in the château. Leisure facilities on site include a swimming pool, children's play area, tennis, volleyball, table tennis and the hire of mountain bikes. Tours of the château grounds and the village by pony and cart are arranged. Games room with baby foot, flipper, pool, draughts, etc. Golf and horse riding 6 km. Good restaurant at Sillé-le-Philippe, a 15 min walk (2 km.) and Savigne L'Eveque (7 km.).

Directions: Site is 15 km. NE of Le Mans. Take D301 Le Mans - Bonnetable road. Sillé-le-Philippe is south of this road and site is well signposted by name.

Charges 1993:
-- Per pitch Ffr. 44.00; adult 23.00; child (under 7 yrs) 12.00; electricity 14.00.

Open:
15 June - 5 Sept.

Address:
Parc de l'Epau, Sillé-le-Philippe, 72460 Savigne l'Eveque.

Tel:
43.76.27.27.
FAX: 43.76.28.28.

Reservations:
No min. length - contact site.

8501 Camping Baie d'Aunis, La Tranche-sur-Mer, nr Les Sables d'Olonne
Small, seaside site with individual pitches and easy access to sandy beach.

Baie d'Aunis really is right by the sea - just walk across a wide car park and you are on a sandy beach which is safer than most here. You can also walk quite easily into town. A special lagoon has been developed in the bay for teaching windsurfing, as La Tranche is a major windsurfing centre. The site, on flat ground, has individual marked-out pitches, mostly about 80 sq.m., and many very sandy. Some small trees give shade and electricity is available (10A). The main sanitary block has been completely rebuilt and is now of an excellent standard, with facilities for the disabled and for babies. There are also facilities in other places, although these may be shut outside the main season and are of only a reasonable standard. Free hot water in basins, showers and sinks; washbasins in private cabins; continental and British toilets. Swimming pool. Shop and restaurant/bar (mid-June - mid-Sept.). A popular site, reservations are essential from mid-June - late August. No dogs accepted in July/Aug.

Directions: Site is on eastern approach to La Tranche; from N747/D46 roundabout turn towards town and site is on left.

Charges 1994:
-- Per unit incl. up to 3 persons Ffr 115.00 - 118.00; extra person 21.00 - 22.00; child (under 7) 15.00 - 15.50; local tax in July/Aug 1.10.
-- Less outside Jul/Aug.

Open:
1 April - 30 Sept.

Address:
85360 La Tranche s. Mer.

Tel:
51.27.47.36.

Reservations:
Made, from March, for exact dates (min. 7 days) with deposit and fee.

166

8502 Camping du Jard, La Tranche-sur-Mer
Neat, developing site, halfway between La Rochelle and Les Sables d'Olonne.

camping du **Jard** ★★★★NN
GRAND CONFORT

- Open 25 May – 15 September
- Free heated swimming pool
- 350 flat grassy pitches
- 700 yds from beach

123, Route de la Faute,
85360 la Tranche-Sur-Mer
Tel: 51.27.43.79 Fax: 51.27.42.92

Du Jard is a well planned, neatly laid out site with shade developing from the many attractive trees and hedges which have been planted. The 350 pitches are flat and grassy, and a minimum of 100 sq.m. Most are equipped with electricity, half with water and drainaway also. The site is 700 m. from a sandy beach and also has its own heated pool (20 x 10 m.), with a small one (5 x 6 m.) for children. There is a good tennis court, minigolf, table tennis and a new sauna, solarium and fitness room. Children's play area and games and TV rooms. The three toilet blocks are well designed and maintained, with excellent facilities for the disabled and for babies. Ample free hot water; mixture of continental and British toilets; washbasins in private cabins. Owner managed, one receives a friendly welcome; English is spoken (in season). Card operated barrier. There is a bar with terrace, restaurant and a small shop for basics (shops and restaurants nearby). Exchange facilities. Car wash. American motorhomes not accepted. Used by two British tour operators.

Directions: Site is east of La Tranche-sur-Mer, 3 km. from the D747/ D46 roundabout, on the D46 road.

Charges 1993:
-- Per pitch incl. 2 or 3 persons 105.00 Ffr, with electricity (4A) l20.00, with 3 services 137.00; extra person (over 5 yrs) 21.50; extra child (under 5) 14.00; electricity 6A 6.50, 10A 10.50; tax 1.10.
-- Less outside 1/7-25/8.

Open:
25 May - 15 Sept.

Address:
123, Route de la Faute, 85360 La Tranche s. Mer.

Tel:
51 27 43 79.
FAX: 51.27.42.92.

Reservations:
Min.1 week, Sat.- Sat. with deposit (Ffr. 500).

8503 Camping La Loubine, Olonne-sur-Mer, nr Les Sables d'Olonne
Friendly site with good atmosphere, near the facilities of Les Sables d'Olonne.

The original mature parts of this site have been added to, giving a total of 260 pitches, including 143 with all services, plus 40 mobile homes for hire. These individual, marked pitches are of particularly large size, on flat grass, and many now have shade. A free heated swimming pool (15 x 8 m.) and children's paddling pool add to its attraction - an indoor pool and toboggan are planned for 1994. Original buildings around a courtyard area have been converted to provide a pleasant restaurant and bar, takeaway and small shop (15/5-15/9). The four toilet blocks are attractively designed and of commendable quality. Tiled throughout, and colour co-ordinated, they have mainly British toilets, large washbasins set in flat surfaces and all in individual cabins, free hot water in basins and sinks, and free pre-set hot showers. Facilities for disabled and babies. Washing machines and dryers. Tennis. Table tennis. Minigolf. Badminton net. Volleyball. Large children's play area (on sand and grass) and children's club in high season. TV with Eurosport channel. Organised activities and sports for adults and children all season. Horse riding and practice golf nearby. The site is under 2 km. from a sandy Atlantic beach, and 5 km. from the lively resort of Les Sables d'Olonne. No dogs taken. Used by 2 tour operators.

Directions: Site lies west of Olonne beside the D80 road.

Charges 1994:
-- Per pitch for 2/3 persons, without electricity 130.00 Ffr, with electricity (4A) 145.00, with all services 155.00; extra child 20.00; extra child (under 7) 10.00; extra car 10.00; electricity (6A) 10.00.
-- Less 30% outside 30/6-21/8.

Open:
1 April - 30 Sept.

Address:
1 Route de la Mer, 85340 Olonne-sur-Mer.

Tel:
51.33.12.92.
FAX: 51.33.12.71.

Reservations:
With deposit and Ffr 120 fee (min. 7 days Jul/Aug.)

8504 Castel Camping La Garangeoire, St. Julien-des-Landes, nr St. Gilles-Croix

Parkland site, with swimming pool, 15 km. from the Atlantic coast.

CASTEL CAMPING – CARAVANNING
LA GARANGEOIRE ★★★★

The peace and tranquility of a private estate, 15 km from the Atlantic coast beaches.
● Large pitches (150-200 sq.m.) ● Restaurant & creperie
● Heated swimming pool ● Lakes and woodland

The village of St. Julien-des-Landes is about 20 km. from Les Sables d'Olonne, and 15 km. inland from the nearest point on the coast, where there are sandy beaches. Set in the parkland surrounding La Garangeoire, a small château, the peaceful, attractive grounds of many acres, where campers may walk, include three lakes, one of which may be used for fishing and boating. The site has a spacious, relaxed atmosphere and many use it as a quiet base. There is a heated swimming pool (200 sq.m.) and child's pool. The camping area consists of three large meadows, edged with mature trees, and a smaller wooded section. The 300 pitches are especially large (most 150-200 sq.m.) and are marked. All have electricity (6A) and some also water and drainage. Sanitary installations are quite satisfactory and are being gradually updated; where complete they are very good. One block, which has been completely modernised, has facilities for the disabled. The site reports a further new block is now open. They have British WCs, basins in private cabins, baby bath, free hot water and laundry facilities. Restaurant, takeaway and crêperie with attractive courtyard. Large play area for children, games room, 2 tennis courts, bicycle hire, table tennis, minigolf and volleyball. Good shop and exchange facilities. Popular with British tour operators (40%) but there is plenty of space.

Directions: Site is signposted from St. Julien; entrance is to the north off D21.

Charges 1994:
-- Per unit incl. 3 persons, with electricity Ffr 141.00; extra person 28.00; child (under 7) 14.00; extra car 10.00; dog 10.00.
-- Less outside 26/6-31/8.

Open:
15 May - 15 Sept

Address:
St. Julien-des-Landes, 85150 La Mothe-Achard.

Tel:
51.46.65.39.
FAX: 51.46.60.82.

Reservations:
Made up to 15/5 (min. 10 days in July/Aug), with deposit (Ffr. 300) and fee (100).

8513 Camping Pong, Landevieille

Pleasant, well kept site 4 km. from the coast at Brétignolles.

This site, situated 12 km. south of St Gilles-Croix-de-Vie, has 162 pitches, of which 112 have electricity (4 or 6A). They are all of a good size with some extra large (130 sq.m.) ones costing a little more. Set on level, grassy/sandy ground with some terraced areas at the lower end, all are separated by shrubs and bushes. There are many mature trees, including attractive weeping willows, which provide shade. Three modern, unisex sanitary blocks provide mainly seatless toilets, free hot water for showers and washbasins (some open plan, some in private cabins), and facilities for the disabled. Separate baby room, washing up under cover and laundry room. Small swimming pool (with water slide), paddling pool and sunbathing area, bar and terrace, fishing, games room, TV lounge, small gymnasium and children's play area on sand and grass. Small shop with bread, milk and takeaway meals. Mobile homes for hire. Tennis 200 m. Golf, markets, vineyards nearby. Site is 2½ km. from Lac du Jaunay (canoes and pedaloes) and 14 km. from Lac d'Apremont and its XVI century château.

Directions: Site is on the D32 St. Gilles-Croix-de-Vie to La Mothe road just south of Landevieille and is signposted.

Charges 1993:
-- Per unit. up to 3 persons Ffr 72.80, with water and drainage 76.80; larger pitch + 5.20 - 8.20; extra person 15.50; child (under 6 yrs) 9.50; electricity 4A 13.50, 6A 18.50; local tax not incl.
-- Less outside 1/7 - 8/9.

Open:
Easter - 21/9

Address:
Rue du Stade, 85220 Landevieille.

Tel:
51.22.92.63.

Reservations:
Contact site.

8505 Camping Les Dunes, Brétignolles-sur-Mer, nr St. Gilles-Croix

Large, busy site with swimming pools and direct access to good sandy beach.

Even in an area like the Vendée, where there are great long stretches of sandy beach, sites where one can walk directly to the beach with no roads to cross are not very numerous. This, however, is one where from several gates in the boundary fence, one can walk over some 150 m. of grass-covered dunes onto the good beach. It is a large site and many of the 760 pitches have been sold for permanent mobile homes, which rather dominate the eye. Additionally some 20% of pitches are occupied by British tour operators. There are, though, about 450 pitches available for tourists and the present intention is that it should remain at this number. Pitches are of at least 100 sq.m. (some over 150 sq.m.), and all have electricity, water connections and drainaway. They are separated by light hedges. About a third is shaded by tall trees, the remainder is without shade and, though closer to the beach, perhaps a little exposed in high winds.

There are 9 identical, modern sanitary blocks of a good standard, with mixed British and continental WCs, washbasins in private cabins with light, shelf, free hot water, pre-set hot showers with pushbutton. They should be an ample provision and each block has a washing machine. Two heated swimming pools (15/5-15/9) with sunbathing areas form an attractive complex. Supermarket (from 15/5), restaurant (from 1/6) and takeaway, 2 tennis courts. Children's playground. Sailing and windsurfing school; boards for hire. TV room. Organised sports programme in July/Aug. for adults and children; some evening entertainments or dancing at times. A good site by a good beach is obviously attractive, and not surprisingly this is popular and full over quite a long period. Perhaps because of its size, it has become a little impersonal.

Directions: Site is 2 km. south of Brétignolles, signposted from main D38 road.

Charges 1994:
-- Prices in brackets outside July/Aug.
-- Per person Ffr. 18.00 (11.00); child (under 7) 10.30 (6.30); pitch 101.00 (66.00); extra car 13.00 (9.30); local tax (over 10s) 2.20.

Open:
Mid-March - 10 Nov.

Address:
85470 Brétignolles-sur-Mer.

Tel:
51.90.55.32.

Reservations:
Made for min. 20 days with deposit (Ffr. 400) and fee (100). Video available from site.

WESTERN LOIRE - Vendée

8506 Airotel Domaine Le Pas Opton, Le Fenouiller, nr St. Gilles-Croix

Well established site with good installations and swimming pool, 6 km. from sea.

Le Pas Opton is family managed and run and much work has been carried out to make it worth considering for a stay in this popular region. It is 6 km. back from the sea at St. Gilles Croix de Vie and quietly situated. With a well established atmosphere, it is a select type of site but at the same time, offers on-site amenities such as a heated swimming pool and childs' pools and an attractive bar with some dancing. There are 184 pitches, most of which have electricity and some hardstanding, water and drainage also. Those in the original part are well shaded by mature trees and tall hedges. The newer areas are developing well with a good, more spacious feel. The four toilet blocks are all of good quality. They have free hot water in all facilities and are kept very clean and in good order, with British toilets, individual washbasins with free hot water, mainly in private cabins for women, partly for men and free hot water in showers and sinks. Laundry facilities available.

Other amenities include a shop, bar, café, takeaway (all open nearly all season), volleyball, table tennis, a children's playground and a car wash area. Entertainment is organised in season. The river Vie runs past the rear of the site (with fishing) and the owners have been improving the access to this. Non-powered boats can be put on the river, but there can be a current at times. A sailing centre close to the site opened in 1993. Chalet and 2 large caravans for hire. Used by a tour operator.

Directions: Site is northeast of St. Gilles, on the N754 about 300 m. towards Le Fenouiller from the junction with D32.

Charges 1993:
-- Per unit, incl. up to 3 persons: without electricity Ffr. 93.00 - 106.00; with electricity 113.00 - 127.00; with water and drainage also 128.00 - 142.00; extra adult 22.00; child (under 7) 11.00; local tax 1.10 per person (over 10 years).
-- Less 20% before 15/6.

Open:
Late May - 15 Sept.

Address:
Route de Nantes,
Le Fenouiller, 85800 St.
Gilles Croix de Vie.

Tel:
51.55.11.98.
FAX: 51.55.44.94.

Reservations:
Advisable for main season,
from Jan. (min. 1 week)
with deposit and fee.

see advertisement in previous colour section

8508 Camping La Puerta del Sol, St. Hilaire de Riez, nr St Gilles-Croix

Well designed, good quality site with swimming pool and other amenities.

La Puerta del Sol, opened in 1986, has been developed on ambitious lines, resulting in a very good, environmentally pleasing site with excellent amenities. It has about 193 individual pitches (and 26 chalets), most of about 100 sq.m., on reasonably grassy ground, with shade developing well from young trees. All pitches have electricity, water and drainaway. The three well designed, identical toilet blocks have mostly British seatless, some continental WCs; washbasins in private cabins with free hot water, shelf, mirror and light; free hot showers (controllable, but operated by pushbutton which runs on for a short time) plus facilities for the disabled, laundry and babies' rooms. The facilities are very well cleaned and the site well regulated, with friendly staff.

The Spanish camp name is reflected in the architectural style of the buildings which contain reception, bar lounge, restaurant and takeaway. A heated swimming pool of over 200 sq.m., with paddling pool, is by the bar with a terrace. There is a mini-market and a general room also used for `animation' events; sports competitions and games. Evening entertainment and dancing (until midnight) and organised excursions in July/Aug. Barbecue area with picnic tables, children's adventure play areas (on sand), tennis and games room with table tennis, amusement machines. The nearest sandy beach is 5 km. and St. Jean-de-Monts 7. American motorhomes accepted in limited numbers and with reservation. Used by one tour operator. Bungalows, chalets and large wooden-floored tents for hire. A good site perhaps for families with teenagers.

Directions: Site is 1 km. north of Le Pissot (which is 7 km. north of St. Gilles Croix-de-Vie on D38) on the D59 road towards Le Perrier.

Charges 1994:
-- Per pitch with up to 3 persons, car and caravan or trailer tent, incl. 3 services Ffr 60.00 - 165.00, acc.to season; tent incl. 2 persons 50.00 - 95.00; extra adult 15.00 - 35.00; child (under 7) 8.00 - 23.00.

Open:
10 April - 25 Sept.

Site address:
Les Borderies,
85270 St. Hilaire de Riez.

Tel:
(from 1/5-30/9)
51.49.10.10.

Reservations:
Made for any period with substantial deposit and fee. Reservations address: 47 Rue de Candale prolongée, 93500 Pantin. Tel: 48.44.33.22.

see advertisement in previous colour section

8507 Camping Les Biches, St. Hilaire de Riez, nr St. Gilles-Croix

Site in a pinewood with good pitches and swimming pools, 4 km. from the sea.

Les Biches is covered by a pinewood, so nearly everywhere has good shade. The 380 individual pitches, which are mostly of very good size (most are equipped with electricity, water and drainaway), are on grassy or sandy ground under the trees and there is a spacious and peaceful atmosphere. This is a popular site and reservations for main season are necessary. There are special parts for tents and caravans, the tent part being particularly shady. The four sanitary blocks are of good quality and size and have been refurbished with colour co-ordinated fittings. They have British WCs, individual basins with mirrors and shelves, many in private cabins with free hot water in all basins and fully controllable showers.Laundry facilities are available.

The camp is not by the sea but several sandy beaches can be reached in a short drive, the nearest being 4 km. away. However, a heated swimming pool of nearly 200 sq.m. has been installed near the entrance, with a little children's pool. Other amenities include a shop with ice service, takeaway, crêperie, tennis courts, volleyball, table tennis and games room with amusement machines. There is a private fishing lake, car wash area, new children's playground, a treatment room, TV room with satellite TV, minigolf and bicycle hire. Mobile homes to let. It is a quiet and peaceful type of site, with not so many camp activities as in some places, but it is popular with British tour operators, so can be busy at times. Site entrance is guarded.

Directions: Site is about 2 km. north of St. Hilaire, close to and signposted from the main D38 road.

Charges 1994:
-- Per pitch incl. 3 persons + car 140.00 Ffr, with electricity (10A) also 165.00; extra person 28.00; child (under 7) 14.00; extra car 10.00; dog 10.00; m/cycle 10.00.
-- Less 20% before 15 June.

Open:
1 June - 15 Sept.

Address:
85270 St. Hilaire-de-Riez.

Tel:
51.54.38.82.
FAX: 51.54.30.74.

Reservations:
Made with dates of both arrival and departure required, with deposit (Ffr. 400) and fee (100).

8511 Camping Le Bois Soret, Notre Dame de Monts, nr Challans
Pleasant, well kept site near beach and with own good swimming pool.

This site, like those at St. Jean de Monts, is separated from the sea by a pine-wood. It is under a kilometre from a good sandy beach, where bathing is said to be safe. One can drive as there is a road which traverses the wood and park by the beach. If you prefer not to make this short journey, a heated swimming pool (135 sq.m.), free of charge, (open late May - late Sept) is on the site, There is an attractive bar/restaurant, takeaway, a shop (late June - end Aug.) and organised activities (sports, special events etc.) in high season. Minigolf, a games room with table tennis, TV, washing machines and children's playground complete the facilities. Le Bois Soret is a well kept, flat site with 250 numbered pitches of good size, separated by attractive hedges and trees; many have electricity, water and drainage. It can be full from early July to late August, when reservation is advisable. The sanitary installations are all at the centre of the site and are well maintained and cleaned. They have mixed continental and British WCs; washbasins with free hot water either in small groups or in private cabins; free hot showers (some pre-set) and free hot water in sinks and baby bath.

Directions: Turn off D38 road towards sea by camp sign at north end of village.

Charges 1993:
-- Per unit with up to 3 persons Ffr 86.50; pitch with electricity 99.50; extra person 20.00; child (under 5) 10.00; local tax (over 15) July/Aug. 1.10.
-- Per unit incl. 2 persons in low season Ffr 50.00, with electricity 60.00.

Open:
2 weeks before Easter - late Oct.

Address:
85690 Notre Dame de Monts.

Tel:
51.58.84.01.

Reservations:
Made for exact dates with deposit and fee.

CAMPING ★★★ NN
LE BOIS SORET
85690 Notre-Dame-de-Monts

● **Heated swimming pool from Whitsun to end September**

● **Sandy beach 900 metres away through the pine forest**

● **Open Easter to 30 September**

8509 Camping L'Abri des Pins, St Jean-de-Monts, nr Challans
Family run, mature site with pool on outskirts of popular resort.

L'Abri des Pins is situated on the outskirts of the pleasant, modern resort of St. Jean-de-Monts and is separated from the sea and long sandy beach by a strip of pinewood. One can walk about 600 m. through the wood to the beach from a back entrance of the site or drive slightly further and park. Bathing is claimed to be safer here than on most of the beaches on this coast, but is nevertheless supervised. The site has 225 pitches, of which some 150 are larger, with electricity, water and drainaway. Electricity is also available in other parts where pitches are around 100 sq. m., fully marked out with dividing hedges and quite shady. The two sanitary blocks have mixed continental and British toilets, washbasins mainly in private cabins; free hot water in basins, the fully controllable showers (no dressing area) and sinks. On site is a heated swimming pool, and paddling pool (open late May - end Aug). Shop. Modern bar and entertainment room with food to eat there or takeaway. Tennis, table tennis, minigolf, TV room, children's playground and exchange facilities. Mobile homes and chalets for hire. Plans for 1994 include a fitness room and a water slide. Riding, sailing and windsurfing hire nearby. Shopping complex near.

Directions: Site is 4 km. from town centre on St. Jean-de-Monts to Notre Dame-de-Monts/Noirmoutiers road (D38).

Charges 1993:
-- Per pitch with tent/caravan and 3 persons 124.50 Ffr; with electricity also 132.00; with electricity, water and drainaway 140.00; extra adult 20.50; child (under 5) 11.50; local tax (over 10 yrs) July/Aug 1.10.

Open:
1 May - 20 Sept.

Address:
85160 St Jean-de-Monts.

Tel:
51.58.83.86.
(winter: 40.71.98.04).
FAX: 51.59.30.47.

Reservations:
Made for min. 2 weeks in main season, otherwise 1 week, with deposit and fee.

8512 Camping Le Bois Masson, St. Jean-de-Monts

Lively, modern site, with many facilities including indoor pool.

Le Bois Masson is a large, lively site with modern buildings and facilities in the seaside resort of St. Jean-de-Monts. As with other sites here, the long, sandy beach is a few minutes away by car, reached through a pinewood. This site, popular with tour operators, offers 480 good sized pitches, all with electricity. They are of sandy grass, mostly separated by hedges, with medium sized trees providing some shade. There are 10 pitches with water and drainage also and an area kept for those who prefer a quieter pitch around a pond used for fishing.

The 4 sanitary blocks are of excellent design, with modern showers with mixer taps, washbasins in cabins and British WCs. They include a dishwashing room (with dishwashers), a laundry, facilities for the disabled and for babies and hot water is free throughout. The comprehensive site facilities are housed in modern buildings which front on to the road. They include a good supermarket, a large, lively bar with entertainment room above overlooking the pools, a restaurant and a crêperie. Plenty of entertainment over a long season. The swimming pool complex includes a large outdoor pool, a child's pool, a separate slide and landing pool and for cooler weather an indoor pool, with sliding doors to the outside. Sauna and fitness room provided together with many other sports including tennis, volleyball, table tennis and bicycle hire. Fishing on small pond and riding, golf, squash, watersports near. No barbecues. Mobile homes and rooms to rent. Very busy in high season, this is not a site for those seeking somewhere quiet, but there is plenty to do for those perhaps with older children.

Directions: From the roundabout at the southeast end of the St. Jean de Monts bypass road, turn into town following signs to 'Centre Ville' and site, which is on the right after 400 m.

Charges 1993:
-- Per unit incl. 3 persons Ffr 100.00 - 139.00, acc. to season, incl. electricity (4A) 118.00 - 158.00, incl. electricity (6A) 126.00 - 164.00, incl. water/drainage also 150.00 - 190.00; extra person 17.50 - 26.00; child (under 5 yrs) 9.00 - 12.50; extra car 9.00 - 12.50; tax (over 10s) 1.10.

Open:
Easter - 30 Sept.

Address:
B.P. 74, 85160 St. Jean-de-Monts.

Tel:
51.58.01.30. (winter and for reservations) 51.58.62.62. FAX: 51.58.29.97.

Reservations:
Write to site for booking form.

8510 Camping Le Bois Dormant, St. Jean-de-Monts

Slightly quieter sister site to Le Bois Masson, with high quality facilities.

Under the same professional management, and situated on the opposite side of the road from Le Bois Masson, this sister site has a slightly quieter air. The 388 pitches here are all of a good size, separated by hedges and many with shade from attractive trees. All have electricity, water and drainage. The bar, with takeaway snacks, has a terrace overlooking the attractive large pool (300 sq.m.) with additional children's pool and water slide. There is a games room here, minigolf and tennis courts near the entrance. The 4 excellent sanitary blocks are very well designed and offer top class facilities including showers with mixer taps, washbasins in cabins with mixer taps, mirrors, shelves and electric point, and British WCs. Baby bathrooms and toilets, plus facilities for the disabled are also provided. Hot water is free to all facilities. Campers may use the restaurant, entertainment facilities and supermarket at Le Bois Masson (200m. away), although there is a small shop here. Only gas barbecues permitted. This site is also popular with tour operators and, while quieter than its sister site can be expected to be very busy in high season.

Directions: As Le Bois Masson, but site is on left.

Charges 1993:
-- Per unit incl. 3 persons Ffr 100.00 - 139.00, acc. to season, incl. electricity (4A) 118.00 - 158.00, incl. electricity (6A) 126.00 - 164.00, incl. water/drainage also 150.00 - 190.00; extra person 17.50 - 26.00; child (under 5 yrs) 9.00 - 12.50; extra car 9.00 - 12.50; tax (over 10s) 1.10.

Open:
15 May - 15 Sept.

Site tel:
51.58.01.30.

Reservations:
Write to Le Bois Masson (address above) for booking form.

WESTERN LOIRE - Vendée

8515 Camping La Yole, Orouet, St. Jean de Monts
Attractive site 1 km. from sandy beach.
This site offers 215 pitches all with 6A electricity and water, some with drainage as well. They are about 100 sq.m. and arranged off avenues of trees, separated by hedges and shrubs. There are 100 static caravans and some British tour operators. Two tiled, fairly modern sanitary blocks have British WCs, free hot water to pre-set showers and washbasins (in private cabins) and the 2 units for the disabled. Laundry room with washing machine, dryer and iron. Outside but under cover are baby baths. Amenities include two swimming pools (one with 2 water slides), children's paddling pool, bar with terrace, restaurant, takeaway and well stocked shop. There is a good sized children's play area on sand and a grassy area for ball games and picnics. Table tennis, pool, electronic games room and entertainment in high season. A pleasant walk through pine trees leads to two fine sandy beaches. St. Jean de Monts is 6 km. which is popular for fishing and watersports and offers 2 golf courses. The campsite has a gate system, closed between 22.00 and 0800.

Directions: Signed off the D38, 6 km. south of St. Jean de Monts.

Charges 1993:
-- Per unit incl. 1-3 persons, electricity and water Ffr 119.00 - 141.00, with drainage also 129.00 - 153.00; extra person 20.00 - 23.00; extra child (under 5) 10.00 - 13.00; extra car 10.00 - 13.00.

Open:
15 May - 15 September.

Address:
Chemin des Bosses, Orouet, 85160 St. Jean de Monts.

Tel:
51.58.67.17.

Reservations:
Advised, particularly for July/Aug.

8517 Camping Le Bois Tordu, St. Hilaire-de-Riez
Small family site 300 m. from sandy beach.
Located near to its sister site, no. 8516, Le Bois Tordu provides comfortable shade, more of a family type atmosphere with a short walk to the beach and a supermarket and bar/restaurant adjoining the site. The beach is across the D123 but there is a heated pool on site, with water chute and children's paddling pool, with a sunbathing area, chairs etc. provided. All of the 104 pitches (100 sq.m) have electricity, water and drainage, and they are clearly marked by hedges and trees. The sanitary block is not as modern as at Sol a Gogo, but provides free controllable hot showers, some washbasins in cabins, the rest in rows. Toilets (continental and British) are at the rear of the block with separate entrance. There are facilities for the handicapped, a bath for children and a laundry room. A children's play area is on sand and table tennis and minigolf on the opposite side of the road. Used by some British tour operators.

Directions: Site is on the D123, midway between St. Hilaire-de-Riez and St. Jean-de-Monts, near Sol a Gogo.

Charge 1993:
-- Per pitch incl. 3 persons and car 154.00 Ffr; extra person 21.00; child (under 5) 11.00; dog 6.00; extra car 6.00; local tax (over 10 yrs) 1.10.

Open:
Late May - early Sept.

Address:
La Pege, 85270 St. Hilaire-de-Riez.

Tel:
51 54 33 78.

Reservations:
Possible **except** between 1-15 Aug.

8518 Le Clarys Plage, St. Jean-de-Monts
Quiet family site with swimming pool, 500 m. from the beach.
Set a little way back from the beach, on the outskirts of the town, the main feature of Le Clarys Plage is its new, attractive, heated pool complex which is imaginatively designed with slides, chutes, bridges, etc. and surrounded by a paved sun bathing area (sun loungers and chairs provided). There is a paddling pool for children and a shaded play area. For 1994 the site is being extended to provide a total of 300 pitches. The original ones, which we have seen, have comfortable shade from attractive trees and brush fences, all with electricity and some with water and drainage also. The single toilet block provides free hot and gives a reasonable provision. The showers are controllable, some with no dividers or hooks, and there are British and continental toilets and a washing machine. Not all the washbasins are in cabins. A `centre commercial' has now been opened. Snacks are available in high season and there are barbecue areas.

Directions: Signposted off the D123 coast road between St. Hilaire-de-Riez and St. Jean-de-Monts.

Charges 1993:
-- Per pitch with 3 persons + car Ffr. 80.00; extra person 16.50; child (under 5) 8.50; extra car 5.00; electricity 13.00; water and drainage 13.00; tax 1.10 (over 10 yrs).

Open:
Early June - early Sept.

Address:
85160 St. Jean-de-Monts.

Tel:
51.58.10.24.

Reservations:
Write to site.

8516 Camping-Caravaning Sol a Gogo, St Hilaire de Riez

Modern site with direct access to the beach and an attractive pool complex.

Sol a Gogo is owned by the family who also own Le Clarys Plage (8518) and Le Bois Tordu (8517). It has a well designed pool complex which also encompasses reception and the bar, and boasts a water chute which seems very popular. The unusually shaped pool with a central water fountain and a smaller children's pool are heated and provide areas for sunbathing, with chairs and sun beds. A sandy beach suitable for windsurfers is reached via the site's private path. Lifeguards patrol in the main season. The restaurant is of a good standard and decor and overlooks the pool. It specialises in grills and salads and offers good value. There is a basic shop and takeaway in season (supermarket, etc. near), tennis (half court), table tennis, pétanque and a play area on sand. Windsurfing is possible off the beach and minigolf near.

The 196 pitches (100 sq.m), on sandy grass, with water, electricity and drainage, are clearly marked by newly planted bushes. These are growing slowly and will eventually provide shade and privacy, but at present the site is rather open and lacks shade, though reed type fencing has been used effectively. The site is used by tour operators so English is evident. There are two modern, well designed toilet blocks, with free hot water, British type toilets, and washbasins in cabins. They should be an adequate provision in the height of the season. Barbecues are permitted.

Directions: The site is on the D123 road, between St. Hilaire de Riez and St. Jean de Monts.

Charges 1993:
-- Per pitch with all facilities, 3 persons and car 154.00 Ffr; extra person 21.00; child (under 5) 11.00; dog 6.00; extra car 6.00; local tax (over 10 yrs) 1.10.

Open:
Mid-May - mid-Sept.

Address:
61 Avenue de la Pege, 85270 St. Hilaire-de-Riez.

Tel:
51.54.29.00.
FAX: 51.54.88.74.

Reservations:
Possible **except** in high season.

see advertisement in previous colour section

N8514 Camping Naturiste Le Colombier, St. Martin-Lars, nr La Roche sur Yon

Countryside site in 125 acres in a valley.

Almost akin to `Camping a la Ferme', but with the benefit of good facilities, this site provides 110 pitches in three different areas, all in unmarked, undulating meadowland. Electricity up to 6A is available at various strategically located points. A bar/restaurant, serving a meal of the day, home baked bread and pizzas, is situated in an old, very attractive converted barn, where there is also a small `library' of local tourist information, table tennis facilities etc. Milk is available from the farm and a grocer/baker calls daily (shop 1 km.). There are facilities for volleyball and boules and a children's paddling pool and playground. Fishing. Bicycle hire.There is no pool here but it is possible to swim in one of the small lakes within the confines of the site, although it is a little muddy and you have to share the water with the fish! For nature lovers the 125 acres in which the site is located provide the opportunity for many walks throughout the attractive, wooded valley. The sanitary installations, at present in two modern blocks although more are planned, are good. They provide hot showers in cubicles, some solar heated, others on a normal system, British WCs.

Directions: From the N148, La Roche sur Yon - Niort road, at St. Hermine, turn onto the D8 eastward for 4 km. Turn left on to the D10 to St. Martin-Lars where there are signs to site.

Charges 1993:
-- Per person Ffr 30.00; child (4-9 yrs) 15.00, (10-16 yrs) 21.00; electricity 12.00.

Open:
All year.

Address:
Le Colombier - Centre de Vacances Naturiste, 85210 St. Martin-Lars en Ste Hermine.

Tel:
51.27.83.84.

Reservations:
Not considered necessary.

WESTERN LOIRE - Vendée

8519 Le Marais Braud, St Hilaire de Riez, nr St-Gilles-Croix

Small, quiet and undeveloped site with swimming pool, near the sea.

Le Marais Braud occupies a peaceful wooded setting with level, grassy pitches, slightly inland from the busy coastal areas. The good sandy beaches are within easy reach by car. The facilities include a swimming pool with a slide and a small children's pool, tennis court and a small lake for fishing. The friendly bar and crêperie incorporate a games area with a small skittle alley and there is a small shop for basics. There are 105 pitches here, of 100 sq.m., half with electricity, with shade and some hedges.

One large and one small toilet block, both with hot water, provide showers and wash cabins with shelves and hooks and mixed continental and British toilets and there is a washing machine. The site has a family atmosphere being managed by the owners, M. & Mme Besseau. Mme Besseau is learning English and is keen to practise! No tour operators. Wooden chalets for rent.

Directions: From St Hilaire de Riez, take the D38 north to Le Pissot, site is signposted from the D59 road from Le Pissot to Le Perrier.

Charges 1993:
-- Per unit, incl. 2 persons 63.00 Ffr; extra adult 17.50; child (2-10 yrs) 13.50, under 2 yrs 7.00; extra car 4.50; electricity (6A) 13.00.

Open:
1 June - 15 Sept.

Address:
298, Route du Perrier, 85270 St Hilaire de Riez.

Tel:
51.68.33.71.

Reservations:
Write to site.

LE CAMPING DU MARAIS BRAUD
298 Route du Perrier
85270 ST HILAIRE DE RIEZ
Tel: 51.68.33.71

On the road from Perrier to St Hilaire de Riez, 10 minutes from the beaches and fishing and pleasure port of St Gilles Croix de Vie and 8 km from St Jean de Monts. Modern sanitary block with hot water and showers, washing machine, ironing room, Swimming Pool with Toboggan Aquatique, Bar, Crêperie, Food Shop, Games and Hot Meals, Tennis, Small Lake for Fishing

Open 1 June to 15 September
Reservations advised for July & August   Chalets for hire

8520 Camping La Petite Boulogne, St. Etienne-du-Bois

Small, attractive site beside the Petite Boulogne river.

The 27 pitches on this small site are set out on semi-terraced grass and are of good size, separated by bushes and shrubs. All have electricity, water and drainage connections. There are 8 mobile homes for hire at the top of the site at the furthest point from the river. Although only in their second season, the owners are justly proud of this attractive little site with its profusion of beautiful rose beds and flowers. Leading from the site, a small wooden bridge takes you across the Petite Boulogne river and, after a few minutes walk, to the village of St. Etienne-du-Bois with its restaurant and bar. St. Etienne is about 24 km. northwest of La Roche-sur-Yon. The modern, centrally heated sanitary block has free hot water to the pre-set showers and the washbasins in both open style and private cabins, and excellent facilities for the disabled. Under cover washing up, small, but adequate, laundry room. Small shop for essentials and fresh bread (supermarket 3 km at Legé). On site facilities are limited at present, with a small children's play area on grass, table tennis and bicycle hire. Horse riding, lake and river fishing nearby. Tennis, volleyball and petanque are available at the local sports centre (300 m.) and an open-air heated pool is near. Large, safe beaches are about 20 km. Al fresco chef speciality nights and wine tasting evenings arranged in peak season.

Directions: From Legé take D978 south towards Palluau for 7 km. then turn left onto D94 towards St. Etienne-du-Bois from where site is well signed.

Charges 1993:
-- Per unit incl. 2 persons Ffr 60.00, with all services 80.00; extra person 10.00; child (under 5 yrs) 5.00; extra vehicle 10.00; electricity 6A 10.00, 10A 12.00.
-- less 25% on pitch fee outside July/Aug.

Open:
All year.

Address:
85670 St. Etienne-du-Bois.

Tel:
51.34.54.51.
Low season: 51.94.97.49.

Reservations:
Made with deposit (Ffr 200) and fee (50).

CORSICA

Corsica is deservedly known as 'the isle of beauty' - about half of its 220,000 inhabitants live in the main towns of Ajaccio and Bastia, leaving much of the 3,400 square mile island (the third largest in the Mediterranean) very thinly populated. Although about half the island is covered with vegetation, pine trees, oaks, chestnut and the famous 'maquis', the variety of scenery is often spectacular, with mountains rising to almost 9,000 feet, 600 miles of coastline and a excellent sunshine record. With an early spring and lingering autumn, Corsica is ideal for early and late holidays.

Travel to and from Corsica by ferry is not difficult, although somewhat expensive, with SNCM Ferries offering a choice of routes from mainland France. We used the SNCM service between Bastia and Marseilles operated by the 'Ile de Beaute' quite one of the best ferries we have ever travelled on, but SNCM's fare structure is quite complicated, and it would seem likely that the most competitive fares are available on their services from Nice. There are also several services to Corsica from mainland Italy and from Sardinia - in fact we arrived in Corsica from Sardinia via the 8 mile (about 45 minutes) Santa Teresa / Bonifacio service, and there can be few more surprisingly spectacular ports in Europe to arrive at than Bonifacio, a real gem of a town. For Ferry information between France and Corsica contact: SNCM Southern Ferries, 179 Piccadilly, London W1V 9DB, Tel: 071 491 4968.

2000 Camping Caravaning U Farniente, Pertamina Village, Bonifacio
Well designed, attractive site only 4 km. from Bonifacio.

Irrespective of whether or not you are using the ferry to Sardinia, Bonifacio deserves a visit and it would be difficult to find a more a more attractive or convenient site than this one at which to pitch for a night stop or longer stay. The 130 pitches, many with electricity, are partially terraced and are hedged with trees and bushes, providing reasonable shade. They are reasonably flat and vary in size, many being well over 100 sq.m. A central feature of the site is the large attractive swimming pool, surrounded by terraces and a bar. There is a good restaurant serving set meals and an a la carte selection at reasonable prices (with a reduced service, ie. shorter opening hours in May, June and Oct). There is a pizzeria and takeaway and a self-service shop. The sanitary facilities are situated in 2 blocks - a new one, not quite finished when we visited in August - the other one with free hot showers (cabins without dividers), washbasins in semi-private cubicles, British and French (Turkish) WCs, dishwashing and washing machines plus ironing facilities. Tennis. Table tennis. Children's play area. TV room. Mobile homes and chalets for weekly hire.

Charges 1993:
-- Per unit incl. 2 persons Ffr. 80.00; extra person 20.00.
Open:
All year.
Address:
Pertamina Village, 20169 Bonifacio (Corse).
Tel:
95.73.05.47.
Reservations:
Contact site.

Directions: Site is on RN198, 4 km. north of Bonifacio on the right. Watch for the sign - you come on it quite suddenly.

2003 Camping Merendella, Moriani
Attractive smaller site with direct access to beach.

This is a smaller, family run, site with the advantage of direct access to a nice beach. It is peacefully situated on level grass, with many trees and shrubs providing shade and colour. There are 140 pitches of a min. 100 sq.m. and electricity is available on virtually all of them, albeit with the necessity for longish cables. The sanitary installations (in one main block plus a couple of very small ones) are modern and include free hot showers in cubicles with partition, and washbasins (H&C) in private cabins. Some British type WCs, plus further 'Turkish' ones. Washing up and laundry facilities, including two washing machines. The site is about 800 m. from the village, but also has its own well stocked shop. Amenities nearby include tennis, riding and various watersports. Snack bar. TV and games rooms.

Charges 1993:
-- Per pitch Ffr. 10.00 - 12.00; person 26.00 - 30.00; child (2-7 yrs) 17.00 - 20.00; vehicle 9.00 - 12.00; motorcaravan 25.00 - 29.00; caravan 11.50 - 14.50; tent 8.50 - 10.00; electricity 14.00 (2A) - 16.00 (5A); local tax 1.00.
Open:
1 May - 15 Oct.
Address:
20230 San Nicolao.
Tel:
95.38.53.47.
Reservations:
Advisable - write to site.

Directions: Site is to seaward of the RN198, immediately (800 m.) south of Moriani Plage.

2001 Camping Arinella Blanca, Ghisonaccia

Very well designed, family run, beach side site on Corsica's east coast.

This site is a tribute to its owners design and development skills as it appears to be in entirely natural 'glades' where, in fact, these have been created from former marshland with a fresh water lake. The 300 marked pitches, all with 6A electricity, are on flat grass among a variety of trees and shrubs, providing ample shade. They are irregularly arranged, but all of good size. The site is right beside a beach of soft sand which extends a long way either side of the attractive central complex of restaurant, shop, bar, amphitheatre, snack bar, etc. which forms the 'hub' of this site. Four open plan sanitary blocks have free pre-set hot showers in larger than average cubicles (some with dressing area), hooks and shelves, washbasins in private cabins and mainly British seatless WCs. Open air washing up areas and a laundry with washing machines and ironing boards. Large range of sports and leisure facilities at or adjacent to the site, including windsurfing, canoeing, volleyball, bicycle hire, tennis, riding, children's play area and a disco. Entertainment programme in the main season.

Directions: Site is north of Porto-Vecchio, just to seaward of main N198 coast road to Bastia - signposted on the main road just south of Ghisonaccia village.

Charges 1993:
-- Per person Ffr. 30.00 - 32.00, acc. to season; child (up to 7 yrs) 15.00 - 16.00; pitch 13.00 - 15.00; car 9.00; motorcaravan 9.00; m/cycle 9.00; dog 6.00; electricity (6A) 16.00; local tax 2.80.

Open:
1 May - 30 Sept.

Address:
20240 Ghisonaccia.

Tel:
95.56.04.78 or 95.56.12.54.

Reservations:
Write to site.

N2004 Camping Naturiste Riva Bella, Aleria

Relaxed, informal naturist site beside glorious beach.

Arguably this is camping and caravanning at its very best. Although offering a large number and variety of pitches, they are situated in such a huge area of varied and beautiful countryside and seaside that it is difficult to believe it could ever become overcrowded. The site is divided into several distinct areas - pitches and bungalows, alongside the sandy beach, in a wooded glade with ample shade, behind the beach, and beside the lake or lagoon which is a feature of this site. The ground is undulating, so getting an absolutely level pitch could be a problem in the main season. Although electric hook-ups are available in most parts, a long cable is probably a necessity. The sanitary facilities, in several blocks, are fairly typical of naturist sites, with British WCs, hot water to open plan washbasins and free hot showers in open plan cubicles. The temperature of the showers is said to be controllable (once you have learned the knack). Besides the beautiful beach, (with sailing school, fishing, sub-aqua and other watersports) there is a wide variety of activities available including volleyball, aerobics, table tennis, archery, half-court tennis etc. You can even spend your time looking at the Llamas. There is an excellent restaurant overlooking the lagoon with reasonable prices, as well as a snack bar beside the beach during the main season. Large well stocked shop (closes 25/9). Facilities are limited at the start and end of the season. There is an interesting evening entertainment programme. Noël Pasqual is fully proud of his site and the fairly unobtrusive rules are designed to ensure that everyone is able to relax, whilst preserving the natural beauty of the environment. There is, for example, a restriction on the movement of cars in certain areas, although there is ample free parking. The police/fire service ban barbecues during the summer as a safety precaution, but generally the ambience is essentially relaxed and informal with nudity only obligatory on the beach itself.

Directions: Site is approx. 8 km. north of Aleria on the N198 (Bastia) road. Watch for signs and unmade road to it and follow for 4 km.

Charges 1993:
-- Per unit Ffr. 50.00 - 87.00, acc. to season; extra person 15.00 - 30.00; child (0-7 yrs) 10.00 - 16.00; extra tent 20.00 - 27.00; electricity 16.00; local tax 1.00

Open:
15 May - 16 Oct.

Address:
20270 Aleria.

Tel:
95.38.81.10 or 95.38.85.97.

Reservations:
Made with deposit (Ffr. 500) and fee/cancellation insurance (160).

SITE BROCHURE SERVICE

The following sites have supplied us with a quantity of their brochures. These leaflets are interesting and useful supplements to the editorial reports and most contain colour photographs or other illustrations of the site which cannot be reproduced in this book. If you would like any of these simply cut out or copy this page, tick the relevant boxes and post it to us. Please enclose a large envelope (at least 9" x 6") addressed to yourself and stamped (on average, 5 brochures will weigh 50 gms). Send your requests to:

Deneway Guides Ltd, Chesil Lodge, West Bexington, Dorchester, Dorset DT2 9DG

0200	Vivier au Carpes	☐	3501	Ville Mauny	☐
0401	Hippocampe	☐	3504	P'tit Bois	☐
0402	Verdon	☐	3701	Mignardiere	☐
0601	St Madeleine	☐	4004	Paillotte	☐
0602	Caravan Inn	☐	4005	Col Vert	☐
0603	Bergerie	☐	4006	Eurosol	☐
0605	Vielle Ferme	☐	4008	Eurolac	☐
0704	Rouveyolle	☐	4404	Parc St Brigitte	☐
1202	Rivages	☐	4409	Château de Deffay	☐
1602	Gorges du Chambon	☐	4603	Les Pins	☐
1405	Colombier	☐	4605	La Reve	☐
1701	Bois Soleil	☐	4701	Moulin du Périé	☐
1703	L'Estanquet	☐	4702	Les Ormes	☐
1704	Bonne Anse Plage	☐	4802	Du Lac	☐
1706	Montravail	☐	5003	Lez Eaux	☐
1707	L'Ocean (Couarde)	☐	5603	Penboch	☐
2201	Les Capucines	☐	5801	Les Bains	☐
2204	Le Chatelet	☐	6201	Bien Assise	☐
2210	Abri Cotier	☐	6402	Ametza	☐
2401	Château Le Verdoyer	☐	6405	Erromardie	☐
2402	Les Granges	☐	6407	Le Ruisseau	☐
2403	Les Périères	☐	6408	Tamaris Plage	☐
2404	Moulin du Roch	☐	6409	La Cheneraie	☐
2405	Hauts de Ratebout	☐	6601	California	☐
2409	Soleil Plage	☐	6602	Ma Prairie	☐
2410	Le Moulinal	☐	8101	L'Entre Deux Lacs	☐
2603	Grand Lierne	☐	8301	Pins Parasol	☐
2905	Orangerie de Lanniron	☐	8311	La Baie	☐
2906	Pil Koad	☐	8312	Du Domaine	☐
2912	Manoir de Kerlut	☐	8502	Du Jard	☐
3003	Abri de Camargue	☐	8503	La Loubine	☐
3201	Camp de Florence	☐	8506	Le Pas Opton	☐
3301	La Dune	☐	8507	Les Biches	☐
3302	Fontaine Vielle	☐	8508	Puerta del Sol	☐
3303	L'Ocean	☐	8518	Le Clarys Plage	☐
3305	Les Ourmes	☐	8519	Le Marais Braud	☐
3403	Napoleon	☐	8601	Le Petit Trianon	☐
			8702	Leychoisier	☐

PLEASE NOTE

We would draw your attention to the fact that these are the sites' own brochures, the contents of which we have no control over. We cannot therefore accept any responsibilities for possible errors, omissions, inaccuracies or misleading information contained therein. Brochures are only available for the sites listed above. We will make every effort to fulfill all requests as promptly as possible, but this offer is subject to stocks being supplied to us and to still being available at the time of receiving your request

REQUESTS FOR INFORMATION OR RESERVATION

For your convenience, we have printed below some slips which you may cut out and fill in your name and address to obtain further information from any of the sites in the guide in which you are interested. Send the slip to the site concerned at the address given in the site report, not to us.

ALAN ROGERS' GOOD CAMPS GUIDE - 1994
ENQUIRY FORM

To (name of site): ....

Please send me a copy of your brochure and details of your conditions for making reservations.

We have our own trailer caravan/motor caravan/tent/trailer tent (delete as appropriate).

Name: ....

Address: ....

....

ALAN ROGERS' GOOD CAMPS GUIDE - 1994
ENQUIRY FORM

To (name of site): ....

Please send me a copy of your brochure and details of your conditions for making reservations.

We have our own trailer caravan/motor caravan/tent/trailer tent (delete as appropriate).

Name: ....

Address: ....

....

ALAN ROGERS' GOOD CAMPS GUIDE - 1994
ENQUIRY FORM

To (name of site): ....

Please send me a copy of your brochure and details of your conditions for making reservations.

We have our own trailer caravan/motor caravan/tent/trailer tent (delete as appropriate).

Name: ....

Address: ....

....

REPORTS BY READERS

We always welcome reports from readers concerning sites which they have visited. These provide invaluable feedback on sites already featured in the Guide, or, in the case of sites not featured in our Guide, they provide information which we can follow up with a view to adding these sites in future editions. Please make your comments either on this form or on plain paper. It would be appreciated if you would indicate the approximate dates when you visited the site and, in the case of potential new sites, provide the correct name and address and, if possible, include a site brochure.

Reports should be sent to: Deneway Guides & Travel Ltd

Chesil Lodge, West Bexington, Dorchester, Dorset DT2 9DG

Name of Site and Ref. No. (or address for new recommendations):

....

....

Dates of Visit: ....

Comments:

Reader's Name and Address: ....

....

....

....

THE REGIONS AND DÉPARTEMENTS OF FRANCE

The map below shows France divided into tourist Regions. These are subdivided into the various `départements' (which correspond roughly to our counties). Each département has an official number which we list opposite. We have used these numbers to prefix our site numbers, eg. a site in Pas de Calais will start 62..

The Regions and
Départements
of France

THE DÉPARTEMENTS OF FRANCE - INDEX

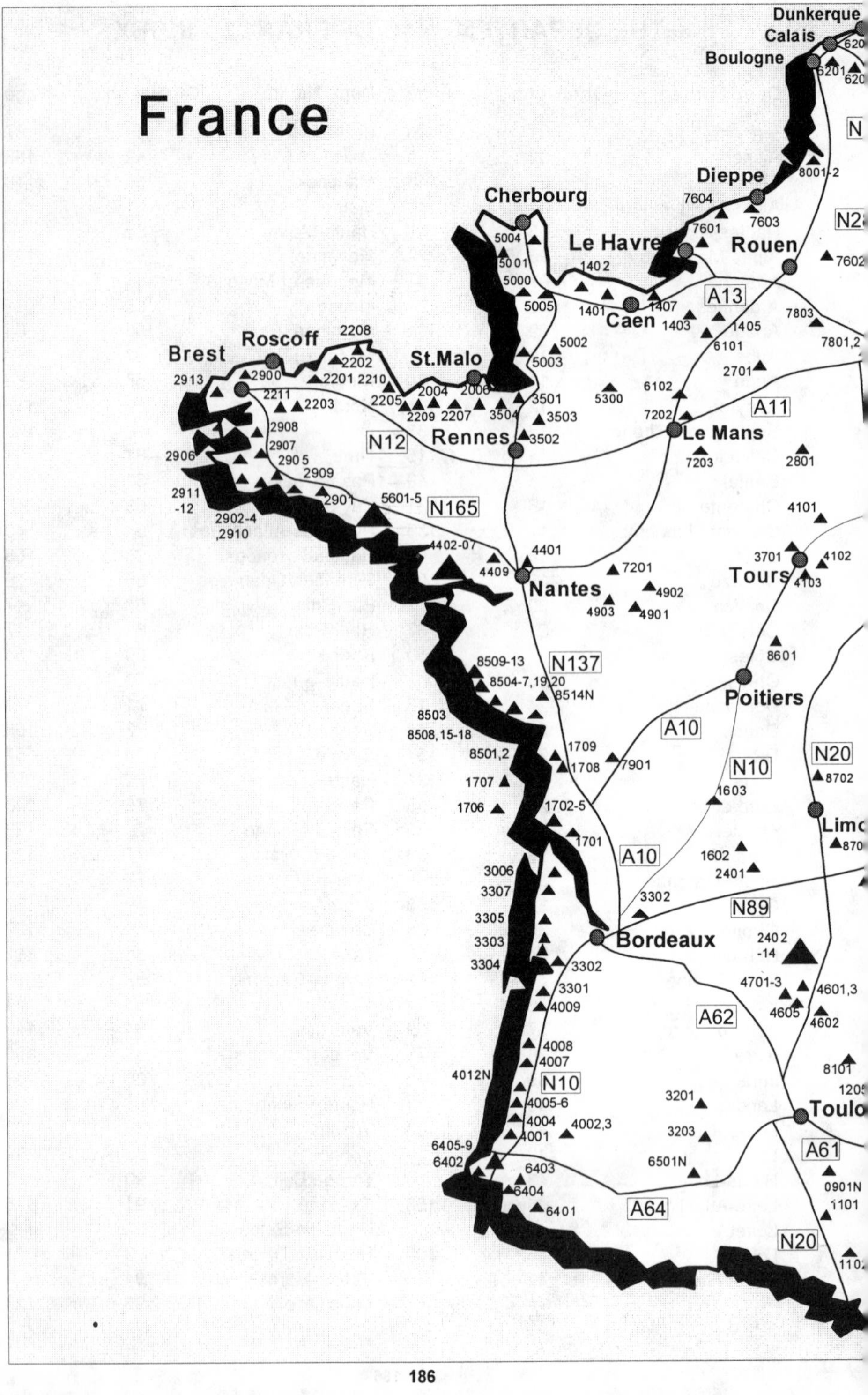

France

Dunkerque
Calais
Boulogne
620
6201 620

N

N2

Dieppe
8001-2
7604
7601 7603

Cherbourg

Le Havre
5004
5001
5000
5005
1402
1401
1407
Caen 1403 1405
6101
2701
7803
7801,2
7602

A13

Rouen

A11

Brest
Roscoff
2208
2202
2201 2210
2211 2203
2900
2913
St.Malo
2004 2006
2205 3501
2209 2207 3504 3503
5003
5002
5300
6102
7202
Le Mans
7203
2801

N12
Rennes 3502

2908
2907
2905
2909
2901
5601-5

N165

2906
2911
-12
2902-4
,2910

4402-07
4409
4401
Nantes
7201
4902
4903 4901

4101

3701 4102
Tours 4103

8601

N137
8509-13
8504-7,19 20
8514N

Poitiers

A10

8503
8508,15-18
8501,2
1707
1706
1709
1708
7901
1702-5
1701

N10
1603

N20
8702

Limo
8701

A10
1602
2401

3006
3307
3305
3303
3304
3302
3302
3301
4009

Bordeaux

N89
2402
-14

4701-3
4605 4601,3
4602

A62

4008
4007
4012N
4005-6
4004 4002,3
4001

N10

3201

3203

8101
1205
Toulo

6405-9
6402
6404
6401
6403
6501N

A61
0901N
1101

A64

N20
110

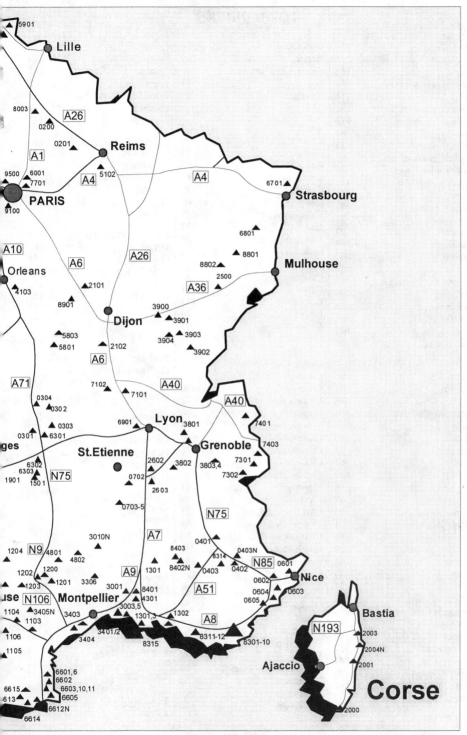

5901

Lille

8003
0200
A26
0201
Reims
A1
9500 6001
7701
A4 5102
A4
6701
Strasbourg
PARIS
9100

6801

A10
8801
A6
A26
8802
2500
Orleans
A36
4103
2101
8901
3900
Dijon 3901
5803
3903
5801
2102
3904
A6
3902
A71
7102
A40
0304
7101
0302
A40
0303
6901
Lyon
3801
7401
0301 6301
Grenoble
7403
ges
St.Etienne
2602
3802
3803,4
7301
6302
0702
7302
6303
N75
1901 150 1
2603
0703-5
N75
3010N
A7
1204 N9 4801
0401
4802
8403
0403N
1202 1200
8314
N85 0601
1201 3306
A9 1301
8402N
0403 0402
Nice
1203
3001
0602
N106 Montpellier
8401
A51
0604 0603
1104 3405N
4301
0605
1103 3403
3003,5
Bastia
1106
3404
1301,3
1302
A8
N193
2003
1105
3401/2
8311-12
8301-10
2004N
6601,6
8315
2001
6602
Ajaccio
6615 6603,10,11
613 6605
Corse
6612N
2000
6614

187

TOWN INDEX

INDEX
of Camp Sites by Region

Note:

To avoid possible confusion, site numbers prefixed with an `N'
are NATURIST sites. In the text, the site name is highlighted.

Note:

To avoid possible confusion, site numbers prefixed with an `N'
are NATURIST sites. In the text, the site name is highlighted.

Note:

To avoid possible confusion, site numbers prefixed with an `N' are NATURIST sites. In the text, the site name is highlighted.